MW01148882

POLITICAL CAMPAIGNING IN THE U.S.

MANAGING THE CHAOS

DAVID A. JONES

James Madison University

ROWMAN & LITTLEFIELD
Lanham • Boulder • New York • London

Executive Editor: Traci Crowell
Assistant Editor: Deni Remsberg
Higher Education Channel Manager: Jonathan Raeder
Interior Designer: Pro Production Graphic Services

Credits and acknowledgments for material borrowed from other sources, and reproduced with permission, appear on the appropriate pages within the text.

Published by Rowman & Littlefield
An imprint of The Rowman & Littlefield Publishing Group, Inc.
4501 Forbes Boulevard, Suite 200, Lanham, Maryland 20706
www.rowman.com

6 Tinworth Street, London SE11 5AL, United Kingdom

British Library Cataloguing in Publication Information Available

Library of Congress Cataloging-in-Publication Data
Names: Jones, David A. (David Adams), 1965– author.
Title: Political campaigning in the U.S. : managing the chaos / David A. Jones.
Other titles: Political campaigning in the United States
Description: Lanham, Maryland: Rowman & Littlefield, 2020. | Includes bibliographical references and index. | Summary: "Provides readers with a comprehensive yet concise and accessible overview of modern U.S. election campaign practices"— Provided by publisher.
Identifiers: LCCN 2019052739 (print) | LCCN 2019052740 (ebook) | ISBN 9781538115183 (cloth) | ISBN 9781538115190 (paperback) | ISBN 9781538115206 (epub)
Subjects: LCSH: Campaign management—United States. | Voting research—United States. | Mass media—Political aspects—United States. | Social media—Political aspects—United States. | Campaign funds—United States.
Classification: LCC JK2281 .J66 2020 (print) | LCC JK2281 (ebook) | DDC 324.70973—dc23
LC record available at https://lccn.loc.gov/2019052739
LC ebook record available at https://lccn.loc.gov/2019052740

Contents

Figures, Tables, and Textboxes

★ ★ ★

FIGURES

TABLES

TEXTBOXES

Preface

DONALD TRUMP'S GENERAL ELECTION victory was a shock, but winning the Republican nomination was even more unlikely. Trump didn't run a single television ad until January 2016, when the primary season was well underway. Through February, he had spent only $10 million on advertising—a miniscule amount compared with "establishment" GOP rivals Jeb Bush ($82 million), Marco Rubio ($55 million), and less even than his fellow upstart Ted Cruz ($22 million) and John Kasich ($14 million) (Confessore and Yourish 2016). Trump was obsessed with his lead in the polls, but did almost no polling of his own. His staff combined youth with inexperience (his twenty-six-year-old press secretary had never worked on a political campaign). His "ground game" was minimal. He made shameful statements that offended many voters, including members of his own party.

Although Trump received an abundance of media coverage, much of it was negative. His nomination was opposed by many Republican party leaders and conservative columnists. Against entitlement spending cuts and free trade agreements, he advocated policy positions that ran counter to conservative Republican orthodoxy. The year 2016 was supposed to be the election of super political action committees (PACs) and big data, but Trump had neither. Not only did he break every nearly rule in the proverbial campaign playbook, he didn't have copy of the book, nor did he seem interested in obtaining one.

By contrast, Trump's top Republican rivals ran relatively conventional campaign operations. They spent millions of dollars on ads aired on television and online. They set up ambitious fundraising operations and formed super PACs to pay for these ads. They opened field offices in key primary and caucus states. They sought endorsements from their fellow Republicans. Some of them employed sophisticated analytics to tailor their messages to targeted audiences. They participated in rigorous prep sessions before each debate. Yet they all lost to a candidate who did none of these things.

Trump's Republican electoral success may prove to be an anomaly. As this book will show, candidates and their campaign organizations usually employ standard practices as they attempt to manage the race in their favor. Sometimes they innovate, but mostly they go with what they know and assume it will work. Yet this book also will show how fruitless these efforts can be. Campaign organizations have very little control over many—perhaps most—aspects of the election. An incumbent candidate can run a nearly flawless campaign operation, but then lose if the economy tanks. A strong challenger can hire energetic and well-trained staffers who employ innovative campaign techniques, but then lose because incumbents nearly always win. Early in the 2016 race for the Republican presidential nomination, Jeb Bush hired top Republican consultants to run his campaign, and his super PAC was flush with cash. He led early polls and secured endorsements from GOP officials. But then Trump entered the race and everything changed. Neither Bush nor any of the other GOP candidates could convert whatever strategic and resource advantages they possessed into a consistently strong showing in the primaries and caucuses. In different ways, all sixteen of them were shown that campaign operations are often more engaged in *managing the chaos* around them than exerting control over predictable events.

The purpose of this book is to provide readers with a comprehensive yet accessible overview of modern election campaign practices. The book is premised on the idea that all students (not just political science majors) and indeed all citizens (not just news junkies) need to understand how campaigns operate—how they collect information about voters; how they attempt to change what voters think about the candidates; and how they encourage voters to think and act in certain ways. The book's analysis will be grounded in dozens of academic studies that assess what works and what does not. Readers will see that campaigns have become remarkably innovative in terms of technology, information management, messaging, communication strategy, and fundraising. But readers also will see that much of what campaigns do is only marginally effective. A campaign might spend hundreds of thousands of dollars on clever, methodically targeted advertising, but their efforts may be matched and therefore cancelled out by their opponent's similar investments. A campaign might build a sophisticated field operation informed by sophisticated analytics, but it cannot recruit enough volunteers who are enthusiastic about the candidate. A campaign might develop constructive relationships with various media outlets, but its candidate gets overwhelmingly negative coverage anyway. Deft campaigning never guarantees positive outcomes.

OUTLINE OF THE BOOK

A campaign organization's inability to control election dynamics will first become apparent in chapter 1, which analyzes the importance of the political landscape—or, what some call the "fundamentals," the "political environment," or the "campaign context." The political landscape consists of the "givens" that the campaigns cannot control at all. Campaigns must plan around and adapt to the conditions that make up the landscape. These fundamentals include the composition of the electorate, especially the percentage of the electorate that identifies with each party. The electorate's demographic composition—race and ethnicity, income and education levels, "religiosity"—also make up part of the landscape. Even more important may be the state of the economy, the mood of the electorate, major external events, and even such specific indicators such as the approval rating of the president. Campaigns also must account for the type of election in which they are running. General elections pitting the two parties against each other have fundamentally different campaign dynamics than intraparty primaries and caucuses. Midterm elections attract different voters than elections held during presidential years. Primaries attract different voters than caucuses. Other consequential "givens" include location-related characteristics such as state-specific election laws and procedures.

How important is the landscape? Political scientists argue that the fundamentals are far more predictive of the outcome than anything the campaigns can control. Models combining indicators of the fundamentals can be used to forecast the results of presidential elections weeks before the general election campaign is underway. These forecasts are accurate enough to prompt the question "Do campaigns matter?" (the title of a seminal political science book on the subject). The answer is yes, campaigns do matter, but usually at the margins, and not nearly as much as campaign operatives like to think, especially at the national level.

We now know that the landscape favored Trump for both the Republican nomination and the general election. The nation's economy had recovered from the 2008–2009 collapse, but income stagnation and sluggishness in the manufacturing sector fueled acute economic insecurity. Americans were in a sour mood, and many of them blamed politicians in general for the sorry state of things. Nontraditional, antiestablishment candidates such as Donald Trump were poised to benefit (as did Bernie Sanders on the Democratic side). Trump thus stood out in a crowded field of seventeen Republicans candidates running for the nomination. He was one of only two non-politicians in the bunch (the other was neurosurgeon Ben Carson, who eventually joined Trump's cabinet), and he was by far the most famous. In addition, the composition of the Republican primary electorate favored Trump in a number of ways. Republican primary voters are overwhelmingly white, and in 2016 a sufficient number of them were anti-immigrant and more reactionary than they were conventionally conservative. These particular Republican voters were receptive to Trump's list of antis: antipolitician, anti-immigrant, and antiestablishment, among others.

If the landscape determines so much of the election outcome, where do campaigns fit in? Mostly they plan around and adapt to the landscape; in essence, that is the primary purpose of a campaign operation. Chapter 2 turns to key concepts that explain how campaigns adapt. In this chapter, readers are introduced to the concept of targeting as well as the processes of persuasion and mobilization. Electoral targeting is the practice of focusing precious campaign resources on particular people and tailoring messages to fit the relevant characteristics of these individuals. People who can be categorized as likely supporters are targeted with messages that are designed to reinforce their predispositions and then mobilize them to actually cast a vote for the candidate they are inclined to support. Undecided voters are targeted with messages aimed at persuading them to support one candidate over the other. Supporters of the candidate's opponents are usually ignored unless the campaign determines that additional votes are needed. Ditto for nonvoters, who might be the targets of mobilization efforts but only if they are identified as likely supporters.

Campaigns target because it saves time and money by reducing wasteful outreach to voters who cannot be moved. It also reduces the likelihood that committed opponents will unintentionally receive the campaign's messages. But as we will see in this chapter, electoral targeting poses serious challenges to a democracy's ability to foster widespread participation and intraparty dialogue. In addition, targeting sometimes fails to meet its strategic objectives. Campaigns have less control over targeting outcomes than they would like to think. Surveys indicate that voters find targeting methods distasteful and they respond negatively when they see targeting in action. They are especially turned off when they accidently receive a mistargeted message—that is, a message aimed at a group to which they do not belong. Overall, voters may prefer broad appeals over narrowly targeted messages (Hersh and Shaffner 2013).

How do campaigns determine which potential voters to target and how to target them? Who is persuadable and who has made up their minds? How do campaigns distinguish between reliable voters and those who needed prodding? They collect data. Chapter 3 focuses on campaigns' information-gathering practices. For many campaigns, especially at the national level, the process of identifying voters has become quite sophisticated. Traditionally, campaigns lean heavily on public voter files, which include key indicators such as voting history, contact information, and—in some states—party affiliation and race. Public data can be augmented (for a price) with consumer data provided by private vendors. Volunteer canvassers can add to and update voters' information in person or by phone. By election day, a well-funded campaigns can build a nearly complete database of politically relevant information about nearly every eligible voter. But as we will see, it turns out that much of that data is either inaccurate or missing. Some of the information is not very useful. And many voters are wrongly classified, resulting in "mistargets" that can backfire, waste the campaign's time, and result in lost opportunities to reach potential supporters.

Polling also is a crucial element of the effort to gather information about prospective voters. In a campaign poll, a randomly selected subset of the population is questioned about candidate preferences, policy priorities, issue positions, and other relevant opinions and behaviors. But whereas a voter database represents an attempt to record and predict the behavior of each individual voter, polling provides an aggregated big picture of the voting population as a whole. Polls help a campaign answer the candidate's favorite question: "How am I doing?" They also help campaigns determine where their strengths and weaknesses are. How is the candidate doing among independent women? Among young voters? Among voters who prioritize national security issues? Poll-supplied answers to these questions can help campaigns focus precious resources on areas of weakness. Polls also can be used to assess the impact of key events such as major ad buys and debate performances.

In addition to collecting data about voters, a campaign also gathers information about the candidates—its opponents, of course, but also its own candidate. Opposition research—or "oppo"—is the systematic effort to collect information about opponents' vulnerabilities and weaknesses. These may include unpopular legislative votes; controversial statements; unfavorable outcomes of policies supported by the candidate; business failures; and scandalous behavior—really, any verifiable documented fact that voters might find objectionable. Oppo usually culminates in a lengthy written report that not only reports the facts but also offers recommendations on how the information may be used by the campaign. Modern opposition research also might include video or links to video showing the opponent making controversial statements or behaving inappropriately. Oppo material is used in television spots and leaked to the media. Campaigns also conduct research on their own candidate to prepare for potential attacks by opponents and damaging news stories.

The media are where most voters experience the election. Chapter 4 is about what campaign pros call "earned" or "free" media. That distinguishes earned from "paid" media—advertising and other forms of bought communication—which is the subject of chapter 5. Earned media include news outlets, talk shows, some forms of social media, and even entertainment programming—any media that might cover the election in some way. Campaigns have very little control over this aspect of election communication, despite their efforts to "manage the news." On one hand, campaigns have become remarkably adept at influencing coverage of the campaign. They hold visually impressive rallies and other events that tend to lead to positive stories. They "spin" reporters' assessment of debate performances and poll results. They selectively leak oppo to resource-starved news outlets. In some ways, increasingly understaffed media outlets are more vulnerable than ever to these news management strategies. Yet every campaign has at least one horror story about a press conference gone wrong, a half-empty rally with a listless crowd, a gaffe that creates a media "feeding frenzy," or a disastrous interview with a reporter. The traditional role of news media as gatekeeper may have diminished, but that does not mean that the campaigns have any semblance of direct control over their media coverage. "Fake news" has only added to the chaos. Earned media can be the most frustrating aspect of the election because so much of it is out of the hands of the campaign.

It may be "free," but there are serious costs in terms of time, aggravation, and relative position in the race.

Trump was a master of earned media. He was a perfect news story: a celebrity who made outrageous, unpredictable statements. He refused to follow the script of a typical politician. He inspired extreme reactions, positive and negative. He openly mocked certain journalists and columnists by name, yet—like one of his Republican opponents, Ted Cruz—he was unusually accessible to journalists for informal interviews. His media coverage was overwhelmingly negative, but the amount of coverage he garnered dwarfed that of his opponents. All this "free" media gave Trump a significant advantage in terms of exposure, and it cost him almost nothing financially.

Campaigns can exert far more control over communication when they buy time and space in the form of advertising. Paid media is the subject of chapter 5. This is where campaigns spend most of the money the raise. Advertising on television is particularly expensive, but online and radio spots also drain campaign coffers. Paid media seems worth the money in part because the campaign has complete control over content and production. As we will see in this chapter, advertising can sometimes fulfill its promise by persuading at least a few prospective voters to change their minds about the candidates. But sometimes ad buys fall short. In highly competitive races, both sides will saturate the airwaves with roughly equal amounts of advertising, giving neither side a paid media advantage. Campaigns may control the content and format of their own ads, but they cannot control the response to these ads. Indeed, paid media's capacity may be overrated. After all, Donald Trump won the Republican nomination despite investing less than $20 million in advertising. Cruz and the independent groups supporting him spent twice that much. Both Trump and Cruz were far outspent by Rubio and Bush (Kurtzleben 2016). Rubio and Bush may have exerted more control over the commercial airwaves, but they did not win more votes.

Trump was far more active on social media, particularly Twitter. In chapter 6, we will examine how campaigns use Twitter, Facebook, and other social media platforms to compensate for some of the shortcomings of earned and paid media. A growing number of voters experience elections through their newsfeeds. For younger voters, social media dwarf other platforms for election-related information. Campaigns know that. Social media enable campaigns to microtarget the kinds of digital advertising in ways that television cannot. Campaigns also use social media to enlist supporters to advocate on their behalf.

They use Facebook status updates and tweets to communicate directly with prospective voters at no cost. Trump, for example, had more than eight million Twitter followers by the end of the Republican nomination campaign. His frequent tweets—he often posted several times a day—potentially reached all of these followers directly, at no cost to the campaign. Yet sometimes his tweets got him in trouble, such as when he posted a pair of photographs: one an unflattering image of Cruz's wife, Heidi, the other an attractive image of his own wife, Melania, with the caption "A picture is worth a thousand words." In response, Cruz called Trump a "sniveling coward" and told him to "leave Heidi the hell alone." Pundits seemed to side with Cruz on this one. For at least one news cycle, Trump had lost control of the story.

Trump was far less invested in the "ground game"—the subject of chapter 7. Also called fieldwork or just "field," this is in many ways the most old-fashioned aspect of the campaign. That is because so much of fieldwork entails one-on-one interaction with potential voters. Field workers spend much of their time canvassing—that is, knocking on doors and talking to citizens in person or on the phone. By outward appearances, the ground game is a low-tech operation.

Looks are deceiving. Actually, the ground game has been at the center of much of the data-driven innovation employed by campaigns since the early 2000s. Advances in fieldwork were triggered in part by political science research showing that door-to-door canvassing actually works—that citizens are more likely to vote if, for example, they are encouraged to do so by a campaign volunteer who encourages them to do so. Intrigued by this evidence, Republicans enhanced traditional canvassing efforts with data that helped them more accurately predict the political orientation of the person answering the door. Democrats caught up and then surpassed Republicans by 2008, when the Obama campaign experimented with a variety of microtargeted voter outreach efforts. These practices have since been employed by many campaigns at the national, state, and even local level.

Even so, a top-notch field operation does not guarantee success. Ted Cruz, for example, led the crowded 2016 GOP field with a state-of-the-art ground game that aimed to identify all likely voters in key primary and caucus states. His campaign's fieldwork may have propelled Cruz to the top tier of candidates in 2016, beyond where he would have stood otherwise. Yet Cruz won only eleven states. Trump wasn't even familiar with the term "ground game" until the February, and his skeletal field operation reflected that. Yet he won the nomination anyway.

How do campaigns pay for all of this? Campaign finance is the subject of chapter 8. Television advertising in particular can quickly drain campaign coffers. So will the expense of hiring paid consultants, polling, staffing field offices, phone banks, and direct mail. Candidates pay for most of their own expenses by raising campaign contributions from individual donors and PACs. This "hard money" aspect of campaign finance is controlled by the campaigns themselves and is regulated by federal and state agencies. Less regulated are outside groups, which absorb some expenditures. But campaigns are prevented from coordinating their efforts with outside groups. And while candidates can count on at least some support from their political party, they first must secure the party's nomination, then hope the party deems the race sufficiently winnable to warrant serious investment. The campaign can control neither the amount of support from the party nor the content of support by outside groups. As we will see, parties and outside groups are sometimes less than helpful. Even campaigns with highly successful fundraising operations can be disappointed by the end result. After all, as we will see in chapter 5, the most expensive aspect of the campaign—television advertising—sometimes has minimal/measurable impact on voters' candidate preferences.

Of course, Trump won both the nomination and the general election without spending much on advertising, field operations, data, or polling. He did not bother raising money because his default strategy—making news by holding massive rallies and saying outrageous things—cost so little. This reality baffled his Republican opponents and their campaigns. Jeb Bush and his super PAC raised tens of millions of dollars and spent much of it on advertising. Ted Cruz built a state-of-the-art field operation. Like Cruz, Marco Rubio possessed strong debate and public speaking skills. Scott Walker's strength as a popular governor in a key state helped him attract a top-notch staff of experts. None of these strategic assets were enough to beat Trump. Trump caused chaos and his opponents were unable to manage it.

Other candidates and their campaign operations are more successful at managing the unpredictable ebbs and flows of modern election dynamics. This book will describe how they do it. By the end, readers will gain an understanding of how campaigns operate and the implications of their practices for representative democracy.

NATIONAL VERSUS STATE AND LOCAL ELECTIONS

Most of the examples used in this book refer to federal elections. Presidential campaigns get more attention than races for the U.S. House and Senate, and all three dwarf the book's treatment of state and local elections. This book draws heavily upon academic research, and the overwhelming majority of election studies center on federal campaigns. I also suspect that students are more familiar with—and interested in—presidential elections.

That said, it is important to acknowledge meaningful differences between the operations of federal campaigns and those for down-ballot candidates. Some of those differences will emerge in the pages that follow. Not surprisingly, presidential campaigns attract the lion's share of campaign contributions, media coverage, and volunteer energy. U.S. House and Senate races also fare well in these areas, but only if they are competitive. Ditto for governor's races. But other state-level and local races will struggle to garner resources and attention. Outside of big cities, mayoral candidates will lack the funds to hire a pollster, conduct opposition research, and build a database. Candidates running for a state legislative seat will rely more on candidate-hosted events than paid media and sophisticated social media operations. Canvassing operations will be more improvisational than the ones described in chapter 7. That said, even local and state campaigns apply the core concepts described in this book, even if the terminology is different and the applications are less elaborate. These campaign operations can be remarkably sophisticated, especially when a race is competitive enough to attract the attention of donors, the media, party organizations, and outside groups.

CAMPAIGN-CENTERED ANALYSIS

This book is written from the point of view of the campaign organization, which consists of the advisers, staffers, and volunteers who report to a candidate. To use the terminology of social science, the campaign organization is the book's *unit of analysis*, which means it is the entity that frames the investigation. This approach makes sense because the people who work for the campaign are charged with carrying out the core functions described in this book. They interact with the media. They work with media consultants to produce and air advertising. They oversee social media outreach. They add to and maintain a voter database, hire pollsters, and sponsor opposition research. They raise money to fund their operations.

The approach reflects the reality that elections have long been more candidate-centered than party-centered. Whereas parties once selected their nominees and actually did much of the campaigning, candidates now typically form their own campaign operations before the party gets publicly involved. This is not to say that parties do not matter. Parties play a variety of crucial roles that will be referenced throughout the book. As we will see, parties are responsible for candidate recruitment. Candidates who get their party's support are more likely to win the nomination. They are the most important source of voter data. And once a candidate secures the nomination, party organizations and affiliated groups play more active supporting roles by spending money on advertising and mobilizing voters to participate. Interest groups carry out many of the same functions. Their support—and the work they do—can be essential. Indeed, it is more useful to think of parties and groups as part of a complex network of organizations that work together to nominate desirable candidates and help them win elections (Masket 2014).

Even so, most of the major strategic decisions are made by the leadership of the campaign organization: the candidate, the campaign manager, various communication staffers, and however many field directors a campaign might need. Their work is the focus of this book. For the most part, they are the campaign. The word "campaign" is commonly used as a shortcut for campaign organization and I have done so here.

ACKNOWLEDGMENTS

The author wishes to thank those who have assisted with production of the book, especially Executive Editor Traci Crowell and Assistant Editor Deni Remsberg. Particularly helpful have been former students who have shared their insights over the years as campaign professionals, including Jane Hughes, Jamie Lockhart, Matt Oczkowski, Eric Payne, Gina Hwang, and Adam Zuckerman. The author also wishes to thank the reviewers of this book: Ryan LaRochelle (University of Maine), Laura Sudulich (University of Kent), Rusty Hills (University of Michigan), Brian J. Brox (Tulane University), Annemarie Walter (University of Nottingham), Nicholas Goedert (Virginia Tech), and Todd L. Belt (University of Hawaii at Hilo).

REFERENCES

Confessore, Nicholas, and Karen Yourish. 2016. "$2 Billion Worth of Free Media for Donald Trump." *New York Times*, March 15: http://www.nytimes.com/2016/03/16/upshot/measuring-donald-trumps-mammoth-advantage-in-free-media.html.

Hersh, Eitan D., and Brian F. Schaffner. 2013. "Targeted Campaign Appeals and the Value of Ambiguity." *Journal of Politics* 75: 520–534.

Kurtzleben, Danielle. 2016. "CHARTS: Sanders Has Spent the Most on Ads, But Trump Has Spent Best." *NPR*, May 19: http://www.npr.org/2016/05/19/478384978/on-ads-sanders-has-spent-most-but-trump-has-spent-best.

Masket, Seth. 2014. "Our Political Parties Are Networked, Not Fragmented." *Washington Post* (Feb. 14): https://www.washingtonpost.com/news/monkey-cage/wp/2014/02/14/our-political-parties-are-networked-not-fragmented/.

About the Author

DAVID A. JONES is professor of political science at James Madison University. He teaches courses on political campaigning, media and politics, and U.S. government. His research has been published in *Political Communication, P.S.: Political Science & Politics*, the *Harvard International Journal of Press/Politics*, and other journals. His book *U.S. Media and Elections in Flux: Dynamics and Strategies* was published in 2016. Dr. Jones has directed the university's Washington Semester program since 2000.

1

The Electoral Landscape

Conservatives rallied behind gubernatorial nominee Ken Cuccinelli at the Virginia Republican convention in 2013. Cuccinelli lost the general election despite a political landscape that favored Republicans. *Source*: *AP Photo/Steve Helber*

LEARNING OBJECTIVES

★ Understand how much of the outcome of a race can be explained by factors that are out of the campaigns' control.

★ Comprehend the differences between nomination contests and general elections and how those differences shape campaign strategy.

- ★ Explore the advantages of being the incumbent candidate as well as the limitations of incumbency.
- ★ Grasp the importance of partisanship in determining the outcome of an election.

WHO IS GOING TO WIN? The final answer to this question won't come until the votes are counted. But the truth is that the outcome of most elections can be predicted with some level of confidence months in advance. The winner will *probably* be the candidate who is favored by the fundamentals of the race, no matter what the campaigns do. All other things being equal, whichever candidate is the incumbent in a legislative race will probably win, especially when the economy is strong. There's a good chance that a House candidate from the president's party who represents a marginal district will lose a midterm race. A Democrat running for the Senate in the deep-red state of Wyoming will probably lose no matter how many hands they shake and ads they run. A Republican is going to win that race nine times out of ten, especially if they are an incumbent.

Where do the campaigns come in? Do they matter? Yes, but they matter less than campaign professionals like to think. But if election results are practically preordained, why bother campaigning? Scholars have been wrestling with this question for decades. Early research—nearly all of it centered on presidential elections—implied that campaigning was a waste of time. It minimized the influence of electioneering, instead emphasizing the predictability of voting outcomes based on factors such as the national economy. But since the early 2000s, studies have isolated the small but sometimes decisive effects of canvassing, earned and paid media, and other campaign activities. We will examine these studies in subsequent chapters. The question has shifted from "do campaigns matter at all?" to "under what circumstances do campaigns matter?" As we will see in the next chapter, campaigns aim to *persuade* the handful of voters who have not committed to a candidate. They also reinforce the predispositions of voters who are inclined to support their candidate, and then *mobilize* these same individuals to cast their vote. There is now plenty of research showing that campaigns can successfully do some of all of these things under certain circumstances.

Even so, campaigning efforts take place within a landscape that nearly always favors one candidate over the other. The landscape is sometimes called the *terrain* or *context* of the race, or perhaps the *fundamentals* of the election. All of these terms describe the same thing: factors that impact the outcome but are beyond the campaigns' control. Campaigns have far more control over the money they raise, the ads they run, the social media posts they share, the fliers they mail, and the doors they knock. They have less control over how the media and their opponents respond. And they have no control over the landscape. Instead, they must adapt to its constraints and, when appropriate, exploit whatever advantages the terrain might provide. Consistent with the theme of this book, campaigns must manage the sometimes chaotic circumstances that are out of their control.

Assessing the landscape is thus a crucial early step during a campaign's planning process. Broadly speaking, a clearly favorable landscape means the campaign can focus on such efforts as shoring up its support, preparing for aggressive attacks by a desperate opponent, and building a field operation limited to mobilizing supporters rather than persuading undecided voters. An unfavorable landscape signals where the disadvantaged campaign should concentrate its resources. For example, if an assessment of the landscape estimates a fifteen-point advantage for the opponent, the campaign enters the race knowing that they must attract at least some voters who tend to support the other party. It therefore must step up its fundraising efforts to pay for primetime television spots aimed at persuading both undecided voters as well as voters who can be cross-pressured to switch sides. A landscape that suggests a tighter race means a comprehensive approach for both campaigns.

NOMINATION VERSUS GENERAL

The landscape varies depending on the phase of the election. Elections happen in two phases: the party nomination and the general election. During the nomination phase, party organizations use a primary election or another method to choose the candidates who will represent the party on the general election ballot. The general election pits the party nominees against each other in contests for all elected government offices—federal, state, and local. Nearly all general elections are held on the national Election Day, which federal law specifies as the first Tuesday after the first Monday in November. Both phases share aspects of the electoral landscape that will be discussed in the general election section of this chapter. But the nomination phase has its own qualities that campaigns must account for when assessing the fundamentals.

The landscape for nomination races can be less predictable than general elections for a number of reasons. Far fewer voters participate, and turnout can vary widely depending on the competitiveness of the race. The main source of uncertainty is the fact that party affiliation is neutralized. In general elections for the presidency, nine out of ten people vote in line with their party leanings. That leaves little room for influence by the campaigns. But during the nomination phase, campaigns can matter quite a bit. Nomination contests are between candidates who tend to agree on core political principles that unite members of the party. Policy differences are minimal compared with the stark ideological contrasts that will emerge during the general election. This can be a challenge for voters who rely on party identification as a shortcut for processing information and a cue for making voting decisions. Party identification is less useful as a cognitive shortcut when all of the candidates share the same party label. Candidates thus must distinguish themselves in other ways— on personal character, for example, or leadership style or governing experience. It is the campaigns—along with the media—that provide voters with information about these candidate qualities.

The neutralization of party identification also makes it more difficult for campaigns to identify likely supporters. In most states, voters provide their party affiliation when they register. Party-based voter registration gives campaigns access to a crucial data point because party affiliation is the most reliable predictor of how people vote in a general election. As we will see in the next chapter, campaigns can thus focus their efforts on mobilizing likely supporters—that is, voters who have been identified as fellow partisans. But during nomination contests, party affiliation does not serve as a candidate preference predictor because nearly everyone identifies with the same party. As a result, "candidates are fighting over primary voters who are difficult to distinguish from one another" (Hersh 2015).

The characteristics described so far generally apply to all nomination contests. Other qualities can vary from race to race. They can be evaluated through a series of questions that campaigns can ask themselves when assessing the landscape. These questions will provide a framework for the rest of the chapter. The first set of questions applies to the nomination phase. Questions specific to the general election phase will follow.

How Competitive Is the Nomination Contest?
Much depends on whether there is an incumbent in the race. An **incumbent** candidate is an elected official who is running for reelection. As

we will see later in this chapter, incumbents enjoy significant advantages during the general election, and they usually win. Most nominations are uncontested, especially when the incumbent is running for reelection. Congressional incumbents rarely face a serious primary challenge. Some never do. As of 2018, U.S. Rep. Rosa DeLauro (CT-3) had never been challenged for the Democratic Party nomination since being elected to Congress in 1990. Ditto for U.S. Rep. Nita Lowey (NY-17). When Alexandria Ocasio-Cortez upset U.S. Rep. Joe Crowley (NY-14) for the Democratic nomination in 2018, it was the first time Crowley had faced a primary challenge in twelve years (Griggs and Pearce 2018).

Even when an incumbent's nomination is contested, the challenger is often a little-known candidate with no chance of winning. These races are more of a nuisance than a serious threat. But more and more incumbents are now being "primaried" by a strong challenger from their party. These candidates tend to come from either the left or the right wing of their respective party, and they often enter the race due to discontent with the incumbent's excessively moderate voting record. Ocasio-Cortez challenged Crowley from the Democratic Party's left flank. A similar challenge from the Republican side ended the congressional career of House Majority Leader Eric Cantor when he ran for reelection in 2014. Cantor was next in line to serve as Speaker of the House, but first he had to defeat Dave Brat for the Republican nomination. Cantor was a reliable conservative, but Brat managed to run to Cantor's right by attacking him for attempting to make deals with President Obama on immigration and the budget. Brat won by 12 percent despite spending less than $200,000 compared with Cantor's $5 million.

Competitive seats can attract multiple candidates, sometimes resulting in a crowded field of potential nominees. The 2018 midterms provided many examples. At least two dozen Republican-held seats were expected to flip, fueling a surge of Democratic candidates vying for their party's nomination. Many of the successful Democratic candidates were women motivated to run in the wake of the election of a president who had, among other outrages, bragged about committing sexual assault. In Virginia's Tenth Congressional District, for example, six Democrats—five of them women—competed to face off against U.S. Rep. Barbara Comstock. In Texas's Seventh Congressional District, seven Democrats vied for the party's nomination to challenge U.S. Rep. John Culberson; the top two vote-getters were women.

Open-seat races also can attract multicandidate nomination races because there is no incumbent. In fact, the opposing party might enjoy a slight boost if the incumbent retired under a cloud of scandal or poor performance. Open seats often result in competitive nomination contests on both sides. U.S. Rep. Darrell Issa's 2018 decision to retire from Congress elicited eight candidates for the Republican nomination and four candidates for the Democrats.

Competitive primaries can be grueling, especially with a crowded field. The challenges do not end once the nomination is secured. The winning candidate's campaign must then grapple with possible "sour grapes" among disgruntled supporters of the losing candidates (Henderson, Hillygus, and Tompson 2010). These fellow partisans must be convinced to "come home" and support the successful nominee during the general election. This can be a tough sell with the losing candidate's most devoted supporters, especially volunteers and activists who may have spent weeks trying to convince others that the eventual winner was the wrong choice. However, primary voters tend to be more partisan and ideological than the general electorate and therefore unlikely to support a candidate from the opposite party. Their existing political leanings just need to be *activated* by the nominee's campaign (Henderson 2015). In other words, they need to be reminded why they usually support the party they do. Research on divisive primaries suggests that thwarted primary voters eventually get over their disappointment and vote for their party's nominee (Atkeson 1998; Henderson 2015; Henderson, Hillygus, and Tompson 2010).

In 2016, supporters of Bernie Sanders had to be convinced to set aside their misgivings about Hillary Clinton and vote for the candidate who was not Republican Donald Trump. These efforts got a boost when Sanders not only endorsed Clinton but also campaigned on her behalf. In the end, about 90 percent of people who voted for Sanders during the primaries "came home" and voted for Clinton in the general election. That was a higher level of party unity than Barack Obama experienced in 2008 when he defeated Clinton after an even more competitive race for the Democratic nomination. Only 71 percent of people who voted for a different Democrat during the primaries ended up voting for Obama during the general election. We later learned that many of the holdouts were not natural Democrats. In both 2008 and 2016, the Democratic primary voters who eventually supported the Republican in the general election were politically out of sync with the Democratic Party (Henderson, Hillygus, and Tompson 2010; Sides 2017). They were unlikely to "come home" unless the party had nominated a politically moderate white male.

BOX 1.1 | How Good Is Your Candidate?

What analysts call "candidate quality" is not usually treated as part of the landscape. But this book analyzes elections from the perspective of the campaigns themselves, and campaigns must treat their candidate as a given—like other aspects of the landscape, they cannot control who the candidate is. They can advise the candidate; they can make adjustments based on the candidate's strengths and weaknesses; they can prod the candidate in particular directions. But the campaign itself cannot replace one candidate for the other. The candidates are in charge; only they can make such decisions. Thus, for the campaign as an organization—and the staffers who work for the campaign—the candidate is part of the landscape. For better or worse, the campaign is "stuck" with its candidate.

Candidate quality includes a number of dimensions. It usually helps to have a candidate with relevant governing *experience*, although sometimes the landscape can favor nonpoliticians like Donald Trump. The recent success of Trump-like celebrity candidates belies the notion that voters demand public sector credentials. Even local celebrities can benefit from the name recognition that comes with being a well-known person in the community. Other aspects of a candidate's *biography* also can matter. A candidate who comes from humble origins might be relatable to some voters and admired by others for overcoming personal challenges. For Democratic candidates, military service (especially in combat) can compensate for the party's disadvantage with voters who have military connections. Republicans might favor a successful entrepreneur over an experienced public servant.

Of course, a candidate's gender and race or ethnicity are also relevant. Most elected officials in the U.S. are white males. But there has been a slow increase in the number of nonwhite, nonmale candidates running for office. The year 2018 saw a significant uptick in women candidates, and a record number of women secured their party's nomination for House and gubernatorial races. Half of the female gubernatorial candidates on the Democratic side were nonwhite women. A record number of LGBTQ candidates also ran for office in 2018. Alexandria Ocasio-Cortez's Puerto Rican heritage may have helped her win the Democratic primary for New York's Fourteenth Congressional District, the population of which was half-Hispanic at the time. But even though success rates can be quite high—women candidates win at comparable and sometimes higher rates than men—some voters resist supporting candidates who do not fit the white male prototype.

(continued)

BOX 1.1 | (*continued*)

A candidate's *personality* can also explain how effectively a candidate can relate to voters. "Retail politics" is the term used to describe interacting with voters face-to-face—"shaking hands and kissing babies," as it is sometimes called. Some candidates are better at retail than others. Most politicians have outgoing personalities, but some can be surprisingly awkward. Chuck Robb represented Virginia in the U.S. Senate for twelve years after serving as governor for four, but he was visibly stiff when talking to voters. Ditto for Republican presidential candidate Mitt Romney, whose personal decency was sometimes overshadowed by awkward behavior and corny jokes during campaign events. Some candidates never master public speaking despite the obvious importance of this skill when running for office. Others are comfortable delivering a prepared speech but struggle when forced to ad lib during a press conference, interview, or debate.

Is the Party's Nominee Chosen through a Primary Election?

Most are. A **primary** is a statewide election between candidates from the same party. The ballot and process are similar to those of a general election: voters choose from a set of candidates and cast a secret ballot typically during a set time frame on a designated day. Nearly half of states hold either *closed* or *semiclosed* primaries, which are open only to registered members of the party or unaffiliated voters who may temporarily choose one party over the other. Most other states hold either *open* or *semiopen* primaries in which all registered voters may participate regardless of party affiliation. Two states—California and Washington—use some form of *blanket* primary, in which the top two vote-getters advance to the general election no matter which party they represent. A similar system is used by Louisiana, which skips a separate primary altogether and uses a general election ballot that lists multiple candidates from each major party.

These distinctions are relevant to the landscape because they shape the nature of the primary electorate. Open primaries can favor centrist candidates because independents can participate as can those who identify with the other party. Campaigns for Republican candidates running in open primaries might be reaching out to an electorate that is less conservative than their party following; Democrats can expect their electorate to be less liberal (Kaufmann, Gimpel, and Hoffman 2003). Campaigns also must concern themselves with the possibility of *strategic crossover voting*—that is, when voters attempt to disrupt the other party's primary results by voting for the weaker candidate or something along those lines, although such efforts rarely have a meaningful effect.

If Not a Primary, Convention or Caucuses?

A handful of state and local party organizations choose their nominees through a party convention. A **convention** is a meeting of party leaders and activists. Because convention attendees tend to be politically engaged and ideological, they can produce ideologically extreme nominees. In Virginia, for example, the Republican Party sometimes chooses its nominees through a convention rather than a primary. That happened in 2013, prompting Bill Bolling to withdraw his gubernatorial candidacy despite having served as lieutenant governor for two consecutive terms. Less conservative than others in his party, Bolling probably would have fared well in a primary, especially since Virginia primaries are open to all registered voters regardless of party (Virginia does not register voters by party). But the state party's central committee opted for a convention, a method that favored Bolling's opponent, Attorney General Ken Cuccinelli—a favorite among conservative activists. Cuccinelli's nomination was confirmed by acclamation at the convention. For the lieutenant governor seat, a ten-hour convention battle between seven candidates resulted in the nomination of Reverend E. W. Jackson, whose controversial statements included a claim that abortions performed by Planned Parenthood made the organization more deadly to African Americans than the Ku Klux Klan. In a landscape that otherwise favored Republicans, Jackson lost to his Democratic opponent by nearly 12 points. Cuccinelli lost the gubernatorial race by 2.6 points.

Presidential campaigns must work around a complex nomination process with rules and procedures that vary state by state. Technically, both major parties nominate their candidates at the national party conventions held during the summer before the fall election. That is precisely what happened until the Democratic Party reformed its presidential nomination rules in the aftermath of its 1968 convention in Chicago, where outrage about the party's candidate selection process resulted in riots outside the convention center and chaos on the convention floor, captivating live television viewers for days. The reforms pressured state parties to open up their convention delegate selection process to regular voters instead of party elites. Most states responded by holding primaries, then using the primary results to determine the number of delegates representing each candidate. Today, forty states hold presidential primaries. To varying degrees, each state uses the results of these primaries to determine the number of convention delegates assigned to support each candidate.

The remaining states rely on **caucuses** to assign convention delegates. Caucuses are party meetings that take place at a certain time in various places across the state. The procedures vary by state and by party. For the landscape, what matters is that caucuses are more like conventions than primaries. Caucus goers tend to be highly engaged and partisan. Mobilizing likely supporters to attend and participate in a lengthy meeting is a tougher sell than encouraging people to take a few minutes to vote in a primary. Many caucuses also require that participants publicly declare their support for a candidate whereas primaries entail a secret ballot. A good example is the Iowa caucuses, which are famous for being the first major contest of the presidential primary season. There are nearly 1,700 Iowa caucuses, one for each precinct. In each precinct on the Democratic side, caucus goers break into groups according to the candidate they support. They then have thirty minutes or so to convince fellow attendees to join their group. Following a head count, candidates with the support of less than 15 percent of attendees are removed from consideration, and their supporters are recruited to join one of the other groups. The final head count signals who won and by approximately how much, but the final delegate allocation is not settled until district and state party conventions are held much later. Needless to say, mastering the intricacies of the Iowa caucuses is a challenge for any presidential campaign.

Do Party Leaders Support Your Candidate?

Party leaders no longer handpick the nominees—voters do, mostly through primaries. But parties still exert a powerful influence on the nomination process. As we saw above, they set the rules for delegate allocation and other such matters. They set the schedule and establish procedures for primaries, caucuses, and conventions. But more importantly, they shape the field of candidates. After all, "political parties have an interest in ensuring that the right election candidate emerges from the party's nomination process to give themselves the best chance to win a majority of seats" (Hassell 2015). That means recruiting promising candidates to run for office. That also means working behind the scenes to discourage weak candidates from entering a race, or quietly tipping the scale against a candidate who does not stack up well against the other party's likely nominee.

Studies indicate that the candidate who was recruited by the party has an edge thanks to endorsements and other positive signals from party leaders, affiliated interest groups, and activists (Broockman 2014; Cohen et al. 2008). This "invisible primary" determines which candidate will prevail long before voters cast their ballots (Cohen et al. 2008). Candidates decide whether to run on their own, and they form their own campaigns. But more often than not, "the party decides" who the nominees will be in the general election for national, state, and local offices (Bawn et al. 2012; Cohen et al. 2008; Hassell 2015; Masket 2009; Niven 2006). In a study of U.S. Senate nominations, political scientist Hans Hassell concluded that parties both dissuade candidates from competing and influence candidates' decision to remain in the race (Hassell 2015). Trump managed to secure the nomination in the face of strong opposition among Republican Party elites (Alberta 2019), signaling that parties shape the field less than they once did. Yet "the party decides" still holds for most subnational races.

Candidate recruitment was reportedly Rahm Emanuel's obsession when he chaired the Democratic Congressional Committee during the 2006 midterms (Broockman 2014). The national landscape favored Democrats, threatening dozens of Republican-held districts with large numbers of Democratic voters. Emanuel thus focused on recruiting centrists who could compete in these "swing" districts. Democrats gained thirty-one seats during that election cycle and took control of the U.S. House as a result.

The landscape also favored Democrats in the 2018 midterm elections. This was two years after Donald Trump's shocking presidential victory, and hundreds of progressive Democrats—especially women—were galvanized to run for office. Many of the most competitive races for the House, Senate, and governorships, saw three or more serious candidates vying for the Democratic nomination. In 95 percent of open-seat races, however, the victor was the candidate who was endorsed by the national party committee. By contrast, the win rate was only 41 percent for candidates endorsed by independent progressive groups that were not connected with the party (Conroy, Rakich, and Nguyen 2018).

In assessing the nomination landscape, candidates thus must account for whether they will have the enthusiastic support of party insiders, government officials from their party, affiliated interest groups, and the relevant party committees. Candidates who lack their party's support often struggle in a crowded primary field. That said, Donald Trump's presidential win may have signaled a diminishment of party influence, at least on the Republican side. In 2016, the

Republican presidential field was extremely crowded; Trump was one of seventeen candidates, several with strong party ties and enough governing experience to secure the party's support. But party insiders waited too long to converge behind a single alternative to Trump. In other words, the Republican Party didn't decide who the nominee would be because the party *couldn't* decide. Since then, outsider Republicans like Trump have fared relatively well in nomination contests against "establishment" Republicans with more governing experience. But that is in part because they secured the support of the leader of their party, President Trump. Meanwhile, Democrats are still mostly nominating candidates supported by their party, even when given multiple nonestablishment options.

GENERAL ELECTION PHASE

The general election landscape is more straightforward. In presidential elections, 90 percent of voters make up their minds in the early stages of the fall campaign. Months in advance, political scientists can estimate the popular vote percentage using simple forecasting models that account for the national economy, the popularity of the current president, and perhaps one or two other variables. But the popular vote does not determine who wins the presidency; the Electoral College does, necessitating that presidential campaigns assess the landscape of each state. Down-ballot campaigns must assess the general election landscape of their state, legislative district, or whatever geographic unit they seek to represent.

Where does the party lean?

An assessment of the general election landscape starts with partisanship. People tend to vote in line with their party identification—even independents, most of whom lean toward one party (see chapter 2). Party identification is pretty stable. It is thus useful to estimate how strongly a geographic area leans toward one political party.

Campaigns can turn to a variety of different measures of what some call **party lean**. Some political media outlets calculate partisan indices that anyone can use because they are available to the public. For example, the *Cook Political Report* calculates a Partisan Vote Index (PVI) for all 435 congressional districts. The PVI uses presidential election results as a baseline. It is a plus-or-minus number that compares how a district voted in the two previous presidential elections with how the nation as a whole voted. For example, the PVI for Texas's Eighteenth Congressional District was D+27 in 2017. That meant the average vote share earned by the two previous Democratic presidential candidates in the district exceeded their average national vote share by about twenty-seven points. This was a very safe seat for Democrats at the time. U.S. Rep. Sheila Jackson-Lee has served the district since 1995, but any Democratic candidate would likely defeat any Republican candidate. By contrast, California's Tenth Congressional District was rated as "EVEN" because the district's presidential vote share matched the national vote share both times. Republican Jeff Denham won the seat in 2010, won reelection by only 3.4 points in 2016, then lost by 4.6 points when the overall landscape favored Democratic candidates in 2018.

An assessment of party advantage provides a starting point. Which party's candidate is favored to win, all other factors being equal? A Republican running in a D+8 district won't necessarily lose. Other fundamentals might be more favorable. A strong campaign might add a few points. But the number does suggest that the race will be an uphill climb.

Partisan lean is a weaker predictor of the outcome in gubernatorial and mayoral races. With elected executives, a candidate's personality or reputation can overcome party for a sufficient number of voters. Voters may also correctly perceive that governors and mayors are themselves less constrained by party dynamics than lawmakers in a legislature or local council. Whereas legislators are pressured by party leaders to vote in line with the interests of the party, executive officeholders can govern with more independence. Massachusetts is a deep-blue state: all nine of its House seats are held by Democrats, and it has voted Democratic in the past eight presidential elections. Yet five of its last six governors have been Republicans. Maryland and Illinois also have Republican governors despite leaning decidedly blue. Louisiana and Montana lean red yet are led by Democratic governors.

Is Your Candidate an Incumbent?
If so, your candidate will probably win the general election. U.S. presidents and many governors face *term limits* that legally prevent them for running for reelection more than once. But term limits do not apply to members of the U.S. House and Senate, many governors and mayors, and most state legislators and local lawmakers. They may run for reelection as many times as they like. When they do, their chances of winning tend to be very high. Although the incumbency advantage

BOX 1.2 | Small Victory

Xochitl Torres Small was not supposed to win. She was a Democrat running in New Mexico's Second Congressional District, which Donald Trump had won by ten points two years earlier. The district's Cook PVI was R+7 in 2017, which made it a solid Republican seat. But other elements of the landscape favored a Democratic candidate. Registered Democrats outnumbered Republicans. And this was the 2018 midterm election, so Republicans were hampered by an unpopular president coupled with the usual "surge and decline" phenomenon that disadvantages the president's party in midterm elections. It also helped that this was an open seat: incumbent Steve Pearce had retired to run for governor.

Initial returns were discouraging for Torres Small. Her opponent, Yvette Herrell, declared victory on election night with a 1,970-vote lead. But more than eight thousand absentee ballots from Democratic-leaning Doña Anna County had not been tallied. Torres Small refused to concede, telling her supporters, "We are waiting until every person's vote is heard." Eighteen hours of vote counting later, Torres Small pulled ahead and eventually won by 3,722 votes (Las Cruces Sun News 2018).

Torres Small benefited from a national political landscape that favored Democrats, but she ran a centrist campaign. She promised to protect the district's oil and gas industry and defend its "rural values." One of her ads showed her loading and shooting a gun on a hunting trip. She highlighted endorsements from Republicans. By contrast, Herrell aimed at mobilizing the Republican base by touting her support for Trump and his border wall as well as endorsements from former House Speaker Newt Gingrich (Contreras 2018). Unfortunately for Herrell, the fundamentals at the time and place did not favor a pro-Trump candidate in this particular congressional district.

SOURCES

Contreras, Russell. 2018. "Republican Who Lost US House Race Seeks to Impound Ballots." *U.S. News & World Report* (Nov. 13): https://www.usnews.com/news/best-states/new-mexico/articles/2018-11-13/republican-refusing-to-concede-us-house-race-questions-vote.

Las Cruces Sun News. 2018. "Xochitl Torres Small Wins Congressional District 2 Race; Herrell Does Not Concede." Nov. 7: https://www.lcsun-news.com/story/news/politics/elections/2018/11/07/xochitl-torres-small-wins-congressional-district-2-race-election-result/1925988002/.

has diminished somewhat, the numbers remain impressive. In the U.S. House, incumbents were reelected at a 97 percent rate in 2016. Incumbents are only slightly more vulnerable in the U.S. Senate, where reelection rates have rarely dipped below 80 percent in recent elections and have reached as high as 96 percent (in 1990 and 2004). Reelection rates are similarly high for state and local lawmakers. A study of more than nine thousand mayoral races between 1950 and 2014 documented an 81 percent reelection rate for incumbents, who received an average of 65 percent of the vote (de Benedictis-Kessner 2018).

Incumbents tend to be favored for a variety of reasons. Legislators tend to vote in line with the majority of their constituents (Butler and Nickerson 2011), who reward them with their support. They are also rewarded for performing *casework*, the term used to describe the services provided by lawmakers to constituents who request assistance. Lawmakers' official duties give them numerous opportunities to use their personalized "home style" when they interact with their constituents (Fenno 1978). They publicize their governing work through local news media, who generally oblige with deferential coverage that can boost public support (Schaffner 2006)—a benefit that challengers usually do not enjoy. Incumbent lawmakers also raise significantly more money than challengers, giving them more funds to spend on paid media and fieldwork. Any of these advantages can be enough to scare off high-quality challengers who possess governing experience or other relevant qualifications (Ban, Llaudet, and Snyder 2016). Less important—although still a factor—is the reality that federal and state legislators tend to hold "safe" seats whose districts lines are drawn to favor either the incumbent or one party (Friedman and Holden 2009). In those cases, incumbents are more worried about a primary challenge from within their party than being defeated in the general election.

The high reelection rates are somewhat misleading. Sometimes lawmakers retire from office and decide against running for reelection when they think they might lose. These are what political scientists Gary Jacobson and Samuel Kernell call "strategic retirements" (Jacobson and Kernell 1981). Ahead of the 2018 midterm elections that favored Democrats overall, thirty-nine Republicans and only eighteen Democrats declined to seek reelection to the U.S. House or Senate. Twenty-six of those Republicans were "pure" retirements, meaning they were not leaving Congress to run for another office. Many retired to avoid the rigors of a competitive and a possible humiliating loss. Ileana Ros-Lehtinen, who represented Florida's

Twenty-Seventh Congressional District, had been reelected fifteen times, but she announced her retirement after Hillary Clinton garnered 20 percent more votes in her district than Donald Trump in 2016. Clinton also carried the district represented by Darrell Issa, who retired after barely winning his reelection bid in 2016. In both cases, a graceful exit was probably more appealing than losing a brutal race in an unfavorable electoral landscape for their party.

Indeed, sometimes incumbency is a disadvantage, or its advantages are diminished. Incumbents can get blamed for a poor economy or a failed policy initiative. During the 2010 midterms, for example, fifty-two House Democratic incumbents were swept away by a "Republican wave" fueled by discontent with the first two years of President Obama's first term (only two Republican incumbents lost their seats that year). Voters are sometimes restless for a change, resulting in slightly higher turnover than usual. In presidential elections, incumbents are at a slight disadvantage when their party has controlled the presidency for two consecutive terms (Abramowitz 2016). That hurt George H. W. Bush, whose 1992 reelection bid was also weakened by an economy that was struggling to recover from a recession. At the local and state level, incumbents can pay a price for dramatic increases in crime rates or visible declines in public school performance.

Sometimes the discontent stems from a national mood that favors outsider candidates who lack governing experience. That sentiment seems to ebb and flow with each election. Antiestablishment moods pose challenges to incumbents running for reelection or seeking higher office. In 2018, five Republicans who retired from the U.S. House to seek higher office ended up losing their primaries. That included four-term Congresswoman Diane Black, who gave up her chairmanship of the House Budget Committee to run for governor of Tennessee. Black was a formidable candidate who secured the endorsement of Vice President Mike Pence, but 2018 was a challenging year for many establishment candidates, and Black finished second behind a businessman with limited political experience.

What Do National Conditions Look Like?

Former Speaker of the House Tip O'Neill was famous for declaring that "all politics is local." The phrase was even the title of a book he authored. What he meant was that politicians do best when they understand and respond to the needs of their constituents. Successful candidates tailor their appeals to the particular and often localized concerns of the people they seek to represent. Even candidates for the U.S. House should be prepared to answer voters' questions about the local schools. But much has changed since O'Neill died in 1994. It remains true that constituent needs are paramount. What has changed is that their priorities are less local than they used to be. To some extent, all elections have become increasingly "nationalized." Assessing national conditions can help campaigns anticipate an electorate's priorities even at the state or local level.

It makes sense that presidential candidates would focus on national issues. There also is nothing new or troubling about U.S. Senate and House candidates being held accountable for their positions on national policy problems. After all, they hold federal offices. What has changed is how rarely voters press them on much else. State and local issues matter, but only when they can be related to national politics (Hopkins 2018). Even local candidates must respond to national concerns. Candidates for county sheriff might be pressed on how vigorously they would enforce immigration laws even if illegal immigrants are scarce in the county. Mayoral candidates might be asked about potential cuts to Medicare, a federal program. Under the Constitution, members of the U.S. House—where Tip O'Neill served for thirty-five years—are expected to respond to the localized priorities of the constituents in their geographically defined district. Yet when *Washington Post* reporters attended fourteen hours of public meetings hosted by congressional lawmakers in winter 2017, only 11 of the 160 constituent questions addressed purely local concerns (Kane 2017).

There are several reasons for this. As we will see in chapter 4, local newspapers are struggling as people get more and more of their news online and on cable television, where national news predominates. That means voters get plenty of news about President Trump and the U.S. Congress, but very little information that helps them cast votes in state and local elections. Political parties fit the same pattern. National party organizations now overshadow their state and local counterparts. Policy is set at the national level with very little variation across states. The policy platform of the Republican Party of South Carolina is not all that different from its equivalent in New Hampshire.

The nationalization of politics means that the electoral chances of all candidates—even for local offices—can be affected by national conditions. Early misgivings about the Affordable Care Act not only contributed to Democrats losing control of the U.S. House in 2010, but also spilled over into gubernatorial and state legislative races. Trump's unpopularity spurred progressives to organize resistance efforts even at the local level, leading to heavy Republican losses in 2017 and 2018. Republicans down to the state level paid a price in 2006 and 2008 for the failures of the war in Iraq. On the other hand, voters rallied behind President George W. Bush and his party in the wake of 9/11, leading to Republican gains in the 2002 midterm elections. A strong economy during Bill Clinton's presidency helped Democrats gain five House seats in 1998, offsetting the usual losses the president's party incurs during midterm elections.

Are Presidential Candidates on the Ballot?
If so, voter turnout will be relatively high. That is especially true if the candidate is running in a battleground state, which practically guarantees personal appearances by both presidential candidates along with heavy investments in paid media and field operations. About 60 percent of the voting eligible population votes in presidential elections, sometimes called *on-year* elections. By comparison, only about 40 percent of eligible voters participate in *midterm* or **off-year** elections, which happen every four years in the even-numbered years between presidential elections. Turnout is even lower for **odd-year** elections, which are held on odd years in between the mid-terms, and *special* elections, which are sometime held to fill vacancies when a lawmaker dies or resigns long before the general election.

The electorate for presidential years is not only larger but also broader. Some people vote only in presidential elections, and these voters tend to be less educated and less informed. They also tend to be less partisan, which means more voters are open to persuasion by the campaigns and more dependent on the campaigns' mobilization efforts. Campaigns for down-ballot candidates also must account for the reality that the presidential race will dominate the attention of media and most voters. All eyes are on the presidential campaign, sometimes to the detriment of crucial but less glamorous state, local, and legislative races.

With midterm elections, attention turns to races for House and Senate seats, and governorships. But even though the president is not on the ballot, midterms are often a referendum for the president currently holding office. The president's approval rating is a stronger predictor of the outcome than the state of the economy. Even with a strong economy, the president's party nearly always loses House and Senate seats during midterm elections. Political scientists call the phenomenon "surge and decline" (Campbell 1960). The party's fortunes surge during on-years when the president wins; it might gain seats in both chambers and pick up a few governorships. But decline occurs two years later when the president is no longer on the ballot and the inevitable disappointment in and backlash to the president's performance sets in. The losses can be heavy. During Obama's first term, Republicans gained sixty-three seats in the U.S. House, recapturing the majority. They also gained six Senate seats, 680 seats in state legislatures, and won twenty-nine of fifty governorships. For Democrats, the decline phase was enormous in 2010. It was not much better midway through Obama's second term, when Republicans made further gains in the House and gained control of the Senate despite a recovering economy. But then the pattern predictably reversed itself during Trump's first term: his party lost forty seats and control of the House in 2018 (for example, see box 1.2, "Small Victory").

Odd-year elections are similarly affected. This is when many local elections occur. Some states such as Virginia and New Jersey use odd years to elect statewide offices and their legislatures. Both states elect their governor one year after the presidential election. By then, disappointment in and backlash against the president has already set in. With one exception, the president's party has lost every Virginia gubernatorial race since 1977. In New Jersey, the president's party has lost every gubernatorial race since 1989. The president's party also tends to take a hit in both state's legislative bodies and other statewide offices. One year after Trump was elected president, Virginia Republicans not only lost all three statewide races but also lost fifteen seats in the House of Delegates and nearly lost the majority.

So, in a way, the president is always on the ballot, even when there is no presidential election. As elections have become increasingly nationalized, even state elections—and sometimes local races—can be referenda on the party in power and the issues they prioritize.

Who Else Is on the Ballot?
The presence of presidential candidates is not the only potentially consequential ballot variable. Each race on the ballot can be shaped by other races on the ballot. A competitive governor's race can boost turnout among supporters of both sides, increasing the number of votes cast for obscure races down the ballot. A lackluster candidate at the top of the ballot can depress turnout on one side, hurting the chances of down-ballot candidates from the same party. An inspiring candidate can have the opposite effect.

Controversial ballot measures can also be impactful. A ballot measure is a piece of legislation that is placed on a ballot to be approved or rejected by voters rather than by elected lawmakers. In 2004, eleven states voted on ballot measures banning same-sex marriage. All eleven passed with an average of 70 percent of voters supporting the measures. Ohio Republicans credited its state's same-sex marriage ballot measure for mobilizing religious conservatives to the polls, helping George W. Bush win the state by a narrow margin (Dao 2004). Subsequent analysis suggests it was more complicated than that, although there appeared to be a strong relationship between support for the measure and voting for Bush (Smith, DeSantis, and Kassel 2006).

Is There a Minor-Party or Independent Candidate on the Ballot?

Independent or minor-party candidates rarely win, but they can influence the outcome of any race. It is common for a general election ballot to list at least a few candidates from neither the Republican nor Democratic party. Some are independent candidates who run on their own without the support of a party. Others secure the nomination of a party other than the two major parties. These are commonly called "third-party" candidates. On the right side of the political spectrum, nineteen Libertarian Party candidates appeared on a general election ballot for the New Hampshire House of Representatives in 2018. On the left, the Green Party had nine candidates running for U.S. House seats in California. Although wins are rare, there are exceptions. Bernie Sanders ran for president as a Democrat and caucuses with Democrats in the Senate, but he has served in Congress as an independent since first being elected to the U.S. House in 1990. The Green Party claimed it had sixty-eight officeholders in California in 2018. The Libertarians claimed it had 186 officeholders nationwide.

Although third-party candidates rarely win, they can siphon off voters from one side over the other. This happened in 2000, when Ralph Nader appeared on the ballot in forty-three states as a Green Party candidate for the presidency. When Al Gore narrowly lost the race to George W. Bush, Democrats accused Nader of "spoiling" the race for Gore by peeling away support from left-leaning voters. Did Nader cost Gore the election? On the one hand, exit polls did show that 47 percent of Nader voters would have voted for Gore if Nader were not on the ballot, whereas only 21 percent would have voted for Bush. In Florida—a state with enough electoral votes to swing the election either way—Nader won nearly one hundred thousand votes, and Gore lost the state by only 537 votes. On the other hand, it is likely that many of Nader's supporters would have stayed home had he not appeared on the ballot (Southwell 2004). Others may have supported another minor party candidate—for example, Pat Buchanan, the similarly famous Reform Party nominee, who secured about seventeen thousand votes in Florida. According to one study, a surprising 40 percent of Nader voters in Florida would have chosen Bush over Gore (Herron and Lewis 2007).

Questions about possible "spoiler" candidates also surrounded the 1994 U.S. Senate race in Virginia. The 1994 landscape strongly favored Republican candidates due to "surge and decline": Bill Clinton was two years into his first term, and indeed his party went on to lose fifty-four seats in the House and eight in the Senate. But the Democrats did not lose Virginia. Incumbent Democrat Chuck Robb fought off a well-funded challenge from Republican Oliver North that garnered national media attention. Both candidates had major weaknesses. Not only was Robb a Democrat running in a Republican year, but he had been accused of attending parties with drug users and having an extramarital affair with a former Miss Virginia USA. North had been convicted of felony charges for his role in the Iran–Contra affair. But North was a more polarizing figure. Fellow Republican Senator John Warner openly opposed him, eventually endorsing Marshall Coleman, a centrist Republican who was running as an independent candidate. Coleman ended up with 11.4 percent of the vote, and North lost by only 2.7 points. Robb might have lost had a second independent candidate stayed in the race: Doug Wilder, a fellow Democrat, a bitter political rival, and a former governor—the first African American governor since Reconstruction. But Wilder dropped out and urged his supporters to vote for Robb. Enough of them did.

It would be stretch to conclude that Coleman cost North the Senate seat in 1994 or that Nader cost Gore the presidency in 2000. Ditto for the possible damage Green candidate Jill Stein inflicted on Hillary Clinton's chances in 2016 (Stein won 1 percent of the national popular vote). But it is safe to say that their major-party opponents had to account for their presence in the race. For example, both Coleman and Wilder were allowed to participate in televised debates, and Wilder's performance seemed to rattle both Robb and North during at least one of the debates. Independent and minor-party candidates can siphon off not only would-be supporters from the same end of the political spectrum but also possible volunteers. They make major-party candidates nervous about possible "spoiler" effects.

They can energize otherwise disenfranchised citizens to cast aside their misgivings and cast a vote. Their ultimate impact may be minimal, but their potential consequences are impossible for opposing campaigns to ignore.

How Do Voters Cast Their Ballots?

Part of the landscape consists of state-specific voter registration and other requirements. All states except North Dakota require that people register to vote before they cast a ballot. The registration requirement can be a significant barrier to voting in states that require people to register two to four weeks before an election. Some eligible voters fail to meet the deadline, which means they will either stay home or be turned away if they try to vote. Some states allow voters who have moved to update their registration address when they show up to vote. Eighteen states and the District of Columbia have lowered this barrier even further through *same-day* or *Election Day registration* (EDR). As the name suggests, EDR allows residents to register when they vote. Studies show that the EDR has a positive impact on turnout (Burden et al. 2014; Brians and Grofman 2001). Turnout is also higher in the three states—Oregon, Washington, and Colorado—where elections are conducted entirely by mail. In all three states, ballots are mailed automatically to all eligible voters, who must return them by mail or deliver them in person. Reforms such as EDR and vote-by-mail seem to have had the intended effect of boosting turnout. Campaigns run in these states know to account for this.

Another practice aimed at making voting easier has actually diminished participation. Some form of *early voting* is allowed in thirty-three states and the District of Columbia. Early voting permits voters to cast ballots prior to Election Day without an excuse. Some states make early voting easy by setting up voting locations in shopping malls and libraries. Others allow early voting on weekends. Early voting made up 30 percent of all votes in 2012. Yet the practice seems to merely make voting more convenient for existing regular voters without stimulating new voters. Early voting diminishes the energy surrounding the practice of voting. "Rather than building up to a frenzied Election Day in which media coverage and interpersonal conversations revolve around politics, early voting makes voting a more private and less intense process." EDR, by contrast, "keeps the focus of social and political activity on a single day" (Burden et al. 2014: 98).

Other states have deliberately made voting more difficult. Twelve states require voters to show their driver's license or a similar form of official identification before casting a ballot. Residents in these states who lack an acceptable form of identification are either turned away at the polls or discouraged from showing up in the first place. Many of these laws are new, and some are tied up in the courts. It remains to be seen whether voter identification laws significantly depress turnout (Highton 2017), but it would surprise no one if it does.

CONCLUSION

Campaigns have no control over the landscape. All they can do is manage it. They can adjust their strategies and modify their tactics to account for the fundamentals that will barely budge during the race. For the most part, the landscape is made up of "givens" that may not change at all. When the landscape is favorable to their candidate, the campaign can build on its intrinsic advantages. A poor landscape is something to overcome, but not alter.

A Republican campaign running in a D+10 congressional district faces an uphill climb no matter how much money it raises and ads it runs on television. Ditto for a legislative candidate from the president's party running in a swing district during a midterm election. A sour national mood can diminish the advantages usually enjoyed by incumbents. Challengers are buoyed when voters are eager for change. The presence of a strong third-party contender from the left wing of the Democratic party can boost the Republican candidate. Strict voting procedures such as requiring government-issued photo IDs can hinder Democrat's voter mobilization efforts. Same-day registration can help. No matter what the campaigns do, turnout will be frustratingly low for primary elections and elections with no presidential candidates on the ballot. The electorate will also be more partisan than it is for presidential elections despite efforts to mobilize centrists.

The intractability of the electoral landscape is humbling for campaigns. Consistent with the theme of this book, much of what happens during the course of an election is out of the campaigns' hands. Their job is often more about managing the chaos than taking control. The remaining chapters are aimed at helping readers understand how campaigns adapt to the landscape they are given.

KEY TERMS

caucus: a local meeting that party members attend to vote on party nominees.

convention: a large gathering of party members who choose the party's nominees and determine its policy platform.

incumbent: an elected official who is running for reelection.

odd-year election: a general election held in a year ending with an odd number (e.g., 2021)—in between elections when presidential elections are on the ballot and midterm elections for U.S. Senate and congressional seats.

off-year election: a general election during which U.S. Senate and congressional candidates are at the top of the ballot. Also known as a *midterm* election.

party lean: a measurement of one party's advantage over the other in a state, congressional district, or other geographic area.

primary: An election to determine a party's nominees for various offices.

DISCUSSION QUESTIONS

1. If election outcomes are often so predictable, why bother campaigning?
2. What explains the "surge and decline" phenomenon? Why does the president's party so often lose seats in Congress, state legislatures, and governorships?
3. Although incumbents tend to win when they decide to run for reelection, the advantages of incumbency are not what they used to be. What has changed? Why are incumbents more vulnerable than they were ten years ago?
4. The election of Donald Trump challenges the theory that "the party decides" who its nominees will be. How did Trump win the nomination in the face of strong misgivings among many Republican officials?

RECOMMENDED READINGS

Hassell, Hans J. G. 2015. "Party Control of Party Primaries: Party Influence in Nominations for the US Senate." *Journal of Politics* 78, no. 1: 75–87.

Complementing Cohen et al.'s The Party Decides, *this article analyzes the extent to which party elites shape the field of primary candidates running for the U.S. Senate. Candidates who fail to secure party support tend to drop out. Those who stay in the race tend to lose.*

Henderson, Michael, D. Sunshine Hillygus, and Trevor Tompson. 2010. "'Sour Grapes' or Rational Voting? Voter Decision Making among Thwarted Primary Voters in 2008." *Public Opinion Quarterly* 74, no. 3: 499–529.

What happens to voters who support a losing candidate in a competitive primary? Do they vote for their party's nominee in the general election? If not, why? Using the 2008 election as the context, this study confirms that most thwarted partisans eventually "come home" and vote along party lines in November. When they don't, it is not due to "sour grapes" about losing the primary but instead because they disagreed with the nominee on a major policy issue.

Hopkins, Daniel J. 2018. *The Increasingly United States: How and Why American Political Behavior Nationalized*. Chicago: University of Chicago Press.

This book challenges the notion that "all politics is local." Hopkins explains how and why American politics has become more nationalized. Candidates running for state-level offices must grapple with the same policy issues as their federal counterparts. Voters assess state-level candidates through a national lens. One explanation is shifting media consumption patterns. People are less likely to get their news from local newspapers and local television broadcasts, instead tuning in to national outlets online and on cable television, where national news naturally prevails.

REFERENCES

Abramowitz, Alan I. 2016. "Forecasting the 2016 Election: Will Time for Change Mean Time for Trump?" *Sabato's Crystal Ball* (Aug. 11): http://www.centerforpolitics.org/crystalball/articles/forecasting-the-2016-presidential-election-will-time-for-change-mean-time-for-trump/.

Alberta, Tim. 2019. *American Carnage: On the Front Lines of the Republican Civil War and the Rise of President Trump*. New York: HarperCollins.

Atkeson, Lonna Rae. 1998. "Divisive Primaries and General Election Outcomes: Another Look at Presidential Campaigns." *American Journal of Political Science* 42, no. 1: 256–71.

Ban, Pamela, Elena Llaudet, and James M. Snyder. 2016. "Challenger Quality and the Incumbency Advantage." *Legislative Studies Quarterly* 41, no. 1: 153–79.

Bawn, Kathleen, Martin Cohen, David Karol, Seth Masket, Hans Noel, and John Zaller. 2012. "A Theory of Political Parties: Groups, Policy Demands and Nominations in American Politics." *Perspectives on Politics* 10, no. 3: 571–97.

Brians, Craig Leonard, and Bernard Grofman. 2001. "Election Day Registration's Effect on U.S. Voter Turnout." *Social Science Quarterly* 82, no. 1: 170–83.

Broockman, David E. 2014. "Mobilizing Candidates: Political Actors Strategically Shape the Candidate Pool with Personal Appeals." *Journal of Experimental Political Science* 1: 104–19.

Burden, Barry C., David T. Canon, Kenneth R. Mayer, and Donald P. Moynihan. 2014. "Election Laws, Mobilization, and Turnout: The Unanticipated Consequences of Election Reform." *American Journal of Political Science* 58, no. 1: 95–109.

Butler, Daniel M., and David W. Nickerson. 2011. "Can Learning Constituency Opinion Affect How Legislators Vote? Results from a Field Experiment." *Quarterly Journal of Political Science* 6: 55–83.

Campbell, Angus. 1960. "Surge and Decline: A Study of Electoral Change." *Public Opinion Quarterly* 24, no. 3: 397–418.

Cohen, Marty, David Karol, Hans Noel, and John Zaller. 2008. *The Party Decides: Presidential Nominations before and after Reform.* Chicago: University of Chicago Press.

Conroy, Meredith, Nathaniel Rakich, and Mai Nguyen. 2018. "We Looked at Hundreds of Endorsements. Here's Who Democrats Are Listening To." *FiveThirtyEight* (Aug. 14): https://fivethirtyeight.com/features/the-establishment-is-beating-the-progressive-wing-in-democratic-primaries-so-far/.

Dao, James. 2004. "Same-Sex Marriage Issue Key to Some G.O.P. Races." *New York Times* (Nov. 4): https://www.nytimes.com/2004/11/04/politics/campaign/samesex-marriage-issue-key-to-some-gop-races.html.

de Benedictis-Kessner, Justin. 2018. "Off-Cycle and Out of Office: Election Timing and the Incumbency Advantage." *Journal of Politics* 80, no. 1: 119–32.

Fenno, Richard. 1978. *Home Style: House Members in Their Districts.* New York: Longman.

Friedman, John N., and Richard T. Holden. 2009. "The Rising Incumbent Reelection Rate: What's Gerrymandering Got to Do with It?" *Journal of Politics* 71, no, 2: 593–611.

Griggs, Troy, and Adam Pearce. 2018. "These 20 Representatives Have Not Had a Primary Challenge for at Least a Decade." *New York Times* (June 30): https://www.nytimes.com/interactive/2018/06/30/us/elections/representatives-running-unopposed-uncontested-primaries.html.

Hassell, Hans J. G. 2015. "Party Control of Party Primaries: Party Influence in Nominations for the US Senate." *Journal of Politics* 78, no. 1: 75–87.

Henderson, Michael. 2015. "Finding the Way Home: The Dynamics of Partisan Support in Presidential Campaigns." *Political Behavior* 37: 889–910.

Henderson, Michael, D. Sunshine Hillygus, and Trevor Tompson. 2010. "'Sour Grapes' or Rational Voting? Voter Decision Making among Thwarted Primary Voters in 2008." *Public Opinion Quarterly* 74, no. 3: 499–529.

Herron, Michael C., and Jeffrey B. Lewis. 2007. "Did Ralph Nader Spoil Al Gore's Presidential Bid?" *Quarterly Journal of Political Science* 2, no. 3: 205–26.

Hersh, Eitan. 2015. "Data Availability Determines Whether Campaigns Focus on Middle or the Base." *FiveThirtyEight* (Aug. 10): https://fivethirtyeight.com/features/data-availability-determines-whether-campaigns-focus-on-the-middle-or-the-base/.

Highton, Benjamin. 2017. "Voter Identification Laws and Turnout in the United States." *Annual Review of Political Science* 20: 149–67.

Hopkins, Daniel J. 2018. *The Increasingly United States: How and Why American Political Behavior Nationalized.* Chicago: University of Chicago Press.

Jacobson, Gary, and Samuel Kernell. 1981. *Strategy and Choice in Congressional Elections.* New Haven, CT: Yale University Press.

Kane, Paul. 2017. "All Politics Is Local? In the Era of Trump, Not Anymore." *Washington Post* (Feb. 25): https://www.washingtonpost.com/powerpost/all-politics-is-local-in-the-era-of-trump-not-anymore/2017/02/25/9a15bc94-fab2-11e6-9845-576c69081518_story.html?utm_term=.4b39eed7bb49.

Kaufmann, Karen M., James G. Gimpel, and Adam H. Hoffman. 2003. "A Promise Fulfilled? Open Primaries and Representation." *Journal of Politics* 65, no. 2: 457–76.

Masket, Seth E. 2009. *No Middle Ground: How Informal Party Organizations Control Nominations and Polarize Legislatures.* Ann Arbor: University of Michigan Press.

Niven, David. 2006. "Throwing Your Hat Out of the Ring: Negative Recruitment and the Gender Imbalance in State Legislative Candidacy." *Politics & Gender* 2, no. 4: 473–89.

Schaffner, Brian F. 2006. "Local News Coverage and the Incumbency Advantage in the U.S. House." *Legislative Studies Quarterly* 31, no. 4: 491–511.

Sides, John. 2017. "Did Enough Bernie Sanders Supporters Vote for Trump to Cost Clinton the Election?" *Washington Post* (Aug. 24): https://www.washingtonpost.com/news/monkey-cage/wp/2017/08/24/did-enough-bernie-sanders-supporters-vote-for-trump-to-cost-clinton-the-election/?utm_term=.66231f3a94df.

Smith, Daniel A., Matthew DeSantis, and Jason Kassel. 2006. "Same-Sex Marriage Ballot Measures and the 2004 Presidential Election." *State and Local Government Review* 38, no. 2: 78–91.

Southwell, Priscilla L. 2004. "Nader Voters in the 2000 Presidential Election: What Would We Have Done without Him?" *Social Science Quarterly* 41, no. 3: 423–31.

2

Targeting, Persuasion, and Mobilization

★ ★ ★

Danica Roem canvasses a Manassas, Virginia, neighborhood shortly after securing the Democratic nomination for the House of Delegates' 13th district
seat. Roem was the first openly transgender person elected to the Virginia
General Assembly. *Source*: *AP Photo/Steve Helber*

LEARNING OBJECTIVES

★ Recognize the distinction between attempts to
  persuade voters versus efforts to *mobilize* them.

★ Comprehend how partisanship and motivated reasoning inhibit efforts to persuade voters.

★ Understand the differences between microtargeting and macrotargeting.

★ Grapple with the implications of targeting practices for democracy.

THIS WAS THE PLAN: Hillary Clinton would win the presidency mostly by mobilizing likely supporters to the polls. Her 2016 campaign would target likely Clinton voters with mobilization messages aimed at boosting turnout among Democrats and Democratic-leaning independents. The campaign had assessed the landscape and concluded that nearly all likely voters had made up their minds about these two widely disliked candidates; changing their minds would be fruitless. Attempts to persuade people would be limited to certain groups of voters—for example, Republican and independent women, who would be targeted with messages aimed at priming their misgivings about Donald Trump's misogynistic behavior (Roarty 2017).

The Clinton campaign's decision to prioritize mobilization over persuasion reflected established assumptions among both practitioners and scholars. It was not controversial at the time. As we saw in the previous chapter, partisans tend to support their party's presidential nominee no matter what. And as we will see in this chapter, *persuading* voters to change their minds is much more difficult than *mobilizing* people who are already inclined to support you. By contrast, the Trump campaign had no choice but to invest in persuasion. Persuasion provided the only path to victory partly because both the campaign and the Republican Party had underinvested in the fieldwork necessary for a mobilization-centered strategy. Its persuasion efforts targeted weak Democrats with messages focusing on such issues as Trump's promise to create manufacturing jobs. The Trump campaign's assumption was that a persuasion-centered campaign could win battleground states with large numbers of white working-class voters who usually voted for Democratic candidates. Trump eventually won the election for a host of reasons, but his shocking upsets in Democratic-leaning Pennsylvania, Michigan, and Wisconsin were what sealed Trump's victory in the Electoral College.

This chapter will introduce readers to three key campaign-related concepts embedded in the scenario described above: persuasion, mobilization, and targeting. In different ways, all three concepts underlay nearly every aspect of campaign communication. Campaign practitioners regularly employ all three terms when they discuss their strategic decision-making. A great deal of academic research tests the effectiveness of campaigns' efforts on all three fronts. It is thus crucial for readers to understand what these concepts mean and how campaigns apply them. The terms will be used frequently throughout the rest of the book.

PERSUASION AND MOBILIZATION

As we will see later in this chapter, successful targeting entails sending the right message to the right voter. Sometimes the targeting is based on group identity, such as when Democrats target nonwhite Americans and Republicans target evangelicals. Other times it centers on policy, such as when a progressive candidate targets college students with messages touting their opponent's opposition to same-sex marriage. Broadly speaking, however, the objectives of targeting are either persuasion or mobilization. To win, the campaign must *persuade* at least some *uncommitted* voters to support their candidate and (most importantly) *mobilize* likely *supporters* to act on their inclination by casting a vote. Understanding these two concepts is crucial to assessing campaign strategy.

Persuasion

Persuasion is the process of changing a voter's mind. That could mean convincing a voter to switch from candidate A to candidate B—a form of persuasion known as conversion. Conversion usually entails luring a partisan away from their predisposition to support the opposing party's candidate. But because conversion is so difficult, campaigns tend to focus their persuasion efforts on convincing undecided voters to support their candidate.

Undecided voters are on the fence for a variety of reasons. For one, they might lack the **party identification** most voters possess to help make sense out of their choices. Party identification is the term political scientists use to describe voters' sense of connection with a political party. It is a loose psychological tie that does not imply formal membership in a party organization. Yet, as we saw in chapter 2, "party ID" is a remarkably robust predictor of vote choice. Two-thirds of registered voters are loyal partisans who nearly always vote for their party's candidate. The percentage of "standpatters"—regular voters who always support their party—is at an all-time high. Even independents and disengaged citizens tend to vote consistently for one party over the other (Smidt 2015). Yet even in today's hyperpartisan political climate, some voters have no meaningful party attachments, depriving them of the informational and decision-making shortcut that partisanship can provide. These voters make up a significant percentage of the undecided electorate. They are up for grabs and therefore susceptible to persuasion.

Traditionally, party identification is measured by asking individuals whether they consider themselves a Democrat, Republican, or independent. The self-identified Democrats and Republicans are then asked whether their partisanship is strong or weak. The independents are asked whether they lean toward either of the two major parties, and most of them will choose one of the two. These "leaners" aren't really independents—they are just as likely as weak partisans to vote for their party's candidate. The remaining 6 to 8 percent of independents lean toward neither of the two major parties. That makes them susceptible to *accepting* a campaign's persuasion messaging. But this is true only if they get the message: because pure independents tend to be less interested in politics than partisans and leaners, they also are unlikely to *receive* a campaign's messaging. That is because they tend to consume less political news and are more likely to tune out campaign advertising than their more partisan counterparts (Zaller 1992).

By contrast, partisans tend to be highly engaged news junkies and therefore more likely to receive campaign messaging. But because their views are more entrenched, they are less susceptible to persuasion. That does not mean persuasion is impossible. They can be converted to vote against their party preference in order to support an incumbent they admire. They also can be persuaded to defect if they disagree with their party's nominee on an issue they care about (Hillygus and Shields 2008). In other words, some voters are undecided about their vote choice not because they lack strong party ties, but rather because there is something they dislike about their own party's nominee. Campaigns are thus incentivized to gear conversion efforts toward people who identify with the other party but are torn about which candidate to support. At the same time, campaigns also engage in **activation** efforts to prevent defections from undecided voters who identify with their party and who might vote for the other candidate—in other words, voters who could be converted by the opposing campaign. In 2016, the Clinton campaign targeted Republican women with messages highlighting Trump's misogynistic statements and behavior. These efforts largely failed: exit polls revealed that 88 percent of Republican women voted for Trump, a level of party loyalty comparable with 2012 when Mitt Romney was the Republican nominee.

Research on the psychological process of **motivated reasoning** sheds light on why partisans rarely defect (or, why conversion is so rare). We would like to think that when voters encounter new information about a candidate—through a news story, for example—they will efficiently update their evaluation of the candidate in response to the new information. There is plenty of evidence suggesting that people do assimilate information in this manner (Gerber and Green 1999). However, according to an opposing school of thought, such rational and unbiased information processing and evaluation rarely happen. That is partly because most people already possess entrenched positive or negative assessments of the candidates and process new information accordingly. Voters tend to cling to their original assessment, no matter what they read, hear, or see. They do so by either explaining away the new incongruent information, counterarguing with it, discounting it, or simply ignoring it altogether.

Through motivated reasoning, people actively process and assess information in ways that confirm their existing beliefs rather than challenge them (Kunda 1990; Redlawsk 2002; Taber and Lodge 2006). Negative information about a candidate is seen as a threat to the convictions of the people who support the candidate. Supporters are likely to argue against the threatening information, "bolstering their existing evaluation by recalling all the good things about a liked candidate even in the face of something negative" (Redlawsk, Civettini, and Emerson 2010: 567). Thus, a campaign's effort to attack its opponent—through an attack ad, for example—can have a boomerang effect among supporters of the attack's target. Rather than converting them, the attack message pushes supporters back toward the candidate they are inclined to vote for anyway. Motivated reasoning also explains why supporters rally behind a candidate treated harshly in a news story rather than shift their allegiances. When the press hammered Trump during the fall 2016 general election campaign, for example, Republicans didn't defect to Clinton; most rallied behind him.

Mobilization

Clearly, persuasion efforts centered on converting partisans to switch sides can be both fruitless and fraught with peril. And persuasion efforts aimed at undecided Americans sometimes fail because these voters are so often tuned out. As a result, campaigns and political parties often focus their resources on mobilizing their "base"—likely supporters—to vote. **Mobilization** is the primary function of what practitioners call GOTV—short for "Get Out the Vote." Mobilization efforts are important because so many eligible voters otherwise fail to participate. About 40 percent of eligible voters did not cast a ballot in the 2016 election—about the same as 2012 and 2008. Turnout is even lower for elections that lack presidential candidates at the top of the ballot. Boosting turnout among supporters who otherwise might not participate can thus be decisive.

Regular voters can be counted on to participate in nearly every election—midterms, primaries, and even special and odd-year elections. For regular voters, campaigns must simply identify which ones are their supporters and reinforce that inclination. But low-propensity or *marginal voters*—people whose decision to participate is influenced by external factors—must be mobilized by the campaigns, political parties, or outside groups. Numerous studies have demonstrated the positive impact of mobilization efforts on voter turnout (Rosenstone and Hansen 1993), especially those that entail personalized, face-to-face interaction with individual voters (e.g., Gerber and Green 2000). Personalized phone calls by volunteers also help (Nickerson 2006)—more so than impersonal robocalls. Campaigns have learned that marginal voters respond to personally delivered messages that emphasize what is at stake and the importance of their individual participation. But relatively impersonal approaches such as text messaging also can help mobilize (Dale and Strauss 2009). Even door hangers reminding people where to vote can boost turnout by a percentage point or two (Nickerson 2005).

As campaigns have embraced mobilization-centered strategies, concerns have emerged about how their efforts may be widening disparities in participation. As we will see in the "ground game" chapter (chapter 7), mobilization strategies are most effective with people who already vote regularly. High-propensity voters just need an extra nudge, and that is what typical mobilization strategies do. Conventional mobilization can also prod certain low-propensity voters during high-turnout elections such as presidential races (Arceneaux and Nickerson 2009). A low-propensity voter who has participated in past elections can also be responsive, as can newly registered voters (Alvarez, Hopkins, and Sinclair 2010). Low-income voters can be activated and mobilized if they live in a battleground state (Gimpel, Kaufmann, and Pearson-Merkowitz 2007). But chronic nonvoters are otherwise hard to reach. Many have not registered to vote. Many pay scant attention to current events. They probably will not answer when a canvasser calls or knocks on door. And when they do, they are less likely than high-propensity voters to resonate with conventional get-out-the-vote messaging, which taps an individual's sense of civic duty. Conventional mobilization efforts do not connect with many of these citizens, who are more likely to be nonwhite and have lower levels of education. Campaigns that tout their turnout practices need to realize that they may be unintentionally aggravating inequalities in political representation (Enos, Fowler, and Vavreck 2014).

Persuasion versus Mobilization
Influenced by this scholarly work and enabled by technological advances, recent presidential campaigns have emphasized mobilization over persuasion. That was the case with the 2012 campaign between Barack Obama and Mitt Romney, which was considered a "base-driven" election because so few voters were undecided (i.e., persuadable). In 2004, the George W. Bush reelection campaign emphasized mobilization over persuasion because voters' opinions toward the president had become so entrenched by the end of his first term. (See box 2.1, "Bush's Base Strategy.") As we saw in the introduction, Hillary Clinton's 2016 campaign emphasized mobilization over persuasion. Both she and Trump were both famous and disliked, leaving very little room for changing minds.

BOX 2.1 | Bush's Base Strategy

When a campaign employs a "base strategy," that means they focus their resources on *mobilizing* likely supporters rather than *persuading* undecided or uncommitted voters. The term was popularized in the wake of George W. Bush's 2004 reelection victory over John Kerry. Bush narrowly defeated Kerry despite weak economic growth and the increasingly unpopular war in Iraq.

The Bush campaign embraced the base strategy because winning would be difficult otherwise. By its calculations, the number of persuadable voters had declined to only 7 percent of the electorate compared with 22 percent two decades earlier. Opposition to Bush had hardened among Democrats. "Pure" independents who leaned toward neither party were split and could not be counted on to vote anyway. Bush could win by mobilizing the millions of people identified as likely supporters but who failed to vote in 2000. His campaign's primary targets were the four million evangelical Christians who were irregular voters. It also macrotargeted precincts and counties that voted overwhelmingly Republican but

BOX 2.1 | (continued)

had a high number of people who could not be counted on to show up on Election Day. In various ways, the campaign's base messaging centered on reminding conservatives why their vote was so important in this particular election. Its self-described "72-Hour Task Force" used the final three days of the election to turn out likely supporters through face-to-face canvassing.

Persuasion was also part of the plan—just a smaller part than usual. "We didn't say, 'Base motivation is what we're going to do, and that's all we're doing,'" said chief campaign strategist Matthew Dowd. "We said, 'Both are important, but we shouldn't be putting 80 percent of our resources into persuasion and 20 percent into base motivation,' which is basically what had been happening up until that point." The decision to instead focus on mobilization "influenced everything that we did," Dowd said. "It influenced how we targeted mail, how we targeted phones, how we targeted media, how we traveled, the travel that the president and the vice president did to certain areas, how we did organization, where we had staff" (Frontline 2005).

Four years earlier, Democrats outnumbered Republicans in the electorate by about three percentage points, according to exit polls. In assessing the effectiveness of its base strategy, the Bush campaign's measure of success was whether self-identified Republicans equaled the number of self-identified Democrats in the electorate. Exit polls indicated that it met that goal: 37 percent of the 2004 electorate labeled themselves as Republicans and 37 percent as Democrats. An impressive 93 percent of Republicans voted for Bush compared with 89 percent of Democrats for Kerry. Self-identified independents evenly split their vote between the two. Bush won the election.

SOURCES

Cook, Charlie. 2001. "Is Obama Copying Bush's 2004 Re-Election Strategy?" *The Atlantic* (Sept. 30): https://www.theatlantic.com/politics/archive/2011/09/is-obama-copying-bushs-2004-re-election-strategy/245955/.

Frontline. 2005. "Interview: Matthew Dowd." *Karl Rove—The Architect*, https://www.pbs.org/wgbh/pages/frontline/shows/architect/interviews/dowd.html.

Persuasion is more important with nonpresidential campaigns. Voters are less familiar with the candidates running for Congress, governor, state legislatures, and local offices—especially candidates who are challenging incumbent officeholders. Opinions toward the candidates tend to be less entrenched and therefore more subject to change. That was the case for Democrat Terry McAuliffe when he ran for governor of Virginia in 2013. His team's persuasion strategy was to "win the middle" by defining his Republican opponent Ken Cuccinelli as an ideological extremist. McAuliffe outraised his opponent by $15 million, an advantage that enabled generous investment in persuasion-centered television and digital advertising. Mobilization was even trickier: the election took place one year after Obama's reelection, and the president's party usually loses these odd-year elections partly due to depressed turnout among its supporters. Anticipating this problem, the McAuliffe campaign enlisted thirteen thousand volunteers to mobilize Democrats who had voted in the previous odd-year election in 2009 but otherwise might not show up for McAuliffe. The campaign used computer modeling to create "heat maps" showing where mobilization efforts should be intensified. It opened field offices in places where volunteers and likely supporters were located. Volunteer canvassers asked voters to complete postcards pledging to vote in November, and then mailed them back the postcards as reminders shortly before the election. McAuliffe won by 2.5 percentage points (Burns 2013).

Both persuasion and mobilization were also apparent during the June 2017 special election to replace Tom Price, whose congressional seat was vacated when Trump appointed him to serve as U.S. secretary of health and human services. Price's affluent suburban Atlanta district leaned Republican, but Trump had won just 48 percent of voters in 2016 compared with the 61 percent Romney secured four years earlier. Democrats seized on the chance to pick up a Republican seat. The first step was the April 18 "jungle primary," for which all candidates from both parties appeared on the same ballot in April. The top two vote getters—Democrat Jon Ossoff and Republican Karen Handel—then faced off in a runoff election in June. Turnout for special elections tends to be very low. But this race was seen as a referendum on the early Trump presidency, and it attracted national attention as well as an astonishing amount of money; it became the most expensive U.S. House race in history, with the candidates and outside groups spending about $55 million.

Ossoff led for much of the race as his campaign seized upon anti-Trump sentiment and galvanized Democrats and independents who had turned against the president. The Handel campaign had to mobilize a Republican electorate consisting of a growing number of

Table 2.1 Persuasion versus Mobilization Tools

Persuasion Tools	Mobilization Tools
Advertising	Door-to-door canvassing
News coverage	Phone canvassing
Social media posts	Direct mail
Direct mail	Text messages
Door-to-door canvassing	Rallies and other candidate appearances

demoralized conservatives. To boost GOP turnout, a group aligned with House Speaker Paul Ryan hired 135 field operators to canvass about thirty-eight thousand Republicans who voted in the 2016 presidential primary but did not turn out for the jungle primary five months later. Mobilizing these particular marginal voters helped Republicans hold the seat (Hohman 2017). Handel won by about ten thousand votes. Both campaigns exceeded their turnout goals, but Republican participation was surprisingly high given what appeared to be a demoralized GOP electorate (Shepard 2017).

In the end, Handel's victory illustrated the limits of persuasion and the importance of the fundamentals discussed in chapter 1, particularly the partisanship of the district. Georgia's Sixth Congressional District leans heavily Republican: although Trump won the district by only 1.5 percentage points, Price won reelection by 24 points, and 1979 was the last time a Democrat had held the seat. To win, Ossoff would have had to persuade Republican voters to defect. Few of them did. He attempted to do so by cautiously presenting himself as a bland, nonobjectionable moderate. That approach didn't resonate with targeted Republicans, who stood by their party's nominee and were mobilized to turn out for Handel in droves (see table 2.1 for a comparison of persuasion and mobilization tools).

TARGETING

Advances in information technology have improved the ability of campaigns to target individual voters with customized messages. Campaigns now have access to data that help estimate each voter's candidate preference and the likelihood that the voter will volunteer, contribute money, and turn out to participate in the election. Campaigns also have at their disposal a wide array of outlets for sending microtargeted—that is, individualized—messages to the right people.

These advances should enable campaigns to achieve what they have long sought to do: aim *persuasion* messages at prospective voters who haven't made up their minds and target firm supporters who might need encouragement with *mobilization* efforts. Through *targeting*, campaigns aim to connect with key voters while reducing wasteful outreach to people who either don't need it, wouldn't respond to it, or wouldn't like it.

Macro versus Micro

Targeting is the term used to describe the campaign strategies and practices aimed at sending particular messages to particular voters. Practitioners and scholars sometimes distinguish between macrotargeting and microtargeting. **Macrotargeting** is targeting based on the aggregate characteristics and interests of particular groups of people: the population of a state, congressional district, neighborhood, or precinct, for example; an audience for a specific television program or cable channel; or an ethnic group or gender identity. When presidential campaigns focus their resources on battleground states (sometimes called "swing" states because they tend to swing back and forth between the two parties from election to election), they are engaging in a form of macrotargeting because they are focusing their efforts on certain groups of voters (battleground state residents) at the expense of others (residents of states that vote reliably for one party over the other). The national party committees are doing a form of macrotargeting when they send prominent campaign consultants, campaign staff, and TV spots to winnable congressional races while ignoring those that appear to be lost causes. Running a pro-Republican advertisement on a cable television program that attracts conservative audience members is another example of macrotargeting.

Microtargeting is more precise than macrotargeting because it is based on the known or predicted characteristics of individuals rather than a group of individuals. It entails sending a narrow message to an individual voter based on these characteristics. For example, a Republican campaign might microtarget persuasion messages to a specific person who has been identified as a weak Democrat but who supports Republican positions on an issue that is important to her or him. A Democratic campaign might microtarget mobilization messages to a registered Democrat who regularly participates in presidential elections but did not vote in the most recent midterm election. Individualized microtargeted messages can be delivered in person, by mail, on the phone, or online (see table 2.2 for a comparison of macro- and micro-targeting outlets).

Table 2.2 Macrotargeting versus Microtargeting Outlets

Macrotargeting	Micro-targeting
Television advertising	Digital advertising
Precinct or neighborhood-based canvassing	Individual-based canvassing
Campaign events	Direct mail
Talk-show appearances	Email

A BRIEF HISTORY OF TARGETING

Campaigns have long engaged in both forms of targeting. There is nothing new about the need to focus precious resources on certain voters while ignoring others. It makes sense for campaigns to classify individual voters based on their level of support, and then adjust their outreach depending on what they know about each voter. Abraham Lincoln sounded like a microtargeting-savvy campaign strategist when, in a campaign circular sent to his fellow Whigs in 1840, he directed county committees to

> make a perfect list of all the voters [and] ascertain with certainty for whom they will vote. If they meet with men who are doubtful as to the man they will support, such voters should be designated in separate lines, with the name of the man they will probably support . . . [then] keep a CONSTANT WATCH on the DOUBTFUL VOTERS, and from time to time have them TALKED TO by those IN WHOM THEY HAVE THE MOST CONFIDENCE, and also to place in their hands such documents as will enlighten and influence them. (Basler 1953: 202)

In 1892, the chairman of the Republican National Committee claimed to have compiled a list of all voters in multiple states along with their age, occupation, residence, and other facts. This information was collected "so that literature could be sent constantly to each voter directly, dealing with every public questions and issue from the standpoint of his personal interest" (McGerr 1986, in Turow et al. 2012).

Traditional canvassing efforts—door-to-door campaigning usually by—also entailed a crude form of targeting. Campaign strategists have long used a rule of thumb of 65 percent: a campaign will blanket the precinct, county, or neighborhood with volunteers if past voting returns indicate that at least 65 percent of households supported the party's candidate. The remaining 35 percent of households might receive the campaign's message as well, but so be it. Many Americans have sorted themselves into either majority Republican or Democratic communities (Bishop 2008), although very few geographic areas meet the 65 percent criterion. It turns out that very few precincts or counties are overwhelmingly Democratic or Republican (Hersh 2015).

These early versions of targeting fell out of favor with the advent of mass media in the twentieth century (Turow et al. 2012). Television and radio advertising enabled campaigns to reach wide swaths of voters with broad and relatively inclusive messages. Mass media advertising was expensive, but its reach was impressive. Whereas individualized targeting required armies of volunteer canvassers to gather information about and communicate with one voter at a time, a single television spot could reach thousands of voters (Hersh 2015). A lot of messaging and imagery could be packed into a thirty-second commercial. Campaigns began investing more resources in broad mass media messaging on broadcast outlets and less in labor-intensive field operations.

The 1960s and 1970s saw the emergence of direct mail for political microtargeting. A key figure was conservative operative Richard Viguerie, who built a database of prospective donors starting with a list of people who donated to Barry Goldwater's 1964 presidential campaign (Burton, Miller, and Shea 2015). Direct mail enabled campaigns to send different mailers to different voters depending on available information. Individuals with children could be sent a direct mail piece touting the candidate's support for local schools. Gun owners could get a mailer reassuring them that the candidate would protect their right to bear arms. Likely supporters could be sent mail with messages affirming their support or encouraging them to vote.

Cable television enabled a form of macrotargeting based on audience composition. Targeting on cable television is not unlike targeting a neighborhood that is 65 percent in your camp. That is because cable shows and even channels attract smaller and more like-minded audiences than programs aired on broadcast television. In 2004, for example, the George W. Bush campaign bought spots on the Golf Channel once it determined that the network's audience was disproportionally Republican (Ridout et al. 2014). The campaign for his opponent John Kerry targeted programs with large African American audiences (Ridout et al. 2014). The popularity of political talk shows, particularly among conservatives, enabled Republican campaigns to reach small but like-minded audiences with messages aimed at reinforcing their right-leaning predispositions and mobilizing them to the polls.

Mitt Romney's successful 2002 Massachusetts gubernatorial campaign was among the early adopters of data-driven microtargeting on a large scale. The campaign combined individual-level data about consumer habits and political preferences with the Republican Party's voter file, then used phone calls and direct mail to target particular voters (Turow et al. 2012). For the 2004 presidential campaign, the Republican National Committee identified thirty target groups—for example, "traditional-marriage Democrats" and "tax-cut conservative Republicans"—and used targeted messaging to convey the stakes of these respective issues in the election. This effort included outreach to Democrats who could be peeled away from the Democratic coalition. For example, security-focused Jewish Democrats were sent a direct mail piece featuring a woman saying, "I remember 9/11 as if it happened yesterday. . . . Like most Democrats, I disagree with President Bush on a lot of issues, but he was right to act quickly and decisively after we were attacked. . . . I've always been a pro-choice Democrat, but party loyalties have no meaning when it comes to my family's safety" (Hillygus and Shields 2008).

It was not until 2008 that microtargeting became viable for a full range of candidates (Hersh 2015). Publicly available data based on voter registration were spotty in quality and difficult to use until Congress passed the National Voter Registration Act of 1993 (also known as the "Motor Voter Law"), which established national standards for voter registration and obligated states to remove the names of ineligible voters. More importantly, the Help Americans Vote Act (2002) required states to create a computerized registration list. The law set a deadline of 2006, which meant that with the 2008 election, "virtually any candidate running for office could easily and cheaply access a complete list of registered voters" (Hersh 2015: 64). These changes enabled campaigns to more fully apply the lessons of political science research that demonstrated the effectiveness of door-to-door canvassing and other individual-based outreach efforts (Gerber and Green 2000).

Since 2008, the capacity for campaigns to microtarget has set off alarm bells and quite a bit of negative press. For example, the 2016 Ted Cruz campaign caught a lot of flak when it sent out a mailer aimed at "shaming" voters into participating in the Iowa caucuses. The mailer was targeted at highly likely Cruz supporters whose odds of voting were estimated at only one in four. The mailer resembled an official document, and its headline read "Voting Violation" with a subhead included the phrase "Official Public Record." The recipient's name was listed along with the names of neighbors, each with a letter grade assessing their rate of participation in past elections (a 55 percent turnout rate earned an F grade). It urged the recipient to "caucus on Monday to improve your score." The Cruz campaign could point to dozens of experiments demonstrating that shame-based social pressure can motivate nonvoters to participate. But this was an unusually aggressive approach, and the media and Cruz's opponents pounced (Issenberg 2016).

Targeting Effects

As more campaigns have embraced targeting, scholars have begun testing its effects on voters. In their seminal study of the 2000 and 2004 elections, Hillygus and Shields (2008) analyzed efforts by the presidential campaigns to target cross-pressured partisans from the opposing party—that is, opposite-side partisans who might be persuaded to defect because they disagreed with their party's position on an issue that was important to them. To lure them, the campaigns used targeted messages to prime these voters to give greater weight to these "wedge" issues than their partisanship. They found that nearly 20 percent of cross-pressured partisans defected in 2000. The fact that defection rates were much higher in battleground states and among highly engaged voters suggested that the campaigns' targeting efforts played a role.

Subsequent research has provided mixed signals about the effectiveness of targeting. On the one hand, campaign spots embedded with religious cues can activate religious considerations among Christian voters (Weber and Thornton 2012). Nonpartisan Spanish-language radio ads can boost Latino voter turnout (Panagopoulos and Green 2011). Women seem to respond positively to campaign advertisements that are crafted to prime their gender identity, although only under certain circumstances (Kam, Archer, and Geer 2017)—that is, if the candidate is a woman (Holman, Schneider, and Pondel 2015). These studies suggest that targeting can yield positive outcomes for campaigns.

On the other hand, targeted messages are sometimes sent to the wrong voters. What happens when certain white voters mistakenly receive a message targeted to black voters? The possibility that some white voters might watch TV spots aimed at African American and Hispanic voters keeps some campaigns from using overt racial and ethnic appeals when they macrotarget certain television programs (Nteta and Schaffner 2013). Although "mistargets" don't always respond negatively (Holman, Schneider, and Pondel 2015), some voters punish the candidate who mistakenly sends a targeted message to a group to which they do not belong (Hersh and Schaffner 2013). Microtargeting promises more precision and therefore fewer mistargets, but the data campaigns and parties possess about individual voters are loaded with erroneous and incomplete information (Endres 2016). In the end, backlash from unintended recipients of tailored messages can offset whatever gains campaigns make among intended targets.

Other negative consequences suggest troubling implications for a democratic society. Because skillfully targeted messages are sent directly to voters, they can escape the oversight of journalists whose job it is to scrutinize campaign rhetoric for accuracy (Jamieson 2013). Targeting also assumes certain voters are more worthy of outreach than others. Targeted voters are inundated with campaign messages. They are contacted multiple times by multiple sources—a situation that is exacerbated by legal prohibitions against coordination between campaigns and outside groups, who often identify the same targets (Nickerson and Rogers 2014). Individuals identified as *persuadable likely voters* are prime targets, whereas individuals who are not even registered to vote are ignored (Hillygus and Shields 2008). Indeed, effective targeting is practically invisible to voters who are left out. Candidates can make claims and promises that are hidden to all except the targeted voters. Their priorities may not be shared by the broader electorate (Hillygus and Shields 2008). "A coalition of voters built quietly by promising narrow benefits to narrow audiences implies a very different kind of democracy than a coalition of voters built on broad principles and collective benefits" (Hersh and Shaffner 2013: 522). Voters are complex, yet data-driven targeting efforts often boil down to a binary division between voters who are valuable to the campaign and those who are not (Hersh 2015). The result is a form of redlining of the electorate that excludes low-propensity voters, exacerbating divisions between the haves and have-nots (Turow et al. 2012).

The datasets used for targeting include information that people would prefer to keep private. A comprehensive voter database will include personal information such as birthdate, home address, phone numbers, email addresses, and even ethnic identity. It also might include sensitive information such as religious orientations, political views, and past voting behavior. The security of these datasets cannot be guaranteed: for two months in June 2017, anyone with the right link could access political data on 62 percent of the U.S. population, thanks to the carelessness of a Republican-affiliated data firm (BBC 2017).

Yet targeting also positive outcomes. Accurately targeted voters are more likely yields to receive information about policies they care about (Turow et al. 2012). Targeted mobilization messages can boost political participation by "ensur[ing] that a voter receives an absentee ballot, knows where her polling place is, or is reminded to vote" (Jamieson 2013: 429). Targeting also may have led practitioners to regain an appreciation for traditional, interpersonal forms of campaign work such as door-to-door canvassing, which requires face-to-face interaction between volunteers and potential voters (Nickerson and Rogers 2014). Finally, targeting motivates campaigns to develop a more precise understanding of what citizens want and need. "When politicians know more about voters, they can pay attention to citizen preferences with a level of specificity that was not before possible" (Hersh and Schaffner 2013: 522).

As we will see in later chapters of this book, campaigns can sometimes target a handful of voters and persuade them to change their minds. Sometimes a handful is all they need, as demonstrated by Trump's 2016 victories in three key states: Pennsylvania, Michigan, and Wisconsin. How do campaigns determine which voters should be targeted with persuasion messages and which voters are better suited for mobilization-centered targeting? They collect and analyze data. The next chapter will introduce readers to campaigns' increasingly sophisticated methods for collecting voter information and using these data to determine whom to target with which message.

KEY TERMS

macrotargeting: targeting based on known or estimated characteristics of a group or collective.

microtargeting: targeting based on the known or estimated characteristics of the individual.

mobilization: the process of encouraging and motivating likely supporters to actually cast a ballot.

motivated reasoning: the process by which individuals evaluate information in ways that confirm their existing beliefs rather than challenge them.

party identification: an individual's psychological connection with a political party.

persuasion: the process of changing voters' minds—either from being undecided to supporting the candidate, or *converting* a voter to shift from one candidate to another.

DISCUSSION QUESTIONS

1. What is the difference between macrotargeting and microtargeting? Explain how advertising on social media platforms is more conducive to microtargeting than it is on cable television.
2. Discuss the pros and cons of targeting for a healthy democracy. What might be lost when campaigns target certain voters over others? What might be gained?
3. How does the concept of motivated reasoning explain the difficulty campaigns sometimes encounter when trying to persuade voters to support their candidate?
4. Let's say you are a campaign volunteer canvassing a neighborhood of likely supporters of your candidate. What questions do you think you should ask of the people who answer the door? What information do you think you should provide?

RECOMMENDED READINGS

Green, Donald P., and Alan S. Gerber. 2008. *Get Out the Vote: How to Increase Voter Turnout*, Second edition. Washington, DC: Brookings Institution Press.

What is the most cost-effective way to increase voter turnout? That is the question that frames this classic book. Informed by scholarly research on the topic, the book provides a how-to guide to managing get-out-the-vote operations. Features chapters on door-to-door canvassing, volunteer versus commercial phone banks, signage and direct mail, and email/texting.

Hersh, Eitan D., and Brian F. Schaffner. 2013. "Targeted Campaign Appeals and the Value of Ambiguity." *Journal of Politics* 75, no. 2: 520–34.

Provides evidence that the risks of targeting can outweigh the rewards. "Mistargeted" voters who unintentionally receive messages targeted for someone else penalize candidates enough to cancel out whatever gains were achieved among intended targets. A good example of the use of an experimental research design to test campaign effects.

Hillygus, D. Sunshine, and Todd G. Shields. 2008. *The Persuadable Voter: Wedge Issues in Presidential Campaigns*. New York: Oxford University Press.

Seminal study of how campaigns use wedge issues to persuade voters to change their minds, even partisans who might otherwise stick with their party. Casts doubt on the idea that presidential campaigns are solely about mobilizing the base. A surprising number of partisans can be persuaded to defect if campaigns prime them to focus on cross-pressured issues.

REFERENCES

Alvarez, R. Michael, Asa Hopkins, and Betsy Sinclair. 2010. "Mobilizing Pasadena Democrats: Measure the Effects of Partisan Campaign Contacts." *Journal of Politics* 72, no. 1: 31–44.

Arceneaux, Kevin, and David W. Nickerson. 2009. "Who Is Mobilized to Vote? A Re-Analysis of 11 Field Experiments." *American Journal of Political Science* 53, no. 1: 1–16.

BBC. 2017. "Personal Details of Nearly 200 Million US Citizens Exposed." June 19: http://www.bbc.com/news/technology-40331215.

Basler, Roy P. (ed.). 1953. *The Collected Works of Abraham Lincoln*. New Brunswick, NJ: Rutgers University Press. Vol. 1.

Bishop, Bill. 2008. *The Big Sort: Why the Clustering of Like-Minded America Is Tearing Us Apart*. New York: Houghton Mifflin.

Burns, Alexander. 2013. "How McAuliffe Mapped His Win." *Politico*, Nov. 6: http://www.politico.com/story/2013/11/terry-mcauliffe-campaign-governor-virginia-2013-elections-099497.

Burton, Michael John, William J. Miller, and Daniel M. Shea. 2015. *Campaign Craft: The Strategies, Tactics, and Art of Political Campaign Management*, 5th ed. Santa Barbara: Praeger.

Butler, Daniel M., and David E. Broockman. 2011. "Do Politicians Racially Discriminate against Constituents? A Field Experiment on State Legislators." *American Journal of Political Science* 55, no. 3: 463–77.

Dale, Allison, and Aaron Strauss. 2009. "Don't Forget to Vote: Text Message Reminders as a Mobilization Tool." *American Journal of Political Science* 53, no. 4: 787–804.

Endres, Kyle. 2016. "The Accuracy of Microtargeted Policy Positions." *PS* (Oct.): 771–74.

Enos, Ryan D., Anthony Fowler, and Lynn Vavreck. 2014. "Increasing Inequality: The Effect of GOTV Mobilization on the Composition of the Electorate." *Journal of Politics* 76, no. 1: 273–88.

Gerber, Alan S., and Donald P. Green. 1999. "Misperceptions about Perceptual Bias." *Annual Review of Political Science* 2: 189–210.

———. 2000. "The Effects of Canvassing, Telephone Calls, and Direct Mail on Voter Turnout: A Field Experiment." *American Political Science Review* 94, no. 3: 653–63.

Gimpel, James G., Karen M. Kaufmann, and Shanna Pearson-Merkowitz. 2007. "Battleground States versus Blackout States: The Behavioral Implications of Modern Presidential Campaigns." *Journal of Politics* 69, no. 3: 786–97.

Green, Donald P. 2004. "Mobilizing African-American Voters Using Direct Mail and Commercial Phone Banks: A Field Experiment." *Political Research Quarterly* 57, no. 2: 245–55.

Hersh, Eitan D. 2015. *Hacking the Electorate: How Campaigns Perceive Voters*. New York: Cambridge University Press.

Hersh, Eitan D., and Brian F. Schaffner. 2013. "Targeted Campaign Appeals and the Value of Ambiguity." *Journal of Politics* 75, no. 2: 520–34.

Hillygus, D. Sunshine, and Todd G. Shields. 2008. *The Persuadable Voter: Wedge Issues in Presidential Campaigns*. New York: Oxford University Press.

Hohman, James. 2017. "Most Republicans in Georgia Special Election Are Willing to Give Trumpcare a Chance." *PowerPost The Daily 202*, June 20: https://www.washingtonpost.com/news/powerpost/paloma/daily-202/2017/06/20/daily-202-most-republicans-in-the-georgia-special-election-are-willing-to-give-trumpcare-a-chance/59484b04e9b69b2fb981dd99/.

Holman, Mirya, Monica C. Schneider, and Kirstin Pondel. 2015. "Gender Targeting in Political Advertisements." *Political Research Quarterly* 68, no. 4: 816–29.

Issenberg, Sasha. 2016. "How Ted Cruz Engineered His Iowa Triumph." *BloombergPolitics*, Feb. 2: https://about.bgov.com/blog/how-ted-cruz-engineered-his-iowa-triumph/.

Jamieson, Kathleen Hall. 2013. "Messages, Micro-Targeting, and New Media Technologies." *The Forum* 11, no. 3: 429–35.

Kam, Cindy D., Allison M. N. Archer., and John G. Geer. 2017. "Courting the Women's Vote: The Emotional, Cognitive, and Persuasive Effects of Gender-Based Appeals." *Political Behavior* 39, no. 1: 51–75.

Kunda, Ziva. 1990. "The Case for Motivated Reasoning." *Psychological Bulletin* 108, no. 3: 480–98.

Nickerson, David W. 2005. "Partisan Mobilization Using Volunteer Phone Banks and Door Hangers." *Annals of the American Academy of Political and Social Science* 601: 10–27.

———. 2006. "Volunteer Phone Calls Can Increase Turnout." *American Politics Research* 34, no. 3: 271–92.

Nickerson, David W., and Todd Rogers. 2014. "Political Campaigns and Big Data." *Journal of Economic Perspectives* 28, no. 2: 51–74.

Nteta, Tatishe, and Brian Schaffner. 2013. "Substance and Symbolism: Race, Ethnicity, and Campaign Appeals in the United States." *Political Communication* 30: 232–53.

Panagopoulos, Costas, and Donald P. Green. 2011. "Spanish-Language Radio Advertisements and Latino Voters Turnout in the 2006 Congressional Elections: Field Experimental Evidence." *Political Research Quarterly* 64, no. 3: 588–99.

Redlawsk, David P. 2002. "Hot Cognition or Cool Consideration? Testing the Effects of Motivated Reasoning on Political Decisionmaking." *Journal of Politics* 64, no. 4: 1021–44.

Redlawsk, David P., Andrew J. W. Civettini, and Karen M. Emerson. 2010. "The Affective Tipping Point: Do Motivated Reasoners Ever 'Get It'?" *Political Psychology* 31, no. 4: 563–93.

Ridout, Travis N., Michael Franz, and Erika Franklin Fowler. 2014. "Sponsorship, Disclosure, and Donors: Limiting the Impact of Outside Group Ads." *Political Research Quarterly* 68: 1–13.

Roarty, Alex. 2017. "Democrats Say They Now Know Exactly Why Clinton Lost." *McClatchy DC Bureau* May 1: http://www.mcclatchydc.com/news/politics-government/article147475484.html.

Rosenstone, Steven J., and John Mark Hansen. 1993. *Mobilization, Participation and Democracy in America*. New Haven, CT: Yale University Press.

Shepard, Steven. 2017. "GOP Turnout Confounds Pollsters in Georgia Election." *Politico* June 21: http://www.politico.com/story/2017/06/21/georgia-sixth-congress-polls-handel-ossoff-239813?cmpid=sf.

Smidt, Corwin D. 2015. "Polarization and the Decline of the American Floating Voter." *American Journal of Political Science* 61, no. 2: 365–81.

Taber, Charles S., and Milton Lodge. 2006. "Motivated Skepticism in the Evaluation of Political Beliefs." *American Journal of Political Science* 50, no. 3: 755–69.

Turow, Joseph, Michael X. Delli Carpini, Nora A. Draper, and Rowan Howard-Williams. 2012. "Americans Roundly Reject Tailored Political Advertising." *Annenberg School for Communication, University of Pennsylvania*. Retrieved from: http://repository.upenn.edu/asc_papers/398/.

Weber, Christopher, and Matthew Thornton. 2012. "Courting Christians: How Political Candidates Prime Religious Considerations in Campaign Ads." *Journal of Politics* 74, no. 2: 400–13.

Zaller, John. 1992. *The Nature and Origins of Mass Publics*. Cambridge: Cambridge University Press.

3

Voter and Candidate Research

★ ★ ★

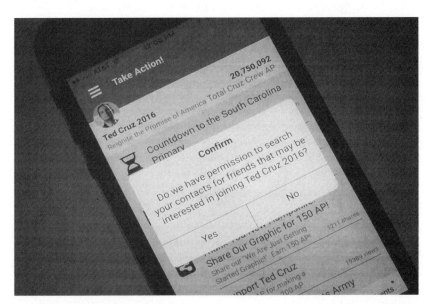

In terms of phone apps and data, the Ted Cruz campaign led a crowded field of candidates running for the Republican presidential nomination in 2016. *Source: AP Photo/J. David Ake*

LEARNING OBJECTIVES

★ Understand the types of information campaigns collect about individual voters, how that information is gathered, and how it is used.

- ★ Grasp the limitations of using voter databases and polling to measure and predict the attitudes and behavior of voters.
- ★ Comprehend the basic mechanics of polling, particularly sampling error.
- ★ Develop a nuanced understanding of opposition research processes and applications.

CAMPAIGNS KNOW A LOT about their voters. Or at least they think they do. They attempt to predict who is likely to vote, who their supporters are, and who can be persuaded to change their minds. They also estimate voters' policy priorities and other politically relevant characteristics. In addition, campaigns know a lot about the other candidates in the race. They can verify some of the information they gather about their opponents; the rest may be hearsay that never sees the light of day. How they obtain knowledge about their voters and their opponents is the focus of this chapter. This chapter is about two of the campaign's most important operations: how they employ data analytics and polling to *know the voters* and how they use opposition research to *know their opponents*. As we will see, they know less about voters than we assume. Much of the information is already in the public domain. The same applies to what the campaigns know about their opponents—and themselves.

DATA

One of a campaign's many objectives is to create a "digital profile" of every possible voter (Hersh 2015). They do so mostly for the sake of targeting, a concept covered at length in chapter 2. Recall that campaigns target certain messages to particular voters in the interest of efficiency. Broadly speaking, individual voters who have been identified as likely supporters are targeted with *mobilization* messages, especially if they cannot be counted on to participate. *Persuasion* messages are typically reserved for uncommitted voters. A campaign would rather not bother with people who either cannot be persuaded to change their minds or will not vote no matter what. Firm supporters of the campaign's opponent are to be avoided altogether.

How do campaigns know who is a supporter, who is persuadable, and who needs a nudge on Election Day? They build a voter database and analyze the data. This is what is known as data analytics.

The voter database serves a number of purposes, including helping campaigns identify and recruit potential volunteers and even rally attendees. But its primary purpose is to provide a list of voters to contact by Election Day. Figuring which voters to contact and how to contact them is challenging. That is why a comprehensive voter database might contain reams of information about each possible voter. That is especially true for resource-rich presidential campaigns, which must create databases for every state. In recent election cycles, voter databases have "become more sophisticated, the sources of data have exploded, and the expertise required for everything from managing technical systems to analyzing data has grown more specialized" (Kreiss 2016: 116).

A typical voter database is built around the public **voter file**—the official list of all registered voters in a state, county, or other smaller geographic area. The *Help America Vote Act* of 2002 mandates that each state maintain its own voter file, typically under the auspices of the secretary of state, the agency that is usually charged with administering elections. Some states' voter files provide more information than others. In addition to the voter's name, address, and age, a voter file might provide a phone number and the individual's gender. It also might track whether the person voted in past elections—including primaries—and whether the voter cast a vote on Election Day or through an alternate method such as voting absentee by mail or in person. In states where voters register by party, the voter file provides the most useful of all predictors of a person's vote choice: the party affiliation for each voter.

Because public voter files are so limited and sometimes out of date—people move, after all—they are often augmented with additional data and updated contact information. Merging the voter file with census data can help estimate such variables as years of education, income, number of children, and ethnicity. A private database vendor can provide updated phone numbers—crucial information for the ground game (see chapter 7)—as well as data on politically relevant variables such as home ownership status and mortgage information (Nickerson and Rogers 2014).

What campaigns really want to know is: Who are their supporters? How likely are they to vote? Who might change their minds? This is where **predictive modeling** comes in—the analysis part of data analytics. Many voter databases contain "scores" that rate voters on a scale of one to one hundred on such variables as the probability that they will vote for the candidate, their likelihood of casting a ballot at all, and how responsive they will be to persuasion efforts. In addition to scores for these variables—campaign professionals call them "support," "turnout," and "persuasion" scores—a database might also include predictive scores for the likelihood of giving money, volunteering, and attending a rally (Nickerson and Rogers 2014). These scores are modeled based on demographic and other characteristics the person shares with other individuals whose preferences are known (Kreiss 2016).

Where do the data originate? The database will probably be provided by the party, a third-party vendor that specializes in data, or a combination of both. The campaign then adds to and updates the data as individual voters are contacted by the field team (chapter 7). Indeed, canvassers make calls and knock on doors not only to persuade and mobilize but also for the purpose of what is known as **voter identification**, also known as "voter ID." Voter ID helps campaigns check the accuracy of the data they possess about the voters and make updates as needed. Canvassing scripts include questions like, "If the election for governor were held today, which candidate would you vote for?" The voter's response may or may not be consistent with the support score predicated in the database. Do the individuals with high support scores confirm that they will vote for the candidate, or did they appear to be on the fence? Can a supporter with a high turnout score be counted on to vote on Election Day? Is a person's persuasion score consistent with what they told the canvasser about whether a decision has been made? Canvassers record what they learn during their interaction with voters, and the database can be updated accordingly (in real time if the canvasser is using a phone or tablet app).

The Role of the Parties

Campaigns are short-term operations. They usually last no more than eight months, perhaps longer if there is a contested nomination. Yet building and maintaining a database is a long-term responsibility. That is why campaigns lean on their respective party organizations and affiliated data vendors for list building. The party's crucial role in maintaining data infrastructure is such that "presidential campaigns value their party organizations primarily as *databases* during election cycles . . . they are first and foremost a voter file and a set of tools for accessing it" (Kreiss 2016: 117; italics in original). Parties have privileged access to states' public voter files. They also can coordinate efforts to incorporate updates across different campaigns within the party. Compared with campaigns, parties are in a better position to maintain long-term relationships with allied consulting firms that augment the public datasets and develop campaigns-specific tools for using the data.

At least until recently, the national Democratic Party has coordinated its data-building efforts more assertively than Republicans. Its existing data infrastructure actually took shape in the wake of John Kerry's loss to George W. Bush in the 2004 presidential election. Bush's campaign had been praised for clever targeting practices that were informed by data about individual voters. Two of Kerry's Democratic primary opponents were Wesley Clark and Howard Dean, whose campaigns were seen as technological innovators (especially Dean's). Dean was appointed chair of the Democratic National Committee in 2005, and the party launched an effort to build a national voter file during his tenure. The result was VoteBuilder, a voter database program since used by every major Democratic campaign. Democrats' nearly universal embrace of a single database facilitated the development of innovative platforms for voter contact around a stable data infrastructure. Volunteers for Democratic campaigns across the country were given access to a data platform that required minimal training to use. VoteBuilder's developer, NGP VAN, launched its own applications that used the data, as did a number of other commercial vendors affiliated with the Democratic Party. All were built around the same stable data infrastructure (Kreiss 2016).

By contrast, the Republicans' hands-off, decentralized approach led to chaos on the data front. The GOP's efforts to build a comparable national database were complicated by competing efforts by private-sector vendors. The most ambitious of these was i360, a massive data platform launched by Charles and David Koch's independent political operation to support conservative causes and candidates. Their goal was to compete with the Democrats' data infrastructure and its many supporting programs. But even though Republican candidates stood to benefit, the project hampered the GOP's effort to build a national data infrastructure.

By the time Barack Obama ran for reelection against Mitt Romney in 2012, Democrats were far ahead of the Republicans in terms of data infrastructure, field tools, and expertise. It did not help that Romney, unlike his opponent, secured the nomination only after a lengthy primary race, leaving little time to build a data infrastructure from scratch. "You can't have a baby in 3 months, that's just the reality of life. I tried," said Zac Moffatt, Romney's digital director (Goldmacher 2016). Making matters worse were the campaign's lengthy vetting process for all digital content and its frugal hiring of technologically savvy staffers. Obama invested four times more than Romney in personnel for the digital team (Kreiss 2016).

Republicans have since caught up. Trump's first presidential campaign may have lacked an extensive field operation, but by 2016 the Republican National Committee had built a national voter database that could be shared across campaigns, party organizations, and groups. Trump should easily secure the Republican nomination in 2020, giving the Republican National Committee plenty of time to enhance its data infrastructure for the general election—an incumbency advantage similar to the timing benefit that Obama enjoyed in 2012.

As with Romney, Trump's Democratic opponent will have to catch up after a lengthy and crowded nomination battle. The Democratic National Committee's recent data-building efforts were also hampered by a dispute with state party organizations over how the party manages and pays for state voter files. The quarrel was resolved in 2019, when the party launched a national "data trust" that would enable campaigns, parties, and groups to share voter data in real time. That means a canvasser knocking on doors for Planned Parenthood in Ohio has the same level of access to the voter file as a volunteer for a Democratic congressional candidate in Florida. Updates to individual voter information are made in real time by any Democratic-affiliated operative or volunteer (Barrow 2019).

Democrats have also wrestled with disputes over who can use the party's data. Some state parties make it difficult or impossible for candidates challenging Democratic incumbents to gain access to VoteBuilder. That happened to Anthony Clark in 2017 when he challenged ten-term incumbent Danny Davis in Illinois's Seventh Congressional District. Illinois had a policy of denying database access to intra-party incumbent challengers, so Clark had to pay a premium for a database produced by a private vendor. Similarly, Washington state's Democratic party denied access to Sarah Smith when she challenged an incumbent in the Ninth Congressional District. Smith was unable to meet the state party's requirement that challengers secure the endorsement of the state party chair and 50 percent of legislative district clubs, plus one (Lapowsky 2017).

How Much Does It Help?

"I have never seen a campaign that's more driven by the analytics," observed one Democratic strategist about Hillary Clinton's 2016 operation. The Clinton campaign used data to determine not only which voters to talk to, how to talk to them, and what to say, but also *when* to say it. Is it best to contact a voter ninety days before the election, or the night before? These are the sort of questions the Clinton team used data analytics to answer (Goldmacher 2016).

By contrast, Trump called data "overrated." Maybe he was right about that. The sophistication and depth of Clinton's data operation may have given the campaign false confidence. Its models predicted victories in so many states that the campaign stopped conducting tracking polls in some states during the final month of the race. The campaign shifted resources to long-shot red states like Georgia and Arizona, underinvesting in Michigan and Wisconsin—supposedly safe states that Clinton eventually lost (Cook 2016). Clinton won 2.87 million more votes nationwide, but Trump secured the majority of Electoral College votes with slim majorities in states where Clinton's data operation projected victories. These upsets serve as a reminder that strategic advantages over one's opponent can mask underlying weaknesses. A superior data operation promises more precision and control than a campaign can deliver.

Problems can start with the data themselves. Some states' voter files are more useful than others. Race is a good predictor of voting behavior, but only eight states, all in the South, ask people to specify their race when they register. The best predictor of how a person will vote is party identification, but voters do not register by party in nineteen states. Some commercial data vendors tout their ability to provide individual data on not only car purchases and home ownership but also voters' shopping histories, gambling tendencies, interest in get-rich-quick schemes, and dating preferences (Duhigg 2012). But consumer data often disappoint when it comes to predicting political behavior, and even consultants who specialize in data analytics are skeptical about their value. "Despite its sex appeal to the media, for the most part consumer data is only helpful at the margins," said Alex Lundry, chief data scientist for Targetpoint (Sides and Vavreck 2014). Dan Wagner, the 2012 Obama campaign's chief analytics officer, said voting history and basic demographic information are more important than voters' magazine subscriptions (Sides and Vavreck 2014). Political scientists John Sides and Lynn Vavreck remind us that "the best predictor of whether you will vote in an election is whether you voted in past elections. And the best predictor of whether you'll vote is not your choice of beer but your party registration" (Sides and Vavreck 2014).

This is why public data are so important, even where direct measures are not available. In states like Texas and Virginia, where voters do not register by party, campaigns can guess party identification by determining whether the individual has participated in one party's primaries. Predicting turnout can simply be a matter of analyzing public data on who voted in recent elections. A "3 of 4 voter" is someone who, according to state-level data, cast a vote in three of the past four general elections. That person might need a nudge from the campaign, but far less than a "1 of 4" voter would need. Old-fashioned precinct-based targeting also entails sound prediction. A campaign can reasonably guess that an individual is a likely supporter if she lives in a precinct in which the party's candidate wins an average of 65 percent of the vote. The odds that they will be wrong about one-third of the time seems worth the risk (Nickerson and Rogers 2014).

But public data have many limitations, and not only in states that do not track party affiliation and race. By design, a state's voter file lists only people who have registered to vote. That matters because research shows that there are meaningful differences between registered and unregistered individuals in terms of demographic characteristics and policy views (Jackman and Spahn 2015). Populations that have lower participation rates are underrepresented in any dataset that is based on a voter file. Voter databases tend to have far more information about regular voters, who tend to be whiter, older, and better educated than individuals about whom little political data exists (Nickerson and Rogers 2014). Hispanics and frequent movers are especially underrepresented in voter databases (Igielnik et al. 2018). According to one study, younger voters are more likely to be categorized as "unlikely" to turn out simply because their voting history is so short (Endres and Kelly 2018). Campaigns that are motivated to reach historically disengaged citizens will struggle to find useful information about them. These would-be voters are often overlooked as a result, which perpetuates the cycle of nonvoting.

Campaigns can turn to commercial vendors for databases with far more information than public datasets can provide, but with mixed results. A Pew assessment of five commercial database vendors revealed that they did a good job predicting turnout, candidate support, and party identification. But other estimates are more problematic. Demographic data such as education and income were accurately predicted only 48 percent (education) and 63 percent (income) of the time (Igielnik et al. 2018). Targeting certain religious voters is tricky because it is difficult to use available data to predict a person's religious affiliation. According to research by political scientist Eitan Hersh, a reputable data vendor for Democratic candidates correctly identified Catholic voters only 38 percent of the time, Protestant voters only 39 percent of the time, and Jewish voters only 25 percent of the time. Guessing a person's race is easier, but still error prone. Predictions of race were accurate 90 percent of the time for whites but only 68 percent for blacks, and 73 percent for Latinos (Hersh 2015).

Such a high error rate has strategic implications. It is common for Democratic campaigns to target African Americans for mobilization (rather than persuasion) because they support for Democratic candidates nine times out of ten. But in the forty-two states that do not record race in their voter files, campaigns must use indicators such as last names and neighborhoods where people live. Yet most African Americans do not live in overwhelmingly African American neighborhoods, and black and white last names are similar. That matters because campaigns risk backlash from voters who are wrongly targeted by race. According to one study, a white voter who mistakenly receives a message targeted to nonwhite voters might decide to vote for the other candidate (Hersh and Shaffner 2013).

Voter data also must be updated from time to time. After all, people move. In 2017, about 16 percent of Americans said they had lived at their current address for less than a year (DeSilver 2018). Sometimes they move to a different state, county, or precinct. People change their phone numbers and email addresses. They also change their minds during the campaign about whom they plan to vote for, or at least their level of commitment. Solid supporters can become weak supporters when a candidates stumbles. Voters who are undecided early in the race might lean one way or the other as they are exposed to campaign messaging. This is why voter ID is such an important part of a field operation; door-to-door and phone canvassing can help campaigns make adjustments when changes are detected and recorded. It also helps when state voter files are updated periodically. Even so, anyone who has canvassed door-to-door has at least one story to tell about knocking on the door of a person who has been misidentified as a likely supporter when they actually support the opponent. Outdated bad data can result in painfully awkward conversations and slammed doors.

Problems aside, campaigns are better off strategically with voter data than without. "Basing campaign decisions on data is certainly a lot better than basing them on gut instinct or hunches, even if those hunches are occasionally right" (Sides and Vavreck 2014). According to one study, predictive modeling helped the Obama campaign target its mobilization efforts at the right voters: individuals with high Democratic support scores but low turnout scores. The 2012 presidential election would have been tighter had Obama not used predictive scores to target certain voters (Nickerson and Rogers 2014).

Even so, exaggerated claims about the transformative power of so-called big data are just that. "The fallacy is that modern campaigns are assumed to have accurate, detailed information about the preferences and behaviors of voters" (Hersh 2015: 11). They do not. Voter datasets are riddled with errors, and it turns out that consumer data is of limited use. But campaigns do have access to useful public data about registered voters. Although some states have more comprehensive voter files than others, campaigns can use analytics to fill in at least some of the holes in the data, and canvassers can help verify and make corrections if needed. By Election Day, campaigns know at least something about the voters they care about the most.

POLLING

As with data, polls also help campaigns know their voters. The key difference is that whereas a voter database represents an attempt to catalog all voters, polls use a subset of the electorate—a sample—to gauge their opinions and behavior. Data help the campaign answer questions about individual voters like, "What issues does this particular persuadable voter care about?" and "What will it take to get this individual supporter to the polls?" With polls, campaigns can measure the issue priorities and turnout barriers of voters *as a whole*. A campaign's voter database serves as a "micro" tool that facilitates direct contact with individual voters. Polls provides more of a "macro" bird's-eye view to guide general strategy, message development, and resource allocation.

A poll is a set of survey of questions asked to a sample of people drawn from a much larger population. The population is whatever group of voters interests the campaign—for example, all registered voters in a legislative district or state. A sample is necessary because it would be impossible to poll everyone in the population. Ideally, the sample is a random probability sample, which means each member of the population has a known chance of being selected. If participants are randomly selected, a poll of about six hundred people can come close to estimating the opinions and behavior of a much larger population. Random probability sampling make it possible to calculate the poll's sampling error, which allows the campaign to precisely estimate how far the poll results are from reality. As we will see, however, pure probability samples are impossible to achieve, forcing pollsters to make adjustments that will be described later in this chapter.

Campaigns use polls to measure how they are doing in the race. They use polls to answers basic "horse race" questions such as who is ahead and by how much. Polls also help campaigns assess what people know about the candidates and their policy priorities. In addition, they serve as tools for mapping strategic communication and tracking opinion change. According to Democratic campaign manager Martha McKenna, polls "help campaign managers analyze candidates' strengths and flaws, give managers snapshots of a candidate's favorable and unfavorable ratings, measure popular views of their job performance, and reveal head-to-head matchups" (Feltus, Goldstein, and Dallek 2019: 52).

Readers are probably familiar with *public polls* because they are the ones that get covered in the media. These are independent polls that are not affiliated with the campaigns, parties, or partisan groups. Some are sponsored by news organizations, often a TV network collaborating with a newspaper, while the poll itself is conducted by a commercial polling company. For example, Langer Research Associates conducts many of the polls for the ABC News/Washington Post poll. Some of the more prominent polls are conducted by colleges and universities at their "polling institutes," with students serving as interviewers. The Marist Poll at Marist College was the first of these; Monmouth University, Siena College, and Quinnipiac University also conduct widely covered polls, as do dozens of other institutions. Companies like Survey USA conduct polls for private-sector and nonprofit sector clients, but also make some of their results available to the public. The Pew Research Center is a respected nonprofit organization that conducts numerous polls and publishes them on its website.

The results of public polls are available to anyone, so cash-strapped campaigns can rely on them if they cannot afford to do much or any of their own internal polling. Public polls can also be useful to campaigns with plenty of resources. Early in Joe Biden's bid for the 2020 Democratic presidential nomination, he embraced a centrist strategy that was premised on the idea that the party's base was not as young and as far left as observers thought. To justify this approach, his campaign pointed to public polls showing that a majority of Democratic primary voters were either moderate or conservative, over fifty, and lacking a college degree (Korecki and Caputo 2019).

But public polls can only help so much. The campaign has no control over the questions being asked in a poll that is designed and conducted by someone else. It also has no access to the dataset of responses, limiting its ability to do serious data analysis. That is why campaigns usually hire a pollster—typically a professional polling firm that specializes in political clients—to do their own **internal polls**.

Internal polls use the same methodologies as public polls. All entail a set of questions posed to each person in the sample. Traditionally they are conducted on the phone by live interviewers, although automated "robocall" surveys are increasingly common. A growing number of polls are conducted entirely online. Nearly all of the questions follow a *fixed-response* format, which means respondents choose from a set of provided answers as opposed to using their own words. But whereas media-sponsored polls are used as fodder for news stories, campaigns use their own internal polls to measure and analyze relevant characteristics of the voters they care about. Typical survey questions fit at least one of the following categories:

- **Demographic** questions measure individual characteristics such as gender and racial identity, education, income, religious affiliation, and occupational status.
- **Knowledge** questions tend to focus on what people know about the candidates. For down-ballot races, it is especially important to measure *name recognition* to determine the extent to which voters are familiar with the candidates.
- **Belief** questions tap into voters' core values—their ideology, their views toward government's role in solving social problems, their religious convictions, and—most importantly—their party identification.
- **Attitude** questions are narrower but crucial because they measure respondents' specific views toward the candidates as well as their opinions on key issues. Attitudes are far more subject to change than core beliefs.
- **Behavior** questions ask respondents to describe their past, present, and future political action. Most importantly, subjects are asked questions aimed at determining which candidate they will cast a ballot for and whether they will vote at all.

Internal campaign polls rarely cover all of these areas. But a comprehensive *benchmark* poll will include at least a few questions from all five. This is the poll campaigns will conduct if they can afford to pay for only one. Benchmark polls are conducted at the beginning of the race. They are sometimes called **baseline polls** because they provide reference points for comparison if and when the campaign conducts shorter follow-up polls later in the race. With sufficient resources,

BOX 3.1 | GOP Holds FL

Republicans liked their chances in Florida in 2018. The political land-scape favored Democratic candidates. After all, this was the midterm election two years into Donald Trump's presidency. The president's party nearly always loses seats in midterms, and 2018 would be no different. But Florida narrowly voted for Trump in 2016. The Repub-lican National Committee attributed that victory to its last-minute data analytics-driven effort to target four hundred thousand likely Clinton voters who also wanted a change in direction from President Obama's policies. Republicans spent the final few days reaching out to these "HRC change voters." A small but crucial number of Florida Democrats voted for Trump (Caputo 2017).

In 2018, Florida featured two high-profile contests: the guber-natorial race between Republican Ron DeSantis and Democrat Andrew Gillum, and the U.S. Senate race between Republican Governor Rick Scott and incumbent Democratic Senator Bill Nelson. Republicans were encouraged by what their polling and voter modeling showed: support for Trump's policy priorities and a desire for Democrats to work with the president. This suggested that the Gillum's and Nelson's opposition to Trump's policies would not go over well with a sufficient number of voters (Caputo 2017).

Public polls did not look good for the Republican candidates. Gillum had won the Democratic nomination despite ranking fourth in preelection polls, and Democrats were excited about the pros-pect of electing the state's first African American governor. When matched up against Republican DeSantis in the general election, polls showed Gillum with a narrow lead throughout the fall. The Senate race was tighter, although Nelson led in most polling. Polling also showed that about 97 percent of voters already had made up their minds about both races by September (Mehta and Velencia 2018). But as Election Day approached, both races tight-ened enough to make them too close to call—that is, within the margin of error. In the end, DeSantis and Scott narrowly defeated their opponents—close enough to trigger recounts in both cases.

SOURCES

Caputo, Marc. 2017. "RNC: Nelson, Democrats Should Fear Republican Data Operation." *Politico* (July 24): https://www.politico.com/states/florida/story/2017/07/24/rnc-nelson-democrats-should-fear-republican-data-operation-113581.

Mehta, Dhrumil, and Janie Velencia. 2018. "Just About Everyone in Florida Has Already Decided Who to Vote for." *FiveThirtyEight* (Sept. 7): https://fivethirtyeight.com/features/just-about-everyone-in-florida-has-already-decided-who-to-vote-for/.

a campaign can also do a series of **tracking polls** to assess opinion change during the course of the race. Shorter **quick-response polls** can be used to assess the impact of a particular event such as a debate performance, a damaging news story, or a series of attack ads on either side. For example, a baseline poll might reveal that a candidate suffers from low name recognition. Subsequent tracking polls will show whether voters are becoming more familiar with the candidate over time. A quick-response poll can assess whether the candidate got a bump from a three-day ad buy.

Campaigns also hold **focus groups** to delve more deeply into voters' thoughts and reactions. Focus groups are not polls. Rather, they are small gatherings of individuals ranging in size from ten to twenty participants who are recruited to discuss their opinions and explain their reactions in depth. Focus groups are led by a facilitator who guides participants through a structured interactive conversation that is recorded and later analyzed. Participants tend to be voters who have not made up their minds and are therefore persuadable. Early in the race, a focus group can be held to hear what a small subset of likely voters have to say about the candidates before campaigning heats up. Focus group are routinely used to gauge reactions to a TV advertisement before it airs. Following a viewing of the ad, the facilitator encourages participants to describe their reactions, being careful to encourage reserved members to speak up and discouraging more assertive individuals from dominating the conservation. The ad might be modified depending on how the focus group reacts, or perhaps it won't run at all. Because focus group participants are not randomly selected, their opinions and reactions do not represent those of the population as a whole. But they do provide rich qualitative information.

Unlike focus groups, polls provide detailed quantitative data for statistical analysis. Although advanced statistics are possible, the analysis also can be quite simple. One of the advantages of polls is their capacity to examine basic relationships between respondents' answers to two different questions. This is where **crosstabs** come in. Short for cross-tabulations, crosstabs provide a visual representation of the relationship between two or perhaps three variables. For example, if the campaign wants to assess how well its candidate is doing among women, it can analyze a crosstab showing the relationship between gender and candidate preference. To explore whether a candidate's top policy priority is associated with voters' candidate preferences, it can examine a crosstab using a question like, "Please

Table 3.1 Policy Preferences among likely Brat and Spanberger Voters

Policy Priority	Candidate Preference (%)	
	Brat	Spanberger
Immigration	27	12
Health care	13	42
Gun control	10	16
Abortion	5	9
Tax	21	8
Job creation	18	6
Other	3	4
Don't know	3	3

Source: Monmouth University Poll of 400 registered voters living in Virginia's Seventh Congressional District who voted in at least one of the last four general or primary elections or had registered to vote since January 2016. Interviews conducted September 15–24, 2018. Margin of error: ±4.9% for full sample.

tell me which one of the following policy issues is most important to you in your vote choice for Congress." That question was posed to a random sample of four hundred registered voters in Virginia's Seventh Congressional District, where Democrat Abigail Spanberger challenged incumbent Republican Dave Brat in 2018. This was a public poll conducted by Monmouth University in mid-September. The crosstab analyzing the relationship between respondents' top policy priority and their candidate preference is shown in table 3.1.

This simple crosstab shows that a plurality of Spanberger supporters—about 42 percent—prioritized health-care policy. That finding made sense because Spanberger focused on health care in her advertising, stump speeches, and in her debate with Brat. Crosstabs cannot prove cause and effect: although it could be that the campaign's messaging primed Spanberger's supporters to prioritize health care, it is also possible that her focus on health care was influenced by voter priorities. In addition, the small sample size yielded a high margin of error of ±4.9 percent, which means it is possible that far fewer actual likely voters prioritized health care. (Margin of error is discussed in more detail in the next section.) Even so, none of the other policy areas even came close, reassuring the campaign that it was on the right track in terms of issue priorities. The poll also revealed a gender gap between support for the two candidates, as shown in table 3.2.

Table 3.2 "Gender Gap" between Brat and Spanberger

Candidate Preference	Male (%)	Female (%)
Brat	48	36
Spanberger	42	51
Other	4	1
Undecided	6	12

Source: Monmouth University Poll of 400 registered voters living in Virginia's Seventh Congressional District who voted in at least one of the last four general or primary elections or had registered to vote since January 2016. Interviews conducted September 15–24, 2018. Margin of error: 4.9% for full sample.

This crosstab suggested a clear preference for Spanberger among women in the sample. Even accounting for the margin of error, women leaned her way a month and a half before Election Day. Spanberger eventually defeated Brat by about two percentage points. National exit polls showed that women voted overwhelmingly for Democratic congressional candidates in the 2018 midterm elections.

Polls do more than help campaigns estimate who is ahead and speculate about why. They also can serve as an earned media tool. In chapter 4, we will examine ways that campaigns "leak" information to media outlets when they think doing so will help their candidate. Internal poll results are common leak fodder. For example, a struggling candidate might let a reporter peek at a copy of an internal poll report showing a tightening race. When a **public poll** shows one candidate widening her lead, the losing candidate's campaign might cite an internal poll showing otherwise. Naturally, campaigns release only the polls that they think will help their candidate (Rakich 2018).

Some internal polls are better than others. In a 2017 special election for a Senate seat in Alabama, Doug Jones's internal polls accurately showed a tight race that he eventually won by one point, whereas public polls were "all over the place" (Klein 2017). In 2012, Mitt Romney's polls had him winning seven states that he eventually lost, overrating his performance by nearly five percentage points, whereas President Obama's internal polls were generally on target (Silver 2012). Hillary Clinton's polls showed her ahead in Midwestern states she eventually lost. According to one analysis, publicly released internal polls for House races between 1998 and 2016 missed the final margin of their race by eight to nine points (Silver 2017). That does not mean internal polls are bad—only that *publicly released* internal polls should be viewed with caution.

How Accurate Are Polls?

Polls sometimes get it wrong. They showed Hillary Clinton ahead of Bernie Sanders by twenty-one points in Michigan, yet Sanders edged Clinton in that state's Democratic primary in 2016. Ralph Northam won the 2017 Virginia gubernatorial election by 8.9 points—5.5 points higher than the average poll projected. Andrew Gillum became the Democratic nominee for Florida governor in 2018 despite ranking fourth in preelection polls. When Ayanna Pressley first ran for Massachusetts's Seventh Congressional District in 2018, she crushed her primary opponent despite polls showing her losing by double digits. Donald Trump won Wisconsin in 2016 in the face of a poll showing Clinton ahead by six points one week before Election Day.

Polling errors may seem increasingly common, but they are no more frequent now than they were twenty years ago (Jennings and Wlezien 2018). Ronald Reagan routed Jimmy Carter in the 1980 presidential election in the wake of preelection public polls showing a dead heat. Between 1998 and 2018, the average error in polls conducted during the final twenty-one days of the race was about six points. In 2017, they were off by an average of 5.1 points compared with 7.5 points in 1998. The error rate is only about four points for presidential general elections but much higher for presidential primaries and races for governor and the U.S. House and Senate (Silver 2018).

Polls fall short partly because we expect more precision than they can deliver. A significant amount of error is part of the process. Error is built into the reality that a sample of voters is being surveyed rather than the population as a whole. Although the objective is to attain a sample that is representative of the whole population, there is always **sampling error**. Sampling error refers to the difference between the estimates provided by the sample and the actual number that would materialize if the entire population could be measured (aka the population "parameter"). The amount of sampling error is expressed as the **margin of error**, which describes the estimated range within which the "true" population parameter lies. Sampling error also includes the **confidence level**, which refers to the degree of certainty that the population parameter falls within the margin of error. For election polls, the typical confidence level is 95 percent.

The larger the sample size, the lower the sampling error. At a 95 percent confidence level, a poll of six hundred people will yield a margin of error of ±4 percent, which is pretty typical. To lower the margin of error to ±3 percent, the pollster would need to survey close to 1,100 people—at added cost to the campaign, and rarely worth it.

Implicit in both sets of figures is the concession that the poll results could be off by quite a bit. If a poll of six hundred Iowans suggests that 44 percent of the sample plans to cast their ballot for Donald Trump in 2020, that means somewhere between 40 and 48 percent of the full population of Iowa voters support Trump. That is a wide range of possible support for reelecting the president. Securing 48 percent of the vote in Iowa might be enough to win the state (assuming a third-party candidate garners a percent or two); Trump loses badly, however, if it's closer to 40 percent. What is more, the 95 percent confidence level suggests that there is a 5 percent chance that the 40 to 48 percent range is off.

The range of possibilities is striking when comparing support across candidates. If that same poll shows Trump's opponent support at 47 percent, it would be tempting to conclude that the Democrat is beating Trump in Iowa. That may be true, but the poll does not demonstrate that. It does estimate that the Democrat's actual support ranges from 43 to 51 percent. If Trump's actual support in the population is 40 percent—the low end of his range—his opponent could be ahead by eleven points if the candidate's support is on the highest end of the range. But it is also possible that Trump is ahead by five points. That is why it is common to hear that a race is "too close to call" because it is "within the margin of error." Most competitive races are. And they sometimes remain so despite the temptation to interpret the ebbs and flows of poll standings as actual change in a candidate's relative position in the race. If one six-hundred-person poll shows a candidate at 40 percent support one week and another poll a week later shows the candidate at 44 percent, that does not mean the candidate is surging. It is possible that the candidate's actual support *dropped* from 44 percent to 40 percent. And by the way: we are only 95 percent sure of these estimates.

That is just sampling error. Poll results can be biased for a host of other reasons. Among them: poorly worded questions. *Leading* questions are worded in a way that encourages one response over the others. Answers to a question like, "Should Donald spend more time solving this country's problems and less time tweeting?" will probably suggest less support for Trump than there really is. *Double-barreled* questions yield worthless answers because they are two questions in one, such as "Are you registered to vote, and do you plan to vote in the next election?" Overly *complex* questions may confuse some people. But a *vague* question like "Do you support Elizabeth Warren's climate change proposal?" will not produce much useful information beyond a broad indication of support for Warren in general. Questions about unfamiliar candidates or issues will introduce bias because some people will respond to survey questions even if they know little or nothing about the topic. When people are polled about voting intentions early in the race, many respondents lack the information they need to make "enlightened voting decisions" (Gelman and King 1993).

The thorniest problem in polling is the decline in the number of people willing to participate in polls and other surveys. The average *response rate* was only 6 percent in 2018—a sharply lower rate than the average in the 1970s, when 80 percent was the norm (Zukin 2015). A low response rate increases the likelihood of *nonresponse bias*, which is when there are systematic differences between the actual participants in the poll and those who either could not be reached or refused to participate. The differences have serious political implications. Nonwhite people are less likely to participate than white people. College graduates are more likely to do a survey than individuals with no college. Retirees are easier to reach by phone than college students. Pollsters compensate for these biases by statistically weighting the sample so that it comes closer to matching the actual demographic composition of the population. They insist that nonresponse bias is a manageable problem (DeSilver and Keeter 2015), and there is at least some research that backs them up (Keeter et al. 2006).

The proliferation of cell phones aggravate the response rate problem. Cell phones have built-in caller ID, allowing people to ignore calls from unfamiliar phone numbers such as those from a polling firm. Younger people are especially unlikely to answer their phone when they don't recognize a number. Unlike with landlines, people can keep their cell phone numbers even when they move away, which detaches area codes from a specific geographic location such as a congressional district or state. But the more costly problem is that cell phones must be dialed manually. When nearly every household had a landline phone, pollsters could use random digital dialing (RDD) to quickly reach a random sample of households, even numbers that were unlisted. RDD automatically calls randomly generated phone numbers until someone answers the call; only then does the interviewer engage the respondent. But RDD is not allowed for cell phones. The 1991 Telephone Consumer Protection Act prohibits the use of automatic dialers to call cell phone numbers. To achieve a sample of one thousand respondents, interviewers hired by a polling firm must manually dial more than twenty thousand random cell phone numbers, most of which are not actual phone numbers (Zukin 2015). That partly explains why telephone polling is more expensive than it used to be. As a result, most telephone polls now call both landlines and cell phones.

These phone-related problems have triggered a shift toward internet polls. Many polls are now conducted fully or partly online. Online polls are less expensive because there is no need to pay interviewers. Response rates also tend to be higher. In addition, there is some evidence that online survey subjects respond more honestly when asked questions on sensitive or potentially embarrassing topics than when speaking to a live interviewer on the phone. For example, internet poll respondents were far less likely than phone poll respondents to agree that there is a lot of discrimination against gays and lesbians, and far more likely to admit being in poor shape financially (Kennedy and Deane 2019). The problem with internet polls is that random probability samples are even more difficult than they are with phones. Despite obvious advances, online polls may be no more accurate than telephone surveys; according to one analysis, telephone polls outperformed internet polls during the 2016 election (Silver 2018).

Many pollsters for campaigns have given up on random samples drawn from the general population. Instead, they use random samples drawn from the registered voters who are listed in their database. Registration-based sampling (RBS) is tricky: the quality of voter files varies, and phone numbers and email addresses are often wrong or nonexistent. Some respondents are turned off by RBS's lack of anonymity and refuse to participate. But RBS can be more cost efficient partly because it works from an existing database that already provides at least some of the information that would otherwise need to be collected through the poll—the respondent's age, for example. And because the typical voter file includes information about turnout in past elections, RBS helps the pollster identify likely voters (Green and Gerber 2006).

Likely voters are the population that interests campaigns the most, and predicting which respondents are likely to vote is a perennial challenge for pollsters (Rogers and Aida 2014). That is in part because so many respondents overstate their intentions to vote, especially when asked by a live interviewer on the phone. Voting is viewed as a civic duty, and some respondents will say they plan to vote but then fail to cast a ballot. Oddly enough, others tell pollsters they do not plan to vote but then end up turning out. Rather than rely on a single indicator of turnout, pollsters have to guess who will vote by creating scales that combine responses to a variety of related questions such as whether the respondent is registered, whether they voted in past elections, and whether they know where people in their neighborhood go to vote. There are many different ways to model voting likelihood, and it is unclear which works best (Zukin 2015). Identifying likely voters is especially difficult during primaries because turnout tends to be low but also ebbs and flows depending on interest. Polling error is higher during primaries as a result. One reason that polls missed Sanders's upset in the 2016 Democratic primary in Michigan is they vastly underestimated turnout among voters under the age of thirty, who typically participate at low rates but showed up for Bernie and voted for him at an 81 percent rate (Bialik 2016).

As with data analytics, it would be a mistake to assume that polls provide precise measures of voter preferences. Polls merely provide rough estimates of what voters think, what they know about the candidates, how they will vote, and perhaps why. There is always uncertainty and error. People change their minds. Their preferences and behavior can be erratic and unpredictable, especially during low-visibility elections. Even so, informed approximations are better than intuitive guesswork when deciding where to spend precious resources. Like voter databases, polls can serve as information-rich tools as long as campaigns keep their expectations in check.

OPPOSITION RESEARCH

Knowing your opponents is quite a bit more straightforward than *knowing your voters*. A candidate will probably face only one serious opponent in the general election: the opposing party's nominee. And although primary races can be crowded with contenders—about two dozen Democrats ran for the party's 2020 presidential nomination—most down-ballot party nominations are uncontested. In other words, a typical candidate will face no more than two serious opponents—one during the nomination phase and one during the general election. Voter research requires building a database of thousands of voters and at least one poll. Yet opposition research shares at least one thing in common with voter research: for both, public information is the most reliable resource. Recall that despite concerns about predicting voting behavior using consumer data, the public voter file is the most valuable data source a campaign can use. Likewise, when campaigns are conducting research about the opposition, the public record will be far more useful than hearsay and gossip about their opponents' misdeeds. Opposition research is more about culling the public record than digging up dirt.

Nicknamed "oppo," opposition research is the practice of investigating political opponents' record and background, usually for the purpose of weakening them. Candidates also do oppo on themselves to prepare for possible attacks (see box 3.2, "Internal Oppo"). In the U.S., candidates have been doing opposition research on each other since the beginning of the republic; they just called it something else. Thomas Jefferson hired "scandalmonger" James Callender to investigate political rivals Alexander Hamilton and John Adams, and then Callender turned against him and reported that Jefferson

---

BOX 3.2 | Internal Oppo

Why would a campaign do **opposition research** on its own candidate? After all, the purpose of "oppo" is to gather damaging information about opponents. The campaign then uses that information to convince voters that the opposing candidates should *not* be elected. But of course the opponents' campaigns are doing the same thing. They also are poring through documents, studying voting records, staring at video footage, and talking to sources— all in an effort to unearth at least one clod of dirt that will lead to their opponent's defeat. To prepare for the possibility that the public will eventually hear about the fruits of that effort, campaigns also do opposition research on themselves. This is what is known as **counter-opposition research,** or self research.

Self research helps the campaign anticipate attacks from opponents. Knowing that an opponent might run an oppo-based attack ad, the campaign can prepare its own response spot in advance. It also can inoculate a candidate against bad press. That is what happened to political consultant Katie LaPotin when she worked for a state House candidate who had failed to pay his taxes on time a few years earlier. "When the story ultimately came out in the fall it managed to last a single news cycle and inflict minimal damage on the candidate," LaPotin said. Self research revealed the problem in advance, and the candidate was ready to immediately release a statement and supporting government documentation (LaPotin 2011).

The process is the same as with opposition research but with one important additional early step: interviewing the candidate. Candidates may not readily disclose embarrassing information about themselves, but talking to them can yield clues that inform a thorough investigation. It helps that opposition researchers are often outsiders hired as consultants; their independence fosters a level of scrutiny that would be awkward inside the campaign. Sometimes opposition researchers discover unwelcome surprises

BOX 3.2 | (continued)

about their candidate. "I can't tell you how many times we've sat down with the candidates after we give them the report, and he or she has said, 'Whose side are you on? I look worse than my opponent in your report,'" said opposition researcher Alan Huffman.

Lee Carter was unusually forthcoming about his dirty laundry. A full year before running for reelection to a seat in the Virginia House of Delegates, Carter took to Twitter to reveal a slew of damning disclosures. He was fired from a job. He was in the midst of his third divorce, one of which involved a child custody dispute. He was arrested for suspicion of assault as a marine. He admitted to being a "terrible student" in high school. He confessed to saying "horrible things" on the internet that were "homophobic, trans-phobic, sometimes sexist or racially insensitive." Carter also tweeted, "Just like everyone else under 35, I'm sure explicit images or video of me exists out there somewhere" (Schwartzman 2018).

A self-described democratic socialist, Carter was considered a long shot when he first ran in 2017 and therefore did not attract much scrutiny, either from the press or his opponent. But he expected that to change for his reelection bid. "To all the Republicans who are tasked with following my social media, enjoy that oppo dump," Carter wrote in his final tweet of the series (Barakat 2018). He was reelected in 2019 by 6.8 percentage points.

REFERENCES

Barakat, Matthew. 2018. "Candid Candidate Voluntarily Airs Dirty Laundry." *Associated Press* (Oct. 19): https://www.apnews.com/af9c9b4af1d440d789324d8f32577462.

LaPotin, Katie. 2011. "A Lesson in Self Research." *Campaigns & Elections* (Nov. 9): https://www.campaignsandelections.com/campaign-insider/a-lesson-in-self-research.

Schwartzman, Paul. 2018. "A Virginia Politician's Novel Approach to Personal Scandal: Tell All Before Opponents Do." *Washington Post* (Oct. 19): https://www.washingtonpcst.com/local/virginia-politics/a-politicians-novel-approach-to-personal-scandal-tell-all-before-opponents-do/2018/10/19/c8ed7ea8-cd65-11e8-a3e6-44daa3d35ede_story.html?utm_term=.ec4d1f5a574a.

had fathered children by his slave Sally Hemmings. Opponents of Andrew Jackson used public marriage records to charge him with adultery for marrying Rachel Robards before she had been legally divorced. Rumors about Grover Cleveland's illegitimate child and Teddy Roosevelt's alleged drunkenness were spread by their opponents during their presidential runs. What is now called opposition research used to be under-the-radar "dirty tricks" operations, often conducted by amateurs who would claim no direct connection to the campaign. Oppo can still be pretty unseemly. But like many aspects of modern campaigning, oppo is now conducted by party organizations and professionals hired by the campaigns themselves.

Today, opposition research is commonly carried out by private consulting firms that specialize in opposition research. Other oppo providers include party committees, which employ their research departments to perform opposition research and share it with their party's candidates. Another source is independent groups, who—like the party committees—support their cause by conducting oppo on opposing candidates in competitive races. For example, American Bridge is a super PAC that supports Democrats by monitoring public appearances by and media coverage of Republican candidates and posting their findings on social media. For Republicans, America Rising PAC produces oppo on Democratic candidates and elected officials. America Rising's efforts to derail the 2020 Democratic presidential candidates began two years in advance. In April 2017, for example, it posted an online video of Elizabeth Warren telling a Chicago audience that she wanted to cut open the bodies of Republicans to see if they have hearts. It was a bad joke intended to criticize Republican lawmakers for attempting to repeal the Affordable Care Act, but the clip attracted some online media attention. By summer, America Rising had filed more than three hundred Freedom of Information requests and monitored more than seven hundred livestreamed events featuring prospective Democratic candidates (Cadelago 2018).

The overarching objective of opposition research to find evidence that the opposing candidate should *not* be elected. Oppo thus centers on opponents' weaknesses and vulnerabilities. It could reveal a pattern of mistakes—or a single mistake—that raise doubts about a candidate's suitability for office. Perhaps the opponent cast a vote for or against legislation that could be framed as proof of hypocrisy or "flip flopping." In primary elections, incumbents could be damaged by evidence that they violated their principles and crossed party lines to support policies proposed by the opposing party. There might be video or audio of a candidate saying or doing something offensive or merely embarrassing. Documentation of an excessive number of missed votes, absences from work, or foreign travel could be used to corroborate charges that opponents have neglected their official duties. Problems in a candidate's private life can be damaging when they suggest serious character flaws.

Opposition research typically culminates in a lengthy written report submitted to the campaign at the beginning of the race, sometimes accompanied by digital video and audio files. Presidential candidates usually warrant a book-length report. A comprehensive report does more than just present raw information. It also provides analysis, advising *how* the campaign can use the information or whether to use it at all. Yet doing oppo need not end when "the book" (as it is often called) is submitted. Opposition researchers continue monitoring what their opponents are saying and doing, watching for mistakes made on the campaign trail. "Some of my competitors research the opponent, submit their report—perhaps nine months before the election—and then walk away," said opposition researcher Terry Cooper in a blog post. "My operating premise is that, if my client's opponent does stupid things—and I've never found one who didn't—then he's not going to stop doing stupid things just because I've submitted my report. In fact, he may commit his dumbest mistakes after I've submitted my report" (Cooper 2014).

The ongoing work entails a combination of media monitoring and tracking. Online software can be used to document any time an opponent is mentioned in the news. Meanwhile, paid or volunteer *trackers* follow opponents everywhere they go in public and film their speeches, rallies, and other public events. With both media monitoring and tracking, the primary objective is to catch the opponent committing a gaffe or saying something that contradicts a previously stated position. Offensive statements can be particularly useful. Senator George Allen's "macaca" gaffe was filmed by a tracker (see chapter 4 for a fuller account of this incident). When Senate candidate Todd Akin said "legitimate rape" victims rarely get pregnant during a television interview, the interviewer did not react. It was media monitoring that caught the gaffe, which then spread online (D'Amico 2017).

Sources

Documentation is key. A serious oppo-based attack is bound to be scrutinized by news outlets and on social media. Documentation strengthens the campaign's hand when the media investigate the charge and when the opponent counterattacks. According to Cooper, the information should be "independently verifiable." It is not enough for the campaign or the opposition researcher they hired to agree that the information is accurate, credible, and relevant. Will it hold up if a reporter checks it out? If the charge goes viral on social media, will it withstand intense online scrutiny?

Oppo that turns out to be inaccurate or misleading can backfire. That happened to Bill Clinton's 1992 presidential campaign when it found evidence that the campaign to reelect President George H. W. Bush was producing campaigns posters in Brazil. The source was promising: a video of a Brazilian TV news story showing Bush–Quayle posters rolling off a printing press located in Brazil. And the potential damage to Bush was irresistible. "Think of it: With millions of Americans out of work the President of the United States was taking his business to South America, undercutting American jobs. Is this the man you want in charge of your economy?" senior Clinton strategist James Carville later said (Matalin and Carville 1995: 430). But Carville leaked the story to CBS News before fully vetting the information. The Bush campaign claimed that an independent operative paid for the operation himself, and CBS could not verify otherwise. The story died, damaging the campaign's credibility with CBS News and the morale of staffers, who had wasted hours on oppo that could not be independently verified.

The infamous "Steele dossier" about Donald Trump also had credibility problems. In April 2016, the Democratic National Committee and a lawyer supporting Hillary Clinton retained a firm called Fusion GPS to conduct opposition research on Donald Trump. A Republican donor had already hired the firm to do research on Trump during the primaries (Entous, Barrett, and Helderman 2017). Fusion subcontracted the investigation to Christopher Steele, a former British intelligence officer and Russia expert, to find out what he could about Trump's connections to the Russian government. Steele summarized his findings in a report that contained serious charges against Trump, including the likelihood that he had cooperated with Russian authorities for years and was vulnerable to blackmail by Russian intelligence operations. Like an intelligence report, however, the dossier was based on unnamed sources. The dossier circulated in the media during the fall of 2016, but the story fizzled because news outlets could not verify the report's claims. It was not until after the election that scrutiny of Trump's Russian connections intensified (Yglesias and Prokop 2018).

The need for documentation partly explains why professional opposition researchers tend to focus on opponents' *public record*. If the opponent served in a legislative body, that means poring over voting records for evidence of unpopular votes, absenteeism, flip-flops, and other inconsistencies. Criminal records could reveal evidence not only of serious crimes but also troubling patterns such as an excessive number of speeding tickets or unpaid parking violations. If the opponent is a developer or landlord, a visit to the local permit office could yield evidence of unscrupulous practices in the area of real estate (Krieger 2017). The revelation that 2008 presidential candidate John Edwards paid $800 for two haircuts originated in one of the candidate's quarterly filings to the Federal Election Commission (FEC). Opposition research based on FEC records also revealed that Kentucky Senate candidate Allison Grimes rented her campaign bus from her father at a below-market rate, a possible campaign finance law violation (Raju 2014). Charges that Mitt Romney profited from companies that outsourced jobs overseas were based on government records from the federal Trade Adjustment Assistance program (D'Amico 2017).

Oppo can also entail scrutiny of formal policy platforms and public statements on issues. An opponent's plan to reform Social Security might be out of step with voter opinion. An ambitious infrastructure program might cost more than the opposing candidate admits. A candidate's statement on an issue might contradict their governing record. For example, when Vermont governor Howard Dean ran for the Democratic presidential nomination in 2004, opposition research leaked to the press revealed that he had signed legislation providing tax breaks to Bermuda-based insurance companies a day after delivering a speech criticizing companies that dodge taxes by incorporating in Bermuda. Dean also got hit with an oppo-based news story reporting that he had attacked President George W. Bush for giving tax breaks to large corporations despite signing legislation giving $80 million in corporate tax relief (Green 2004). Policy-related attacks are usually developed elsewhere in the operation, but opposition research can lay a foundation.

The emphasis on public information does not mean that opposition researchers ignore opponents' private lives. Opposition researchers can and do investigate charges of adultery, drug use, sexual misconduct, and any other behavior that could raise doubts about the opponent's character. It is up to the campaign to decide whether to use this kind of information. More often than not, this kind of oppo gets quietly leaked to the media. Ohio gubernatorial candidate Ed FitzGerald blamed opposition researchers for leaking a police report showing him in a car with a woman who was not his wife at 4:30 a.m. in an otherwise empty parking lot, which led to the revelation that he had lacked a permanent license for more than a decade (WLWT5 2014).

The FitzGerald story may have been unseemly, but the information was legally obtained. It was based on a police report, which is public information. Lawful opposition research means "you don't break into your opponents' offices and take files or plant bugs," wrote Democratic political operative Steven D'Amico in a *Politico* piece. Instead of digging for dirt, "a good opposition researcher assembles the case against their opponent by lawfully compiling the best portfolio of evidence"—similar to "an attorney preparing for a trial." That means poring through public records, news stories, and court cases. Operatives who use illegal methods to gather information risk prosecution. A Democratic researcher was charged with misdemeanor representation when he obtained a Republican Senate candidate's Social Security number from a court document, and then illegally used it to obtain the candidate's credit report. It is possible that Donald Trump Jr. broke the law when he invited the Russian government to dig up dirt on Hillary Clinton obtained by the Russian government (D'Amico 2017).

CONCLUSION

Campaigns do opposition research because they think it helps. Oppo provides the fodder for negative campaigning, and most campaign professionals are convinced that "going negative" is a must. The fruits of opposition research can be seen in much of what the campaign produces. Campaigns routinely perform "oppo dumps"—a nickname for the practice of leaking opposition research to media outlets. A TV commercial attacking a candidate for flip-flopping on policy will likely display direct quotes from the candidate and corroborating documentation, complete with citations of sources—all drawn from oppo. During a debate, a candidate might surprise her opponent with a damaging tidbit discovered during opposition research.

The effectiveness of negative campaigning is a matter of academic debate. A number of studies suggest that attack ads do diminish support for the targeted candidate under the right conditions (Fridkin and Kenney 2011). For example, one study shows that negative messages are effective if they are perceived as legitimate, focused on a relevant topic, and centered on policy rather than personal attacks (Fridkin and Kenney 2004). However, a meta-analysis combining the results of more than one hundred different studies concluded that there is no consistent evidence that "negative campaigning 'works' in achieving the electoral results that attackers desire." Although attacks can diminish support for the candidate they target, they can also result in backlash against the attacker (Lau, Sigelman, and Rovner 2007: 1185).

Clearly campaigns should be careful when they use opposition research to attack their opponents. The safest bet is to rely on public information that lends itself to documentation. The attack will likely get scrutinized by news outlets and on social media. If the information behind it cannot be independently verified, the campaign could pay a political price. Negative campaigning is risky enough as it is.

KEY TERMS

baseline poll: a comprehensive survey conducted in the early stages of the campaign.

confidence level: the degree of certainty that the poll's estimates fall within the margin of error. Typically 95 percent.

counter-opposition research: the process of collecting information about the campaign's own candidate, mostly for the purpose of preparing for attacks and media coverage.

crosstab: short for cross-tabulation, a table that presents the relationship between responses to two poll questions, for example, the relationship between gender and a preferred candidate.

focus group: a small gathering of prospective voters who are recruited to discuss their opinions and explain their reactions to campaign events and activities.

internal poll: a poll conducted by a campaign for its own use.

margin of error: the estimated range within which the actual population lies. Expressed in plus or minus terms (e.g., ±4 points).

opposition research: the process of collecting information about opponents, usually for the purpose of revealing their weaknesses and vulnerabilities.

polling: the process of estimating the attitudes and behavior of a voting population by surveying a random sample drawn from that population.

predictive modeling: the process of using data to estimate likely outcomes, for example, whether a person will vote (turnout) and how they will vote (support).

public poll: a poll whose results will be released to the public; usually conducted by a media outlet, university polling center, or think tank.

quick response poll: a brief survey conducted to gauge

public reaction to a specific event or campaign activity.

sampling error: the difference between the estimates provided by a poll's sample and the actual number that would materialize if the entire population could be measured.

tracking polls: a series of polls that gauge opinion change over time by asking the same questions at various points during the campaign.

voter file: the official public list of all registered voters in a state, county, or other smaller geographic area.

voter identification: the process of collecting political relevant information about individual voters.

DISCUSSION QUESTIONS

1. Does it concern you that campaigns collect and use so much data about voters' political preferences and behavior? Why or why not?
2. What are the consequences of "bad data"—that is, when the information campaigns have about a voter turns out to be inaccurate?
3. Why are cell phones such a problem for pollsters?
4. Critics equate opposition research with digging up dirt, but practitioners say it merely helps them inform voters about the legitimate shortcoming of opposing candidates. What do you think?

RECOMMENDED READINGS

Hersh, Eitan D. 2015. *Hacking the Electorate: How Campaigns Perceive Voters.* New York: Cambridge University Press.

This book provides a comprehensive assessment of how campaigns use databases to microtarget particular messages to specific voters. Closely assesses the accuracy of the information. Reveals that the most reliable information comes from public data collected by state governments. But because states vary in terms of the information they collect, some states' campaigns have better data than others. Consumer data can help, but this information is less useful to campaigns than people think.

Issenberg, Sasha. 2013. *The Victory Lab: The Secret Science of Winning Campaigns.* New York: Broadway Books.

This book documents the influence of political science and psychology research on campaign tactics. Journalist Sasha Issenberg vividly portrays how the 2008 and 2012 presidential campaigns used field experiments and other empirical methods to test what works and what does not. What they discover about the effectiveness of various voter turnout methods is particularly fascinating.

Zukin, Cliff. 2015. "What's the Matter with Polling?" *New York Times* (June 20): https://www.nytimes.com/2015/06/21/opinion/sunday/whats-the-matter-with-polling.html.

In this brief New York Times *article, political scientist Cliff Zukin explains why election polling is so often wrong. His analysis centers on two trends: the prevalence of cell phones and the decline in the number of people willing to participate in surveys. Internet polls can help, but they have their own shortcomings.*

REFERENCES

Baldwin-Philippi, Jessica. 2015. *Using Technology, Building Democracy.* New York: Oxford University Press.

Barrow, Bill. 2019. "Democrats to Launch New Voter Database with Dean at the Helm." *Associated Press* (Feb. 13): https://www.apnews.com/9a47a0def9234e338bc72053e86f221f.

Bialik, Carl. 2016. "Why the Polls Missed Bernie Sanders's Michigan Upset." *FiveThirtyEight* (Mar. 9): https://fivethirtyeight.com/features/why-the-polls-missed-bernie-sanders-michigan-upset/.

Cadelago, Christopher. 2018. "Inside the Mission to Blow Up the 2020 Democratic Field." *Politico* (July 23): https://www.politico.com/story/2018/07/23/2020-democrats-opposition-research-republicans-735563.

Cook, Charlie. 2016. "How Analytical Models Failed Clinton." *National Journal* (Dec. 26): https://www.nationaljournal.com/s/646194/how-analytical-models-failed-clinton.

Cooper, Terry. 2014. "Why Should Your Campaign Pay a Professional to Do Opposition Research?" *In the Know* (Sept. 16): http://aristotle.com/blog/2014/09/professionally-op-researched-campaigns-are-better-campaigns/.

D'Amico, Steven. 2017. "I Ran Oppo Research against Donald Trump. He Has No Idea What He's Talking About." *Politico* (July 15): https://www.politico.com/magazine/story/2017/07/15/i-ran-oppo-research-against-donald-trump-he-has-no-idea-what-hes-talking-about-215381.

DeSilver, Drew. 2018. "Q&A: The Growing Use of 'Voter Files' in Studying the U.S. Electorate." Pew Research Center (Feb. 15): https://www.pewresearch.org/fact-tank/2018/02/15/voter-files-study-qa/.

DeSilver, Drew, and Scott Keeter. 2015. "The Challenges of Polling When Fewer People Are Available to Be Polled." Pew Research Center (July 21): https://www.pewresearch.org/fact-tank/2015/07/21/the-challenges-of-polling-when-fewer-people-are-available-to-be-polled/.

Duhigg, Charles. 2012. "Campaigns Mine Personal Lives to Get Out Vote." *New York Times* (Oct. 13): https://nyti.ms/2pddKLM.

Endres, Kyle, and Kristin J. Kelly 2018. "Does Microtargeting Matter? Campaign Contact Strategies and Young Voters." *Journal of Elections, Public Opinion and Parties* 28, no. 1: 1–18.

Entous, Adam, Devin Barrett, and Rosalind S. Helderman. 2017. "Clinton Campaign, DNC Paid for Research That Led to Russian Dossier." *Washington Post* (Oct. 24): https://www.washingtonpost.com/world/

national-security/clinton-campaign-dnc-paid-for-research-that-led-to-russia-dossier/2017/10/24/226fabf0-b8e4-11e7-a908-a3470754bbb9_story.html?utm_term=.2a6f2937ce6f.

Feltus, William J., Kenneth M. Goldstein, and Matthew Dallek. 2019. *Inside Campaigns: Elections through the Eyes of Political Professionals*, 2nd ed. Thousand Oaks, CA: CQ Press.

Fridkin, Kim Leslie, and Patrick J. Kenney. 2004. "Do Negative Messages Work? The Impact of Negativity on Citizens' Evaluations of Candidates." *American Politics Research* 32, no. 5: 570–605.

———. 2011. "Variability in Citizens' Reactions to Different Types of Campaigns" *American Journal of Political Science* 55, no. 2: 307–25.

Gelman, Andrew, and Gary King. 1993. "Why Are American President Election Campaign Polls So Variable When Votes Are So Unpredictable?" *British Journal of Political Science* 23, no. 4: 409–51.

Goldmacher, Shane. 2016. "Hillary Clinton's 'Invisible Guiding Hand.'" *Politico* (Sept. 7:): https://www.politico.com/magazine/story/2016/09/hillary-clinton-data-campaign-elan-kriegel-214215.

Green, Donald P., and Alan S. Gerber. 2006. "Can Registration-Based Sampling Improve the Accuracy of Midterm Election Forecasts?" *Public Opinion Quarterly* 70, no. 2: 197–223.

Green, Joshua. 2004. "Playing Dirty." *The Atlantic* (June): https://www.theatlantic.com/magazine/archive/2004/06/playing-dirty/302960/

Hersh, Eitan D. 2015. *Hacking the Electorate: How Campaigns Perceive Voters.* New York: Cambridge University Press.

Hersh, Eitan D., and Brian F. Schaffner. 2013. "Targeted Campaign Appeals and the Value of Ambiguity." *Journal of Politics* 75, no. 2: 520–34.

Igielnik, Ruth, Scott Keeter, Courtney Kennedy, and Bradley Spahn. 2018. *Commercial Voter Files and the Study of U.S. Politics.* Pew Research Center (Feb. 15): https://www.pewresearch.org/methods/wp-content/uploads/sites/10/2018/12/final-voter-file-report-2.15.18.pdf.

Jackman, Simon, and Bradley Spahn. 2015. "Unlisted in America." Unpublished manuscript (Aug. 20).

Jennings, Will, and Christopher Wlezien. 2018. "Election Polling Errors across Time and Space." *Nature Human Behaviour* 2 (April): 276–83.

Keeter, Scott, Courtney Kennedy, Michael Dimock, Jonathan Best, and Peyton Craighill. 2006. "Gauging the Impact of Growing Nonresponse on Estimates from a National RDD Telephone Survey." *Public Opinion Quarterly* 70, no. 5: 759–79.

Kennedy, Courtney, and Claudia Deane. 2019. "What Our Transition to Online Polling Means for Decades of Phone Survey Trends." Pew Research Center (Feb. 27): https://www.pewresearch.org/fact-tank/2019/02/27/what-our-transition-to-online-polling-means-for-decades-of-phone-survey-trends/.

Klein, Ezra. 2017. "The Inside Story of Doug Jones's Win in Alabama." *Vox* (Dec. 26): https://www.vox.com/policy-and-politics/2017/12/26/16810116/doug-jones-alabama-polls-roy-moore.

Korecki, Natasha, and Marc Caputo. 2019. "Biden Gambles on a High-Risk Primary Strategy." *Politico* (June 10): https://www.politico.com/story/2019/06/10/joe-biden-democrats-2020-strategy-1358530.

Kreiss, Daniel. 2016. *Prototype Politics: Technology-Intensive Campaigning and the Data of Democracy*. New York: Oxford University Press.

Krieger, Hilary. 2017. "An Introduction to the Dark Arts of Opposition Research." *FiveThirtyEight* (Oct. 31): https://fivethirtyeight.com/features/an-introduction-to-the-dark-arts-of-opposition-research/.

Lapowsky, Issie. 2017. "Progressive Democrats Fight for Access to the Party's Voter Data" (Dec. 11): https://www.wired.com/story/justice-democrats-denied-access-party-voter-data/.

Lau, Richard R., Lee Sigelman, and Ivy Brown Rovner. 2007. "The Effects of Negative Political Campaigns: A Meta-Analytic Reassessment." *Journal of Politics* 69, no. 4: 1176–209.

Matalin, Mary, and James Carville. 1993. *All's Fair: Love, War and Running for President*. New York: Simon & Schuster.

Nickerson, David W., and Todd Rogers. 2014. "Political Campaigns and Big Data." *Journal of Economic Perspectives* 28, no. 2: 51–74.

Raju, Manu. 2014. "The Grimes Family Discount." *Politico* (Aug. 19): https://www.politico.com/story/2014/08/alison-lundergan-grimes-kentucky-2014-elections-110130.

Rakich, Nathaniel. 2018. "Internal Polls Are Usually Bunk." *FiveThirtyEight* (May 7): https://fivethirtyeight.com/features/is-don-blankenship-really-surging-in-west-virginia/.

Rogers, Todd, and Masahiko Aida. 2014. "Vote Self-Prediction Hardly Predicts Who Will Vote, and Is (Misleadingly) Unbiased." *American Politics Research* 42, no. 3: 503–28.

Sides, John, and Lynn Vavreck. 2014. "Obama's Not-So-Big Data." *Pacific Standard* (June 14): https://psmag.com/social-justice/obamas-big-data-inconclusive-results-political-campaigns-72687.

Silver, Nate. 2012. "When Internal Polls Mislead, a Whole Campaign May Be to Blame." *FiveThirtyEight* (Dec. 1): https://fivethirtyeight.com/features/when-internal-polls-mislead-a-whole-campaign-may-be-to-blame/.

———. 2017. "Why You Shouldn't Always Trust the Inside Scoop." *FiveThirtyEight* (Feb. 27): https://fivethirtyeight.com/features/why-you-shouldnt-always-trust-the-inside-scoop/.

———. 2018. "The Polls Are All Right." *FiveThirtyEight* (May 30): https://fivethirtyeight.com/features/the-polls-are-all-right/.

Vogel, Kenneth P., and Byron Tau. 2014. "How Oppo Took Over the Midterms" (Sept. 19): https://www.politico.com/story/2014/09/2014-election-stories-111114.

WLWT5. 2014. "FitzGerald is on the Defensive in Ohio Governor's Race." Aug. 9: https://www.wlwt.com/article/fitzgerald-is-on-defensive-in-ohio-governor-s-race/3545469.

Yglesias, Matthew, and Andrew Prokop. 2018. "The Steele Dossier, Explained." *Vox* (Feb. 2): https://www.vox.com/2018/1/5/16845704/steele-dossier-russia-trump.

Zukin, Cliff. 2015. "What's the Matter with Polling?" *New York Times* (June 20): https://www.nytimes.com/2015/06/21/opinion/sunday/whats-the-matter-with-polling.html.

4

Earned Media

Democratic presidential candidate Elizabeth Warren fields questions from reporters at a 2019 campaign event in New Hampshire. *Source*: *AP Photo/Elise Amendola*

LEARNING OBJECTIVES

★ Understand why journalists consider some topics more newsworthy than others.

★ Grasp the implications of the media's tendency to *interpret* and *analyze* the news rather than merely report objective facts.

- ★ Assess the impact of commercial pressures on election news.
- ★ Evaluate the strategic thinking behind campaigns' attempts to shape their media coverage.

"WHY IS TRUMP SURGING? Blame the Media" read the July 2015 headline in the *Washington Post*. The story was authored by political scientist John Sides, and it conveyed the widely held sentiment that Trump led in the polls during the Republican primaries because the news media focused on him rather than the other sixteen candidates running for the party's nomination. It is worth noting that the story ran six months before the first primary. But the pattern observed then held until Trump secured the Republican nomination: his media coverage dwarfed that of his opponents, and the discrepancy partly explained Trump's success. In other words, the news media were partly responsible for Trump winning the Republican nomination. Absent his party's nomination, there would be no Trump presidency.

This blame-the-media-for-Trump sentiment ascribes a great deal of power to the news media. Yet the media's capacity to shape election results is far more limited than many people think. During the general election phase of any election, the nominees for both parties tend to garner comparable amounts of media coverage. Even if the media cover one candidate more favorably than the other—and sometimes they do—most people vote in line with their partisanship or perhaps support the incumbent, subconsciously resisting the influence of external messages. As discussed in chapter 2, voters reason away information that challenges their inclination to support their party's nominee. They are nearly impervious to unfavorable news coverage of a candidate from their own party. And although they embrace a damning story on a candidate from the opposite party—they might even share the story on their Facebook feed—their negative impressions of the offending candidate are merely reinforced, not fundamentally changed.

Primaries are different, which is why Sides's blame-the-media headline rings true. During the nomination phase, voters are choosing among candidates in the same party, neutralizing party identification as a reliable shortcut for processing information and making decisions. Primary voters are more susceptible to persuasion by external messaging—by the campaigns, of course, but also by media coverage. What is more, some candidates do garner more media attention than others during the primaries, especially when there is a crowded field—as there was in 2016. Whereas general election coverage tends to be relatively balanced, primary coverage tends to focus on front-runners and viable challengers, especially those who represent "good stories" by journalism standards. During the primaries, the news media provide only minimal coverage of hopeless candidates who stand no chance of winning.

The focus of this chapter is what campaign professionals call **earned media**. The term refers to strategies and practices that campaigns employ to gain publicity without paying for it. By contrast, the subject of chapter 5 is **paid media**, which includes advertising and other forms of campaigning that require specific financial costs. Earned media is sometimes called "free media," but that nickname is misleading: earned media strategies may not come with a price tag, but the costs are significant in terms of time, stress, and frustration for candidates and their staffs. Traditionally, earned media entails working with the *news media* and results in stories in newspapers, on television, and their online equivalents. That will be the focus of this chapter. The classic earned media relationship is between a campaign's press secretary and the reporters assigned to cover the campaign. Another typical earned media interaction is a press conference during which the candidate is inundated with questions from reporters. But earned media strategies also include working with media outlets that fall outside of what constitutes journalism. For example, presidential candidates now routinely appear on late-night talk shows, during which the host—usually a comedian—is expected to lob softball questions and avoid controversial topics. Some candidates try to avoid the news media entirely, especially Republicans. That is one approach to earned media.

Did Trump actually get more media coverage than his Republican opponents? Yes. In a follow-up analysis, Sides summarizes two data sources to conclude that Trump got up to one-half of Republican primary news coverage and the remaining sixteen candidates split the rest. Why? Trump was—and is—an irresistible story by the standards of modern journalism. He regularly created controversy with shocking statements and outright lies. His outrageousness triggered responses from opponents that also warranted media coverage. He refused to behave like a regular politician, which set him apart from his opponents. He was entertaining. In other words, "Trump [knew] how to align his behavior with the values of news organizations" (Sides and Leetru 2016). No wonder the media could not resist. And since Trump led in the polls and won most of the primaries, the tone of his coverage was less negative than that of his opponents. That is because election news coverage tends to focus on the "horse race"—who is ahead and who is behind—and Trump fared well on this front, partly by consistently beating expectations that he would eventually be vanquished by his more conventional rivals. He kept winning. It helped that his Republican opponents were reluctant to attack Trump because they feared backlash from his large and growing base of supporters. Republican hesitancy mattered because "attacks are often what helps generate unfavorable coverage as the media quotes these attacks, investigates the claims and uncovers more dirt" (Sides and Leetru 2016). For much of the primaries, critical news coverage of Trump was lacking because so few Republicans were willing to talk to reporters about their misgivings.

Trump was a master of earned media. But, of course, he was not a typical candidate. Most candidates are experienced politicians who behave in relatively predictable ways. Unless they are running for the presidency or a statewide office, they will struggle to attract media attention except when they make a mistake or get caught up in a scandal. Candidates would prefer predictable, favorable coverage that highlights their positive attributes and issue priorities. Yet news outlets are more interested in **newsworthy** stories that are more likely to center on the candidates' shortcomings, their relative position in the race, or the latest controversy. Candidates want certainty; news outlets want novelty. Down-ballot candidates may get no news coverage at all. Campaigns are constantly reminded that journalists are not interested in providing free publicity to candidates. Candidates hoping for help from the news media will nearly always be disappointed if not infuriated. That's why earned media isn't really free. In other words, this is a classic "managing the chaos" situation.

NEWSWORTHINESS

What do media outlets consider newsworthy? Not a candidate's policy platform unless it's controversial. They probably don't want to cover a candidate's stump speech either; after it's been covered once, it's no longer news because it does not change much over time. Scripted responses to interview questions probably won't make the cut either. Journalists are motivated to make their stories *interesting*. That sounds obvious, but political scientist David Niven (2012) explains why the "interesting bias" drives journalists' decision-making:

> Interesting means getting a better position in the paper, perhaps the front page. . . . Interesting means people will start reading your piece and might even finish it. Interesting means walking into a coffee shop and

> overhearing someone discussing your article and seeing bloggers praise
> or attack you. Without interesting, you're not in the paper. You're not
> read. Nothing you write matters. (p. 260)

Today, interesting also means getting your story clicked on and shared
on social media, perhaps virally. Niven is a political scientist, but in
2006 he was hired as a reporter by a newspaper in Columbus, Ohio.
Niven confirmed that journalism is a source-driven process. That is,
stories are shaped by reporters' dependence on interviews with people
who are relevant to the story. But some sources are more interesting—
and therefore more quotable in the story—than others. In the quest
to make their stories interesting, journalists favor "sources who say
something unexpected, something that perhaps they would later wish
they hadn't" (p. 262).

Predicting what news outlets will find newsworthy—or interesting—can be a frustrating guessing game for campaigns. But several
overlapping priorities emerge. As Niven suggests, *unexpected* or *surprising* events or comments can be interesting to journalists, especially when they entail some sort of *controversy*. So when candidates
depart from their usual scripted answers during an interview and say
something provocative, that can be news. A related criterion is *novelty*, which favors new developments that change from one day to the
next. The novelty criterion explains why news outlets might ignore a
candidate's polished stump speech after covering it once: its delivery
might be impressive, but the speech hasn't changed since they covered
it the first time.

Other criteria stem from natural human tendencies. The importance of *drama* explains why tight races between two serious candidates warrant more news coverage than noncompetitive contests
between a safe incumbent and a hopeless challenger. All elections
entail *conflict* between two opposing parties, but candidates who
aggressively attack their opponents are especially newsworthy.
Candidates who have an interesting *human interest* story to tell may
also fare well. In 2006, for example, media outlets ran numerous stories about the many veterans who ran as Democratic candidates for
Congress after returning home from service in the ongoing wars in
Iraq and Afghanistan.

Horse Race Journalism

Clearly, newsworthiness favors certain topics over others. Voters will
benefit from stories that cover the candidates' issue positions, their
qualifications and record, and relevant biographical information. Those

topics get some coverage, but they usually fall short on newsworthiness for the reasons described above. Instead, news outlets will provide voters with a great deal of coverage of what media critics have dubbed the "horse race" aspects of the campaign. The term is used to describe the media's tendency to focus on who is ahead, who is behind, and why. It is now a truism that election news is dominated by stories reporting and analyzing poll results, fundraising numbers, and—perhaps most importantly—the strategies campaigns employ to get ahead or catch up. This "game" or "strategy" frame has dominated election news since the late 1980s (Patterson 1993). In 2016, for example, horse race stories was the primary topic of 42 percent of news stories, outpacing issue-centered coverage by more a four-to-one ratio (Patterson 2016).

Why so many stories about the horse race? For starters, horse race stories meet several of the newsworthiness criteria. The state of the race—who is winning and who is losing—can change from week to week if not day to day. "Polls are a snap to report and provide a constant source of fresh material" (Patterson 2016). A candidate's unexpected surge in the polls creates an element of surprise and adds drama to the story. There is a human interest angle to a "dark horse" candidate who beats expectations or a struggling candidate who is flaming out. A campaign's strategic decision to step up its attacks warrants coverage because of the conflict story it tells. By contrast, a candidate's policy positions rarely change, and they tend to be predictable and lack drama.

Voters seem to agree that horse race stories are compelling. In a study of the 2000 presidential election, about two hundred voters were presented with news reports on a variety of subjects during the weeks immediately before the election. It found that respondents gravitated toward the stories that focused on the horse race and strategy and practically ignored reports on the issues. In other words, "the horse-race sells" (Iyengar, Norpoth, and Hahn 2004: 157). Horse race stories also are easier to produce than policy stories. They lend themselves to straightforward reporting of factual information such as poll results, ad buys, and fundraising totals. By contrast, policy differences are complex and difficult to analyze without betraying a preference for one option over the other. Because costs are low and clicks are high, an abundance of horse race stories makes sense from a news business perspective.

Gaffes

Fox News founder Roger Ailes once grumbled about what he called the Orchestra Pit theory of politics. It went like this: "If you have two guys on stage, and one guy says, 'I have a solution to the Middle East program,' and the other guy falls into the orchestra pit, who do you think is going to be on the evening news?" (Page 2017). Ailes's rhetorical question refers to the truism that news outlets are far more interested in candidates' blunders than their policy ideas. In politics, a mistake is commonly called a **gaffe**—a term that describes an embarrassing statement or act, usually unintentional. Candidate gaffes tend to be verbal—an offensive statement, for example, or a remark that suggests ignorance about the subject matter. Others are physical blunders, such as Ailes's fictitious example of a candidate falling into the orchestra pit.

Gaffes are newsworthy because, as with the horse race, they represent a diversion from the repetitive routine of covering a campaign. Candidates tend to deliver the same stump speech over and over, eliciting yawns from the reporters who are assigned to follow them around. Interviews and press conferences promise more spontaneity, but candidates are coached to provide canned responses to questions their campaign anticipates in advance. That is why reporters pounce when a candidate gets stumped by a question and responds with a gaffe-worthy answer. Ditto when a candidate diverges from the script and says something offensive or incoherent during a speech. Even better is if the candidate falls off the stage (if not into the orchestra pit), as Bob Dole did after a campaign event when he ran for president in 1996.

Like all human beings, candidates make mistakes on a regular basis. And not all gaffes result in a "feeding frenzy" of days and days of media coverage (Sabato 1993). Which gaffes resonate with the media and their audiences? Gaffes hit a nerve when they crystalize a candidate's familiar weaknesses. To reverberate with the news media, a gaffe must exemplify a negative stereotype associated with the candidate rather than undermine it. When Dole fell off a stage, it reinforced the perception that the seventy-three-year-old candidate was too feeble to run for president. In 1992, Vice President Dan Quayle already had a reputation for below-average intelligence when he and President George H. W. Bush ran for reelection. That perception was reinforced during a visit to a New Jersey elementary school, where Quayle jumped in to help judge a spelling bee and proceeded to misspell the word "potato." His mistake was adding an "e" to the end of the word—exactly how the word was spelled on a flashcard provided to him by the school. Rather than being seen as a common mistake precipitated by the school's misspelled flashcard, the "potatoe" gaffe solidified Quayle's image as an intellectual lightweight.

Other well-known gaffes also exaggerate and sometimes distort perceived weaknesses:

- Howard Dean's reputation for being temperamental came to life toward the end of his run for the Democratic presidential nomination in 2004. Having finished a disappointing third place in the Iowa caucuses after weeks of leading the field, Dean attempted to buck up his supporters with a fiery speech that concluded with what sounded like a deranged scream. Dean claimed he was merely trying to elevate his hoarse voice above a noisy crowd. But on television, the microphones amplified Dean's growling and screaming delivery and dampened the sound of the cheering crowd, resulting in video footage of what appeared to be an unhinged losing candidate.

- Dean lost the 2004 Democratic nomination to John Kerry, who made his own share of gaffes. His most resonant blunder was made shortly after he secured the nomination when, in explaining his voting record on funding for the Iraq war, he said, "I actually did vote for the $87 billion—before I voted against it." This was a clumsy way of justifying his decision to vote against the final version of a bill after supporting earlier drafts. But the gaffe clicked because it underscored his opponent's accusation that Kerry was an indecisive "flip-flopper." At the campaign headquarters of his opponent, President George W. Bush, "there was a clear ripple of excitement that rolled through the campaign—not quite as big as the Dean scream, but there was a ripple," said Bush media strategist Mark McKinnon (Wilgoren 2004). The media pounced, as did the Bush campaign.

- For years there had been rumors and a few news accounts about U.S. senator George Allen's history of racially insensitive behavior, but a single event during his 2006 reelection campaign brought that concern to the surface. As is typical with major campaigns today, Allen's public appearances were being filmed by a "tracker" from the opposing party, whose job it is to trail to candidate with a camera in hopes of capturing the candidate making a gaffe. That's exactly what happened, although the particulars are ambiguous. During a rally, Allen singled out the tracker, S. R. Siddarth—a college student of Indian descent, who stood out in the all-white crowd in rural Virginia. Pointing to Siddarth, he twice called him "macaca," a racial slur in some contexts. Allen later claimed he made up

the word and was therefore unaware of its racial underpin-
nings—a plausible explanation, but not one that panned out
given Allen's reputation for racial insensitivity.

- Barack Obama magnified his reputation for being a holier-
than-thou elitist when he was caught on audio tape fretting
over working-class voters who "get bitter . . . and . . . cling to
guns or religion, or antipathy toward people who aren't like
them, or anti-immigrant sentiment, or, you know, anti-trade
sentiment [as] a way to explain their frustrations." It didn't
help that Obama was speaking to wealthy donors at a fundraiser in San Francisco. His full remarks reveal that he was
trying to explain to supporters why he was struggling to gain
traction among voters in industrial states such as Ohio and
Pennsylvania. But the "bitter" and "cling to guns or religion"
reverberated because it fit the elitist narrative about Obama.

- Obama made the "bitter" gaffe during the late stages of the
Democratic nomination race in 2008, and his opponent was
Hillary Clinton. Interestingly, Clinton inflamed some of the
same voters eight years later when running for president
against Donald Trump. In what became known as the "deplorables" gaffe, she told a crowd of supporters: "You know,
to just be grossly generalistic, you could put half of Trump's
supporters into what I call the basket of deplorables. Right?
The racist, sexist, homophobic, xenophobic, Islamophobic—
you name it." No matter that Clinton went on to express em-
pathy for the "other basket of people" who "feel the government has let them down, the economy has let them down."
The "basket of deplorables" phrase hit a nerve because it
underlined the perception that Clinton was condescending
toward white working-class voters who were inclined to support Trump.

- Similarly, Mitt Romney was trying to make sense out of why
his support was so weak among certain voters when he uttered his famous "47 percent" gaffe during his 2012 challenge
to Obama's reelection. At a fundraiser, he explained to donors
that "there are 47 percent of the people who will vote for the
president no matter what . . . who are dependent on government, who believe they are victims, who believe the government has a responsibility to care for them, who believe they
are entitled to health care, to food, to housing. . . . I'll never
convince them they should take personal responsibility and

care for their lives." This was a closed-door event with no media present, but a bartender secretly filmed Romney's remarks on his phone and leaked the footage to *Mother Jones* magazine. Romney's remarks were directed toward donors, and he seemed to be rationalizing his campaign's strategic decision to focus its resources on mobilizing likely supporters rather than persuading likely Democrats to switch. But once the footage went viral, the "47 percent" gaffe fed the narrative that Romney was an out-of-touch plutocrat.

- U.S. Senate candidate Bill Braley's reputation for arrogance and political ineptitude was solidified when he insulted farmers while running in Iowa, a farm state. A Democrat, Braley warned that if his party lost the Senate majority, a "farmer from Iowa who never went to law school" would become the next chair of the Senate Judiciary Committee. What Braley said was true: fellow Iowan Chuck Grassley was indeed in line to chair the committee, and Grassley did own a farm. But so did thousands of other Iowans. Besides, Grassley had represented Iowa in the U.S. Senate for thirty-three years, and many Iowans were pleased when he assumed the Judiciary Committee chairmanship a few months after Braley lost to Republican Jodi Ernst.

What about Trump? Throughout his presidential run, Trump made numerous gaffes that would doom a typical candidate. A *Politico* headline quipped that there were "37 Fatal Gaffes That Didn't Kill Donald Trump"—and that was six weeks before Election Day. By October 2016, Trump had already:

- Accused Mexico of "sending" immigrants who are "rapists" and are "bringing drugs [and] crime."
- Dismissed Senator John McCain's wartime heroism by saying McCain "was a war hero because he was captured. I like people who weren't captured." McCain was a former Navy pilot who was tortured during his five years as a POW during the Vietnam War.
- Mocked the physical disability of a *New York Times* reporter.
- Called for banning all Muslims from entering the U.S.
- Challenged the credibility of a U.S.-born judge for a Trump-related lawsuit on the grounds that he was "Mexican."
- Labeled President Obama as "founder of ISIS."

Even before running for president, Trump had spent years promoting the "birther" myth that Obama was not born in the U.S.—a lie for which he never apologized. Why didn't such gaffes doom Trump? It is worth pointing out that we have no way of knowing whether gaffes ever doom candidates. Many gaffes "just don't register to busy American who have more things to do than follow every jot and tittle of the news" (Sides 2012). Romney lost the 2012 election, but the 47-percent remark had no measurable impact on his support at the time. Obama won the 2008 election despite the "bitter" gaffe. Dean screamed after—not before—a loss in the Iowa caucuses that already signaled the end of his campaign. Allen was one of six Republican senators who lost in 2006; it was a bad election for most Republicans not because of anybody's gaffe but largely due to dissatisfaction with President Bush's handling of the Iraq war. Rarely does a single event determine the results of an election, much less an isolated gaffe.

With Trump, however, there was no single gaffe; there were dozens. Perhaps the sheer volume of mistakes—and the media's coverage of them—explains their lack of impact. Even before he ran for president, Trump had a reputation for saying offensive things; each gaffe merely reinforced that narrative. For Trump, offensive remarks were not mistakes—he was simply speaking his mind. A sufficient number of Americans admired him for that.

Scandals

A political scandal should be far more consequential. A gaffe is a single statement or stumble. It may be part of a larger pattern of similar missteps, but an individual gaffe is unlikely to doom a candidate. A scandal involving a candidate's public or personal misdeeds could be more far-reaching. A scandal is the disclosure of an unethical or unlawful act that raises questions about the politician's suitability for office. Sometimes the disclosure originates from the politician's political opponents; other times the media initiate the investigation. Misbehavior becomes a full-blown scandal when a media "feeding frenzy" ensues, which political scientist Larry Sabato describes as "the press coverage attending any political event or circumstance where a critical mass of journalists leap to cover the same embarrassing or scandalous subject and pursue it intensely, often excessively, and sometimes uncontrollably" (1993: 6).

Scandal stories are appealing to journalists because they epitomize their watchdog function. Democracies thrive when news outlets scrutinize the behavior of politicians and others in positions of power. Political corruption certainly deserves the light of day. It is also true that scandalous behavior checks many of the boxes of newsworthiness. Scandals interrupt the tedium of routine campaign events and repeated speeches. They are controversial by nature. They tell a story about human failings. A scandal can create drama because it promises to shake up the race.

What constitutes a media scandal? Politicians are routinely accused of misbehavior by their political opponents. News outlets are drawn to controversy. Which malfeasances trigger enough media coverage to warrant a full-blown scandal? The straightforward ones involve some form of corruption or other public misconduct—a lawmaker pressuring a company to hire a family member, for example, or a candidate spending campaign funds on personal items. Others center on misbehavior during a politicians' past life—before they ran for office. Shady business deals, disastrous real-estate investments, provocative political statements or actions—all can become scandals once a person decides to enter the public arena.

What constitutes scandalous behavior has broadened considerably since the Watergate scandal in the 1970s. Until then, the media limited their scrutiny to politicians' public actions carried out as part of their jobs as government officials or candidates. Politicians' private lives were considered off-limits and irrelevant. Thus, reporters covering the John F. Kennedy White House looked the other way when the president engaged in extramarital affairs. But Watergate convinced journalists that a politician's personal failings were worth investigating because they predicted and sometimes explained public behavior. President Richard Nixon had approved a "slush fund" to silence operatives engaged in "dirty tricks" supporting his reelection campaign, which included a burglary of the Democratic National Committee headquarters in the Watergate office complex. Ensuing press coverage and congressional hearings revealed a slew of troubling character flaws. Taped recordings of Nixon's White House conversations exposed a president who was anti-Semitic, racist, and paranoid—a crank who was determined to destroy his political opponents. Had the media more aggressively analyzed Nixon's character flaws and paranoid personality when he ran for president in 1968, there would be no Nixon presidency and therefore no Watergate scandal, no Pentagon Papers, no constitutional crisis, and no resignation. The lesson for journalists was that "character matters"—that personal shortcomings can lead to public misdeeds (West 2001).

Republican Roy Moore's character—and his behavior—certainly mattered when he ran for one of Alabama's U.S. Senate seats in special election in 2017. During the closing weeks of the campaign, the *Washington Post* reported that Moore had initiated a sexual encounter with a fourteen-year-old girl when he was a thirty-two-year-old assistant district attorney. Eight other women also shared their stories of inappropriate sexual misconduct, including several who were teenagers at the time. Moore denied knowing any of the women, and most of the incidents were said to have taken place in the 1970s. Yet media reports persisted as questions emerged about Moore's preference for very young women or girls. Eventually, several Republican leaders called for Moore to withdraw from the race. Trump did the opposite and strongly endorsed Moore. Even so, Moore lost to Democrat Doug Jones in a state Trump won by twenty-eight points.

One particular scandal plagued Trump's 2016 opponent, Hillary Clinton. The controversy centered on Clinton's use of a private email server for official email communication while serving as secretary of state. It is not unusual for politicians to use a private email address for at least some professional email correspondence, but the extent of Clinton's reliance on a private account was remarkable. About one hundred of Clinton's emails included classified information, and about three thousand others were later categorized as confidential. To critics and some in the media, Clinton's behavior was not only a careless act of governing malpractice. Her insistence upon a private email server suggested a serious character flaw, reinforcing the perception that Clinton had a tendency to exercise poor judgment, especially when her privacy was at stake. The FBI launched an investigation that concluded that no "reasonable prosecutor" would bring a criminal case against Clinton. But FBI director James Comey criticized Clinton and her aides for being "extremely careless," then released the famous "Comey letter" eleven days before the election announcing the investigation of a new set of emails.

Media coverage was brutal, especially during the final two weeks of the campaign. According to one study, media coverage of Clinton during the 2016 campaign was dominated by references to the email scandal—double the amount of coverage of her policy positions (Faris et al. 2017). The percentage of Clinton coverage dedicated to scandal more than doubled during the final two weeks of the campaign, and 91 percent of those stories were negative in tone (Patterson 2016). During one six-day period shortly before Election Day, the *New York Times* ran as many front-page stories about Clinton's emails as they did front-page stories about her policies during the final two months of the campaign (Watts and Rothschild 2017). Trump had actually been embroiled in far more scandals in the campaign, none more troubling than the release of a videotape showing Trump lewdly bragging about committing sexual assault, followed by numerous women accusing him of sexually assaulting them. All received extensive media coverage, but none that came close to the amount dedicated to Clinton's email scandal (Watts and Rothschild 2017). In terms of media coverage, Trump benefited from being embroiled in multiple scandals rather than just one.

How much can extensive scandal coverage damage a candidate? Clinton's lead in the polls dropped by three points immediately following the release of the Comey letter, which was "*the* dominant story of the last 10 days of the campaign." Undecided and late-deciding voters appeared to break toward Trump (Silver 2017; italics in original), who eventually won the election. More broadly, a study of congressional elections indicated that incumbents charged with corruption lose about 10 percent of the vote in a general election, and 25 percent of them lost their race (Welch and Hibbing 1997). Still, it is unclear how much of the damage is caused by the scandals themselves or by the media coverage investigating them. Joe Trippi, Doug Jones's media strategist, suggested that harsh media coverage may have actually rallied some Republicans behind Roy Moore because they saw the episode as a case of the national media "out to get" a conservative Republican (Klein 2017). Scandal may alarm voters, but awareness of them may not affect their vote choice (Cobb and Taylor 2015). All we know is that scandal—like the horse race as well as candidate gaffes—is an irresistible topic for media outlets.

ANALYTICAL JOURNALISM

One source of frustration for campaigns is the perceived lack of objectivity in modern journalism. Journalists are criticized for injecting their own personal opinions into their stories rather than merely reporting objective facts. There is some truth to this complaint. Decades ago, the norms of journalism shifted away from the goal of pure objectivity and toward news analysis that provides context. Journalists now *interpret* the news rather than merely report facts. Today, a typical news story combines objective reporting of *what* happened with analysis that explains *why* it happened (West 2001). Since journalists are the ones who are providing the analysis, it is inevitable that their personal political orientations become part of the story.

There are many reasons for the shift away from the goal of objectivity (West 2001). Objective journalism may strive for fairness and balance, but a "straight news" story can lack the context readers need to make sense out of the facts being reported. Facts alone can be confusing and even misleading. The shortcomings of objective reporting had become apparent by the 1970s. Objective reporting from Vietnam failed to shed light on military failures there because news coverage relied so heavily on rosy assessment from official Pentagon sources. News coverage of the 1988 presidential election was criticized for slavishly reporting each campaign's "message of the day" without analyzing its veracity and relevance. Analytical journalism promised to "read between the lines" to unearth the true meaning behind the statements and actions of politicians. By the 1990s, the journalist had become "a solo author of the news, whose own analysis was more newsworthy than what the candidate had to say" (Iyengar 2011: 72).

For election news, the rise of analytical journalism means more scrutiny of the actions of candidates and their campaigns. The analysis typically carries a negative tone. Many Republicans are convinced that the news media have a "liberal bias" and that journalists are determined to bury them with unfavorable coverage. The reality is, politicians from both parties tend to be burdened with more negative stories than positive stories. In 2016, for example, whereas 56 percent of Trump's news coverage was negative, Clinton fared worse: her coverage ran 62 percent negative (Patterson 2016). The news media have a "preference for the negative" rather than a consistent liberal bias (Patterson 2002: 374). In recent elections, negative stories about the Democratic and Republican presidential nominees doubled the number of positive stories (see figure 4.1).

Why so negative? Much of the negativity can be explained by the post-Nixon scrutiny of politicians' personal lives described above. Whereas journalists were once inclined to give official sources the benefit of the doubt, news coverage now conveys an assumption that politicians are more concerned with getting reelected than making sound policy. Another explanation lies in the coinciding increase in negative campaigning. Election news coverage is shaped by what campaigns say and do, and the reality is that candidates spend much of their time and advertising attacking each other. It also matters that negativity does not violate journalistic norms. "Although norms of American journalism dissuade reporters from taking sides in a partisan debate, there is no rule that says they can't bash both sides" (Patterson 2013: 16). In any case, this **negativity bias** means that

Figure 4.1   Tone of Presidential Nominees' News Coverage, 1960–2016

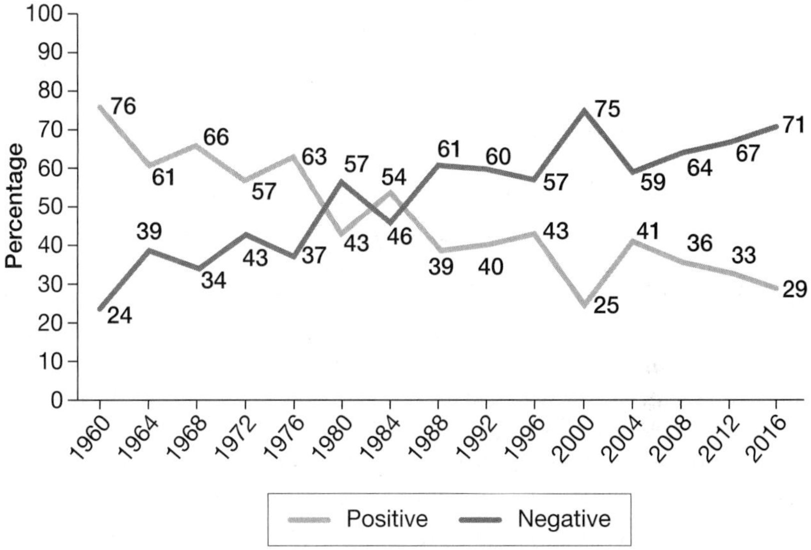

Source: Patterson 2016
Note: Neutral stories were excluded. Percentages were the average for each election for the two major-party nominees.

candidates can expect unfavorable coverage and just hope that their opponent fares worse.

There are exceptions. When Barack Obama first ran for president in 2008, positive stories about him outnumbered negative stories. But that advantage can be explained by other journalistic priorities that stacked up in his favor. Obama was on track to be the first African American president of the United States, which made his candidacy a remarkably newsworthy story. He led for most of the race after defeating the establishment candidate, Hillary Clinton, for the Democratic nomination. His campaign's innovative use of social media also made good copy. That said, Obama's Republican opponent also represented a great story by journalistic standards: John McCain was a war hero who survived over five years of captivity as a prisoner of war in North Vietnam. McCain's problem was that he had already run for president; he was a familiar face in Washington by 2008 and he ran a relatively conventional campaign. That was not the case eight years earlier when McCain challenged George W. Bush for the

Republican nomination with a campaign that broke new ground in terms of media strategy and online fundraising. Like Obama in 2008, the 2000 version of McCain was a fresh face and a serious challenger to the establishment candidate. His campaign bus was nicknamed the "Straight Talk Express," which captured his reputation for speaking his mind and eschewing canned sound bites. To reporters, McCain was very interesting the first time he ran for president; not so much eight years later.

COMMERCIAL PRESSURES

Heightened commercial pressures explain some of the disconnect between the journalistic priorities and the needs of candidates running for office. Nearly all media outlets in the U.S. are businesses that must make healthy profits in order to thrive. Most of their revenue comes from advertising, and nearly all news outlets have seen declines in this source since their peak in the 1990s. Declining revenue has led to cost cuts, usually at the expense of reporting resources. With tight newsroom budgets, media outlets are more sensitive to the preferences of their audiences, especially those that attract advertisers. Election news has thus taken a hit, particularly at the local level, which translates to limited coverage of all but national and a handful of statewide and congressional races. What little election news there is centers more than ever on topics that can deliver advertisers. A story comparing both candidates' plans for entitlement reform will not make the evening news.

Local newspapers have been hit especially hard. Between 2004 and 2017, total newspaper circulation dropped by about 40 percent. Advertising revenue plummeted by 65 percent during that same time. Newspapers have offered online versions of their product for two decades now, but increased returns from digital advertising have failed to compensate for the sharp decline in display advertising by department stores and other struggling industries, not to mention the near disappearance of classified advertising due to the advent of Craigslist and other online competitors. According to one study, for every $1 gained in online advertising revenue, newspapers lost $7 in print advertising (Pew 2013). In response, personnel cuts have been severe: between 2004 and 2017, the number of people employed in a newspaper newsroom plummeted from 71,640 to 39,210 (Pew 2018). The *Denver Post* cut nearly one-third of its newsroom staff in March 2018. The *Oregonian*, the largest daily newspaper serving the

Pacific Northwest, underwent six rounds of staff reductions between 2010 and 2018. The *Charleston Gazette-Mail* filed for bankruptcy shortly after winning a Pulitzer Prize for a story about the opioid epidemic in West Virginia.

The decline of the local newspaper hurts because print journalists provide the lion's share of reporting used by other outlets. The consequences for elections are real. The closure of the *Seattle Post-Intelligencer* and the *Rocky Mountain News* in 2009 may have resulted in decay in various forms of civic engagement in the markets they served (Shaker 2014). A study of local newspaper coverage of U.S. House races in 2010 indicated that uncompetitive races saw a smaller amount of coverage, and with less substance, than hotly contested contests. As a result, citizens were less capable of assessing the candidates and less likely to vote. "When local news outlets like daily newspapers provide less coverage, and less substantive coverage, to politics—whether it be about a House race, state legislative contest, or municipal election—there are few alternative sources to which citizens can turn" (Hayes and Lawless 2015: 460).

Local television news outlets could pick up the slack since their audiences and advertising revenue are holding steady. But their reporting output pales by comparison. According to one study, 92 percent of local news broadcasts during the month before the 2004 elections contained no stories at all about campaigns for congressional, state, and local offices. The same study showed that television stations ran five times more paid advertisements by House and Senate candidates than news stories about their races (Kaplan, Goldstein, and Hale 2005). Another study showed that local news broadcasts in California practically ignored the gubernatorial race in 2002 (Iyengar 2011).

To be clear: there is plenty of election news online and on television. Local newspapers are dying in part because audiences are gravitating toward national news outlets. CNN and especially Fox News are holding steady despite declining cable subscriptions, and MSNBC is thriving during the Trump presidency. Many young adults are embracing online versions of national newspapers. Although people between the age of 18 and 29 are far less likely to regularly get their election news from a local daily newspaper, they are twice as likely as people over the age of sixty-five to seek out a "national" source such as the *New York Times* or the *Washington Post* (Barthel and Gottfried 2017). Both are local newspapers that have benefited from massive increases in online readership, thanks in part to changes in how people get their news online. Although many readers go directly to sources' websites, many click on individual stories as they appear on their social media news feeds. Clicks originating from social media generate only a fraction of the financial returns than when the user navigates directly to the news outlet's website; the social media outlet that hosted the link claims a huge chunk of the revenue. Even so, the *Times*, the *Post*, the *Wall Street Journal*, and other online sources have dramatically expanded their audiences even as local newspapers struggle to attract online readers (Lee 2016). That is because Americans "are substituting Fox News . . . for the *Fayetteville Observer*, and the *New York Times* 'website for the *Nevada Appeal*" (Hopkins 2018). Online-only news sources such as *Politico, Huffington Post, FiveThirtyEight*, the *Daily Caller*, and *Vox* also attract small but highly engaged and loyal audiences (who are therefore attractive to advertisers).

All of this means that the average citizen will be saturated with media coverage of the only national race in town: the presidential election, held every four years. During midterm years and off-year elections, when there is no presidential election, there will be plenty of stories about the races deemed newsworthy by the national media— that is, competitive statewide races for governor and U.S. Senate seats as well as a handful of hotly contested congressional contests. They won't see many stories about candidates who are facing an entrenched incumbent. They will have to look hard for coverage of candidates running for local offices or seeking a seat in a state legislature. No wonder then that turnout for state and local races has declined while remaining constant for presidential races (Hopkins 2018).

PARTISAN MEDIA

Daily newspapers and local TV news programs are losing some audience members to national media outlets that lean to the left or right, particularly the latter. Partisan media are outlets "that not only report the news but offer a distinct point of view on it as well" (Levendusky 2013: 2). The most notable example is Fox News, which was launched in 1996 as a cable network with twenty-four hours of news programming and talk shows aimed at conservative audiences. Also on the right are national syndicated talk shows on the radio hosted by Rush Limbaugh and Sean Hannity (who also hosts Fox's top-rated prime-time talk show on TV). Other popular right-leaning websites include *The Drudge Report* and the *Daily Wire*, a website founded by podcaster and radio talk show host Ben Shapiro. On the left, the MSNBC cable network features prime-time talk shows hosted by progressives such as Rachel Maddow and Chris Hayes. Websites such as the *Huffington Post* and *Buzzfeed* provide news with a left-leaning point of view.

Partisan media attract small but growing audiences. They are important to campaigns because viewers and listeners are highly engaged in politics and vote regularly. Audience members tune in to have their existing views reinforced, not challenged. They tend to be like-minded and therefore somewhat predictable in terms of general partisan leanings. Republican candidates can usually count on the support of conservative talk show hosts; what they want is full-throated, enthusiastic support to help mobilize turnout on Election Day. Persuasion is not only unlikely; it is unnecessary because members of the audience are unlikely to switch sides. Partisan media are more likely to have a persuasive effect during the primaries, when talk shows hosts can serve as kingmakers by endorsing one Republican over another. That happened in 2014 when economics professor Dave Brat secured the support of radio hosts Laura Ingraham, Mark Levin, and Glenn Beck, and appeared on all three of their programs. These endorsements may have contributed to Brat's shocking primary victory over then-Majority Leader Eric Cantor.

MANAGING THE NEWS

Campaigns are not helpless victims of the press they get. To some extent, they are in a position to "earn" their media coverage. They attempt to do so through practices that fall under the category of **media management**—that is, strategies aimed at shaping media coverage by those who are its subjects. These strategies are increasingly sophisticated as campaigns have become more reliant on trained communications—"comms"—professionals to carry them out. But perhaps more so than other aspects of electioneering, earned media is mostly out the campaign's control.

The effectiveness of a campaign's media management efforts depends on an awareness of and adaptation to the patterns described in this chapter so far. Campaigns must account for the media's preoccupation with topics—the horse race, for example—that are out of sync with the priorities of the candidate. The economic struggles and changing priorities of daily newspapers and other local news outlets mean a local campaign can expect only sparse news coverage. The media's negativity bias means the campaign should expect more unfavorable than favorable news stories no matter what it does. These are some of the realities facing campaigns hoping to gain an advantage through their earned media efforts. Adjusting to those realities is vital even if such efforts appear futile.

ASSISTING REPORTERS

A big part of earned media is helping reporters do their jobs. Journalists hate being manipulated, and they resent this part of the relationship. But their dependence is not as insidious as it sounds. First and foremost, campaign reporters are accountable to their bosses—editors, producers, and the news organizations they all work for—and their audiences. But they also rely on the campaigns for information, access, and some logistical support. This dependence is even more acute now for local news outlets that increasingly lack sufficient resources to assign experienced reporters to cover local races.

For most high-profile races, the primary point-of-contact is a *press secretary* or equivalent. (Down-ballot campaigns may turn to the campaign manager or another staffer to fulfill these responsibilities.) The press secretary's primary responsibility is to interact with reporters, producers, and other media figures. Their duties range from corralling reporters between campaign events to strategically releasing information to particular media outlets. They might oversee the production of *press releases*—written documents produced in the style of news articles that can serve as a quick-reference information resource for time-strapped reporters. They also serve as a spokesperson on behalf of the candidate for most media inquiries. When a scandal erupts or a gaffe is uttered, the press secretary and the rest of the "comms" staff are tasked with doing "damage control."

Interactions with the press can take various forms. *Interviews* allow reporters to ask questions relevant to the story they are preparing. Reporters would prefer a one-on-one interview with the candidate; instead, they'll probably get a few minutes with the press secretary or equivalent. *Press conferences* are more efficient because they allow the candidate or spokesperson to answer questions from multiple reporters simultaneously. Some campaigns avoid press conferences because they can be chaotic and unpredictable, with reporters shouting over each other to ask sometimes antagonistic and surprising questions. More common are press *avails* (short for availability), which are brief, informal question-and-answer sessions announced on short notice. For all of these formats, candidates are coached to provide tame responses while deflecting reporters' attempts to create unwanted controversy.

Photo ops are preferred by most campaigns because there is no expectation that the candidate will answer questions. Short for "photo opportunities," photo ops are staged events that give news outlets the visuals they need without sacrificing the campaign's preference for predictability. They typically involve the candidate performing a praiseworthy, image-friendly task—visiting wounded soldiers in the hospital, for example—while the cameras are rolling. For the campaign, the goal is for voters to see and respond positively to the visuals; what the candidate says (or does not say) is beside the point. Reporters see photo ops as manipulative and contrived. But the pictures often appear on the news somewhere.

Photo ops imply a dependence on campaigns that journalists resent. But journalists also rely on campaigns for substantive information. As we saw in chapter 3, opposition research reports are chock-full of information about the opposing candidate's weaknesses and vulnerabilities. An oppo report might include detailed information about an unsavory or unethical act that has not been previously reported. Oppo provides fodder for a campaign's advertising and other forms of paid media. But it is not uncommon for a campaign to secretly release oppo to select news outlets. All the news outlet has to do is verify and perhaps dig deeper. Many scandal stories originate as oppo.

These "oppo drops" are a type of *leak*—a secret, off-the-record release of information to the media. Campaigns leak to the media when they want information to be made public but don't want to be identified as the source. Oppo drops are one example. Another is when a struggling campaign leaks internal poll results to demonstrate that its trailing candidate is actually catching up. This sort of leak satiates the media's hunger for **horse-race** data while satisfying the campaign's need to reassure worried supporters, as would the leaking of encouraging fundraising numbers before they are publicly disclosed. In all of these cases, both sides must establish ground rules for sourcing and attribution. Speaking to a reporter "off the record" means no direct quotes or source attribution in the story, whereas "on background" buries any reference to a source. "Not for attribution" allows the reporter to use direct quotes as long as the source is described in generic terms (for example, "a campaign spokesperson").

SPINNING THE ANALYSIS

One earned media challenge is adapting to the media's tendency to interpret and analyze the news rather than objectively report straight facts. A candidate debate will not merely be described; it will be analyzed in terms of: Who won and who lost? Which candidate landed the most effective rhetorical blows? What were the defining moments and why did they matter? A horse-race story will not merely report the relative position of each candidate in the polls; it will analyze why the front-runner is ahead and how the trailing candidate is trying to catch up. A scandal will be interpreted in terms of how badly the candidate will be damaged and how effectively the campaign responded.

Campaigns try to shape this analysis through **spin**. Over time, the word "spin" has taken on a vague, clichéd meaning that includes any form of manipulative communication. But spin is a useful concept when defined as *strategic attempts to shape media interpretation of political events*. Journalistic norms provide opportunities here. Recall that political scientist David Niven's study confirmed that journalism depends on sources. A reporter might interview dozens of people for background information, substantive guidance, and interesting comments. The final story will be loaded with direct quotes from relevant sources. Inevitably those conversations with sources will shape the analysis with the direct quotes serving as "evidence" and color.

Sources for campaign-related news stories might include expert observers (such as political scientists!), but more importantly the campaigns themselves—if not the candidate, then a press secretary or other spokesperson. Knowing that reporters need sources—and that their analysis is shaped by what their sources say—campaigns can take the initiative by making their candidate or a spokesperson available for an interview. These sources can be prepped so that they respond to interview questions in ways that advantageously inform the analysis. For a horse-race story, a struggling candidate's spokesperson might talk about the advantages of being the underdog, or point to improving fundraising or poll numbers. A lackluster debate performance can be spun as a surprising victory on the grounds that the superior candidate fell short of lofty expectations. Debate spin is so commonplace that organizers sometimes set up a "spin room" where reporters and cameras congregate for postdebate interviews with campaign spokespeople. (See box 4.1 for more analysis of debate coverage.)

BOX 4.1 | Mediated Debate Effects

Presidential debates are powerful earned media events. They are hosted by media outlets and are moderated by TV news personalities. That means journalists usually ask the questions and therefore control what the candidates will discuss. They set the agenda. As moderators, they determine who gets to talk and when. Although the candidates do most of the talking, the moderators orchestrate the flow of the conversation, sometimes cutting off candidates who speak too long and probing candidates whose answers fall short.

Televised debates provide voters with a rich opportunity to watch the candidates perform and talk policy for about ninety minutes. Viewers can see how well the candidates think on their feet and explain themselves. Debates are thus far less mediated than a typical election news story, during which the correspondent will talk more than the candidates. But make no mistake: presidential debates are fundamentally shaped by the media.

TV moderators are not the only sources of media influence. Postdebate news coverage of the debates can also be impactful. Not everyone watches the debates; some rely on news coverage. That matters because, as we have seen in this chapter, the media will not only report what the candidates said and did, but also analyze how well they performed. Campaigns attempt to "spin" that analysis, but they cannot control it. They know that postdebate news coverage can reshape voters' impressions of the candidates. One study of the 2004 presidential debates found that people who watched the third debate evaluated John Kerry more positively afterward and declared him the winner over George W. Bush. Yet Kerry's postdebate news coverage was significantly more negative than Bush's across multiple news outlets. That tone differential mattered: it diminished the boost Kerry received for performing well. People who relied solely on postdebate news coverage were led to believe that Kerry underperformed (Fridkin et al. 2008).

What about the debates themselves—do they have a broader impact separate from media analysis? There are reasons to be skeptical about the effects of the general election debates in the fall. By then, most voters are committed to their party's presidential nominee. Viewers tend to be highly engaged partisans who watch the debates to affirm their predispositions. But some viewers are still up for grabs. Even though the number of persuadables is small in a presidential general election, a minor postdebate boost can influence the results of a tight race. If nothing else, a strong debate performance can help partisans feel better about

(continued)

BOX 4.1 | (continued)

the candidate they are already supporting. A weak performance can raise doubts, but not enough to keep partisans from voting for their party's nominee.

Primary debates are potentially far more consequential. Partisanship is neutralized, so viewers are more open to changing their minds. Some watch the debates for the purpose of picking a favorite. Academic research indicates that debates are most consequential early in the election cycle when the candidates are not well known. They also matter more when the field is crowded with candidates—far more likely during the nomination phase. Under those circumstances, lesser-known candidates can demonstrate their electability with a debate performance that sets them apart from the rest of the pack. The effects: a bump in the polls and an uptick in fundraising.

SOURCES

Azari, Julia. "What We Know about the Impact of Primary Debates." FiveThirtyEight (June 24): https://fivethirtyeight.com/features/what-we-know-about-the-impact-of-primary-debates/.

Best, Samuel J., and Clark Hubbard. "'Maximizing 'Minimal Effects': The Impact of Early Primary Season Debates on Voter Preferences." *American Politics Quarterly* 27, no. 4: 450–67.

Fridkin, Kim L., Patrick J. Kenney, Sarah Allen Gershon, and Gina Serignese Woodall. 2008. "Spinning the Debates: The Impact of the News Media's Coverage of the Final 2004 Presidential Debate." *International Journal of Press/Politics* 13, no. 1: 29–51.

Holbrook Thomas M. 1999. "Political Learning from Presidential Debates." *Political Behavior* 21, no. 1: 67–89.

McKinney, Mitchell S., and Benjamin R. Warner. 2013. "Do Presidential Debates Matter? Examining a Decade of Campaign Debate Effects." *Argumentation and Advocacy* 49(spring): 238–58.

CONTROLLING ACCESS

Campaigns can attempt to spin the analysis, but their efforts may be futile: reporters and the news organizers they work for are the ones who produce the story. Yet the media's reliance on sources gives campaigns one area of control. Campaigns are the ones that decide how much *access* each media outlet is granted. Access control gives campaigns a tool for constraining the media's negativity bias. Campaigns are inclined to give more access to media outlets whose coverage they like. Outlets perceived as hostile might be penalized with limited or no access. A favored network or reporter might get an exclusive one-on-one interview with the candidate. Another might be the only outlet to secretly receive a leaked video showing the opposing candidate committing a serious gaffe.

A reporter who has angered the candidate with an inflammatory question or harsh story can be "cut off" from future interviews or press conferences. That happened in 2000 to NBC's Alexandra Pelosi when she asked then-candidate George W. Bush what he described as a "below the belt" question about the number of executions in his home state of Texas. His campaign responded by cutting off access, which hindered Pelosi's ability to do her job and therefore put her network at a competitive disadvantage. The incident is depicted in *Journeys with George*, a documentary for which Pelosi filmed her experience covering the Bush campaign with a handheld video camera. This event aside, Bush's relationship with Pelosi and other reporters appeared to be friendly. Pelosi's (and NBC's) access was restored soon afterward.

Many Republicans are so fed up what they call the "liberal media" that they limit access to a handful of friendly outlets. Fox News is an obvious choice for presidential candidates, as are nationally syndicated talk shows on the radio. Republican candidates for state and local office may seek out an array of online outlets that cater to conservative audience. Media outlets that are perceived as hostile still cover the campaign, but they must do so from a distance, without much (if any) direct access to the candidate.

The negativity bias is particularly acute with the national media, prompting even Democrats to avoid them in favor of friendlier outlets. Bill Clinton was the first presidential candidate to appear on daytime talk shows to reach new audiences with friendly banter. His campaign also used a "go local" strategy," eschewing the national press and granting exclusive interviews to daily newspaper reporters and local television stations along the campaign trail. Hillary Clinton did the same when she ran for president in 2016. Presidential candidates "go local" because they expect softer questions from inexperienced reporters who are enamored by the presence of a national figure. Local media are likely to cover the candidate's stump speech because, unlike the national media, it is actually news to them.

CONCLUSION

Does it matter? Working with the media is one of the most frustrating functions of a campaign. The campaign's priorities are completely out of sync with the media's. An innocent gaffe can result in days of unwanted and embarrassing press. Even friendly outlets can be unpredictable. Local media seem like a safe bet, but they may no longer have the resources to send a reporter to cover a campaign rally.

Earned media outreach is worth the effort because of the potential damage of extraordinarily poor news coverage. But in presidential elections, the negativity bias means that both candidates will get hammered in the press. Voters are so saturated with news, advertising, and other messages that it is unusual for a single outlet or story to have a measurable impact. For decades, research on "media effects" cast doubt on whether news messages did much more than reinforce voters' existing attitudes. There was plenty of evidence of a **priming** effect, through which the media shaped the criteria voters use to evaluate candidates by focusing on certain issues and events (Iyengar 1991). But the capacity of the media to persuade voters to support one candidate over the other appeared limited. That began to change as researchers employed richer datasets and methodological advances (Bartels 1993; Dalton, Beck, and Huckfeldt 1998). Recent studies suggest that a media outlet can affect people's vote choice when it favors one side over the other (DellaVigna and Kaplan 2007; Zaller 1996).

Media messages are even more likely to have an impact during primary elections, when there are sometimes multiple candidates vying for attention and voters cannot rely on their partisanship as a decision-making shortcut. Primary election news is even more centered on the horse race than during the general election, resulting in more favorable coverage for strong frontrunners as well as viable challengers. During the 2016 primaries, the media's Trump obsession inhibited Republican voters' ability to inform themselves about the other sixteen candidates. The imbalance seemed to help Trump in the polls (Reuning and Dietrich 2018).

Down-ballot races also see one candidate getting more favorable coverage than the other. The consequences can be significant. That happened in 2000 when Democrat Mark Dayton challenged incumbent Republican Rod Grams for one of Minnesota's seats in the U.S. Senate. News coverage in the Minneapolis *Star-Tribune* was slanted toward Dayton, which affected voters' candidate evaluations and may have impacted their vote choice (Druckman and Parkin 2005). A study of multiple Senate races revealed that voters favored candidates that were endorsed by their local newspaper (Kahn and Kenney 2002).

For campaigns, what is frustrating is how little control they have over the media coverage they receive. Their earned media efforts may be sophisticated and based on logic, but they are often for naught. The next two chapters will examine media strategies that afford more control over at least the content and production of media messaging (if not their delivery). Paid media and social media may not be "free," but at least they are more predictable.

KEY TERMS

earned media: strategies and practices that campaigns use to gain publicity without paying for it.

gaffe: an embarrassing statement or act, usually unintentional.

horse-race journalism: reporting that focuses on the strategic or "game" aspects of politics, such which candidate is winning the race.

media management: strategies aimed at shaping media coverage by those who are its subjects.

negativity bias: the media's tendency to focus on undesirable aspects of politics.

newsworthy: a topic that is suitable for news coverage under the standards and needs of journalism.

photo op (aka photo opportunity): an event staged by a campaign primarily for its visual appeal to media outlets.

priming: when the media shape the criteria voters use to evaluate candidates by focusing on certain issues and events.

spin: strategic attempts to shape media interpretation of political events.

DISCUSSION QUESTIONS

1. Why is election news coverage so negative? Do you think the news media are more negative than they should be?
2. Research casts doubt on the notion that the news media have a "liberal bias" toward Democratic candidates. Then why do conservatives think otherwise?
3. Local newspapers are in serious decline. What are the consequences for candidates running for local and state offices?
4. The growth of partisan media means people can limit their news consumption to sources that reinforce their existing political views. Is this a problem? Why or why not?

RECOMMENDED READINGS

Patterson, Thomas E. 2016. "News Coverage of the 2016 General Election: How the Press Failed the Voters." Harvard Shorenstein Center on Media, Politics, and Public Policy. December: https://shorensteincenter.org/wp-content/uploads/2016/12/2016-General-Election-News-Coverage-1.pdf?x78124.

Author of the seminal book Out of Order *documents how the lessons from that book still apply: election news coverage is overwhelmingly negative and preoccupied with the horse-race aspects of the election rather than candidates' policy differences. Reports a number of surprising differences between Trump's and Clinton's media coverage.*

Hayes, Danny, and Jennifer L. Lawrence. 2016. *Women on the Run: Gender, Media, and Political Campaigns in a Polarized Era.* New York: Cambridge University Press.

Challenging conventional wisdom, this study of 2010 and 2014 congressional races finds that women candidates fare about as well as their male counterparts in terms of attracting media attention, raising money, and winning over voters. Only 0.3 percent of news stories referred to a female candidate's physical appearance.

Niven, David. 2012. "An Interesting Bias: Lessons from an Academic's Year as a Reporter." *PS: Political Science and Politics* 45, no. 2: 259–64.

Fascinating brief article analyzing the author's participant-observer experience as reporter for a local newspapers. Helps explain why journalists favor novelty over in-depth descriptions of policy. The lesson: if a candidate wants news coverage, they should say or do something unpredictable and avoid canned answers to reporters' questions.

REFERENCES

Bartels, Larry M. 1993. "Messages Received: The Political Impact of Media Exposure." *American Political Science Review* 87, no. 2: 267–85.

Barthels, Michael, and Jeffrey Gottfried. 2017. "For Election News, Young People Turned to Some National Papers More Than Their Elders." *Pew Research Center,* February 17: http://www.pewresearch.org/fact-tank/2017/02/17/young-people-national-newspapers-for-election-news/.

Cobb, Michael D., and Andrew Taylor. 2015. "An Absence of Malice: The Limited Utility of Campaigning against Party Corruption." *American Politics Research* 43, no. 6: 923–51.

Dalton, Russell, Paul Beck, and Robert Huckfeldt. 1998. "Partisan Cues and the Media: Information Flows in the 1992 Presidential Election." *American Political Science Review* 92, no. 1: 111–26.

DellaVigna, Stefano, and Ethan Kaplan. 2007. "The Fox News Effect: Media Bias and Voting." *Quarterly Journal of Economics* 122, no. 3: 1187–234.

Druckman, James, and Michael Parkin. 2005. "The Impact of Media Bias: How Editorial Slant Affects Voters." *Journal of Politics* 67, no. 4: 1030–49.

Faris, Robert, Hal Roberts, Bruce Etling, Nikki Bourassa, Ethan Zuckerman, and Yochai Benkler. 2017. *Partisanship, Propaganda, & Disinformation: Online Media & the 2016 U.S. Presidential Campaign.* A report by the Berkman Klein Center for Internet & Society at Harvard University.

Hayes, Danny, and Jennifer L. Lawrence. 2015. "As Local News Goes, So Goes Civic Engagement: Media, Knowledge, and Participation in US House Elections." *Journal of Politics* 77, no. 2: 447–62.

Hopkins, Dan. 2018. "All Politics Is National Because All Media Is National." *FiveThirtyEight,* June 6: https://fivethirtyeight.com/features/all-politics-is-national-because-all-media-is-national/amp/?__twitter_impression=true.

Iyengar, Shanto. 1991. *Is Anyone Responsible?: How Television Frames Political Issues.* Chicago: University of Chicago Press.

———. 2011. *Media Politics: A Citizen's Guide,* 2nd ed. New York: Norton.

Iyengar, Shanto, Helmut Norpoth, and Kyu S. Hahn. 2004. "Consumer Demand for Election News: The Horserace Sells." *Journal of Politics* 66, no. 1: 157–75.

Kahn, Kim Fridkin, and Patrick J. Kenney. 2002. "The Slant of the News: How Editorial Endorsements Influence Campaign Coverage and Citizens' Views of Candidates" *American Political Science Review* 96, no. 2: 381–94.

Kaplan, Martin, Ken Goldstein, and Matthew Hale. 2005. *Local News Coverage of the 2004 Campaign: An Analysis of Nightly Broadcasts in 11 Markets.* A report by the Lear Center Local News Archive, a project of the USC Annenberg School and the University of Wisconsin.

Klein, Ezra. 2017. "The Inside Story of Doug Jones's Win in Alabama." *Vox* (Dec. 26): https://www.vox.com/policy-and-politics/2017/12/26/16810116/doug-jones-alabama-polls-roy-moore.

Lee, Timothy B. 2016. "Print Newspapers Are Dying Faster Than You Think." *Vox* (Nov. 2): https://www.vox.com/new-money/2016/11/2/13499004/print-newspapers-dying.

Levendusky, Matthew S. 2013. "Why Do Partisan Media Polarize Viewers?" *American Journal of Political Science* 57, no. 3: 611–23.

Niven, David. 2012. "An Interesting Bias: Lessons from an Academic's Year as a Reporter." *PS: Political Science and Politics* 45, no. 2: 259–64.

Page, Clarence. 2017. "Roger Ailes, a Polarizing Pioneer in Political Media." *Chicago Tribune* (May 19): https://www.chicagotribune.com/columns/clarence-page/ct-roger-ailes-fox-trump-perspec-20170519-story.html.

Patterson, Thomas E. 1993. *Out of Order.* New York: Knopf.

———. 2002. "The Vanishing Voter: Why Are the Voting Booths So Empty?" *National Civic Review* 91, no. 4: 367–77.

———. 2013. *Informing the News: The Need for Knowledge-Based Journalism.* New York: Vintage.

———. 2016. "News Coverage of the 2016 General Election: How the Press Failed the Voters." Harvard Shorenstein Center on Media, Politics, and Public Policy. December: https://shorensteincenter.org/wp-content/uploads/2016/12/2016-General-Election-News-Coverage-1.pdf?x78124.

Pew Research Center. 2018. *The State of the News Media:* http://www.pewresearch.org/topics/state-of-the-news-media/.

Pew Research Center's Project for Excellence in Journalism. 2013. "Newspapers Turning Ideas into Dollars: Four Revenue Success Stories." http://www.journalism.org/2013/02/11/newspapers-turning-ideas-dollars/.

Reuning, Kevin, and Nick Dietrich. 2018. "Media Coverage, Public Interest, and Support in the 2016 Republican Invisible Primary." *Perspectives on Politics* 17, no. 2: 326–39.

Sabato, Larry. 1993. *Feeding Frenzy: How Attack Journalism Has Transformed American Politics*. New York: Basic.

Shaker, Lee. 2014. "Dead Newspapers and Citizens' Civic Engagement." *Political Communication* 31, no. 1: 131–48.

Sides, John. 2012. "Breaking: Many Americans Don't Have Any Idea That All-Important Political Gaffes Even Happen." *The Monkey Cage* blog (June 21): http://themonkeycage.org/2012/06/breaking-many-americans-dont-have-any-idea-that-all-important-political-gaffes-even-happen/.

———. 2015. "Why Is Trump Surging? Blame the Media." *Washington Post* (July 20): https://www.washingtonpost.com/news/monkey-cage/wp/2015/07/20/why-is-trump-surging-blame-the-media/.

Sides, John, and Kalev Leetru. 2016. "A Deep Dive into the News Media's Role in the Rise of Donald J. Trump." *Washington Post* (June 24): https://www.washingtonpost.com/news/monkey-cage/wp/2016/06/24/a-deep-dive-into-the-news-medias-role-in-the-rise-of-donald-j-trump/?utm_term=.353eb9325eda.

Silver, Nate. 2017. "The Comey Letter Probably Cost Clinton the Election." *FiveThirtyEight* (May 3): https://fivethirtyeight.com/features/the-comey-letter-probably-cost-clinton-the-election/.

Watts, Duncan J., and David M. Rothschild. 2017. "Don't Blame the Election on Fake News: Blame It on the Media." *Columbia Journalism Review* (Dec. 5): https://www.cjr.org/analysis/fake-news-media-election-trump.php.

Welch, Susan, and John R. Hibbing. 1997. "The Effects of Charges of Corruption on Voting Behavior in Congressional Elections, 1982-1990." *Journal of Politics* 59 (1): 226–39.

West, Darrell. 2001. *The Rise and Fall of the Media Establishment*. New York: St. Martin's.

Wilgoren, Jodi. 2004. "The 2004 Campaign: Political Memo; Kerry's Words, and Bush's Use of Them, Offer Valuable Lesson in '04 Campaigning." *New York Times* (May 8): https://www.nytimes.com/2004/05/08/us/2004-campaign-political-memo-kerry-s-words-bush-s-use-them-offer-valuable-lesson.html.

Zaller, John. 1996. "The Myth of Massive Media Impact Revived: New Support for a Discredited Idea." In *Political Persuasion and Attitude Change*. Edited by Diana C. Mutz, Paul M. Sniderman, and Richard A. Brody, 17–18. Ann Arbor: University of Michigan Press.

5

Paid Media

★ ★ ★

Flyers for candidates running for one of Texas' U.S. Senate seats in 2012 are placed on a chair before a debate in Houston. *Source*: *Marjorie Kamys Cotera/ Bob Daemmrich Photography/Alamy Stock Photo*

LEARNING OBJECTIVES

★ Critically assess the impact of campaign advertising on voters' attitudes and behavior.

★ Grasp the differences between airing spots on television versus posting digital advertisements.

★ Comprehend the distinctions between positive and negative advertising.
★ Understand message development.

BERNIE SANDERS'S "AMERICA" AD is remarkably simple. It begins with quiet scenes of American life: farmers inspecting their cows and baling hay; a child embracing her mom; a woman ordering coffee; office workers chatting and tapping on their computers. There is soft humming and a strumming guitar playing in the background. Then the camera cuts to Sanders speaking to a small group of people. As the music builds, the camera shifts to campaign rallies filled with swelling crowds of supporters, all cheering for Sanders. The song is Simon and Garfunkel's "America," and when the duo sings the chorus, "They've all come to look for America," the scene shifts to a mosaic of hundreds of photos of individual Americans. The sixty-second video ends with a scene showing Sanders standing at the podium in a packed auditorium. There is no dialogue—just music and cheering crowds. The message seems to be that Sanders is no typical candidate; his campaign represents a movement made up of ordinary Americans seeking inspiration.

Did "America" help Sanders? It seemed to make people who saw it feel happy and hopeful. That was one of the conclusions of two political scientists, Lynn Vavreck and John Geer, who ran a weekly experiment in which they randomly assigned a representative sample of one thousand people to watch various ads during the course of the 2016 election. Even Republicans seem to like the spot, as did independents. The ad lifted Sanders's favorability rating. More than half of viewers recommended that the campaign run the ad a lot (Vavreck 2016).

But did the ad result in votes for Sanders? That's what campaigns want to know. Linking ad viewership with voting behavior is difficult to do. We do know that people liked the video. And millions of people watched it. The video had more than a million online views within twenty-four hours of the campaign posting it onto YouTube (Gold 2016). The ad was aired on television in New Hampshire and Iowa shortly before their nomination contests, and Sanders won New Hampshire by twenty-two points and nearly upset Clinton in Iowa. Even so, we don't know how much of Sanders's electoral success can be explained by "America."

Uncertainty about effectiveness does not discourage campaigns from spending more than half of their budget on advertising. Whereas earned media strategies exemplify the "managing the chaos" theme of this book, advertising and other forms of *paid media* promise more control. As we saw in the last chapter, campaigns can control *some* aspects of earned media. Candidates can prepare for and tightly manage an interview with a reporter. The campaign can do damage control when a scandal breaks or the candidate commits a gaffe. Staffers can attempt to spin a lackluster debate performance or disappointing poll results. But neither the candidate nor the campaign has any control over the media coverage that ensues. Earned media is frustrating in part because its content is produced by someone outside the campaign, usually a news outlet that is not motivated to help out.

By contrast, paid media content is in the hands of the campaign. As the name suggests, paid media is strategic communication that comes with a price tag. It includes all forms of advertising: television, digital, and radio. Advertising is the focus of this chapter. Direct mail, billboards, and posters also belong in this category. Paid media is attractive because the campaign or other sponsor—not the news media—controls the content, production, and timing of the message. A typical television spot is half a minute long. For that thirty seconds, the campaign has complete control over what they say and how they say it—for a price.

And the price tag can be huge. On average, campaigns spend about half of their budget on television advertising alone. Some spend even more. For example, Barack Obama's 2012 reelection campaign spent 71 percent of its budget on paid media, and his opponent Mitt Romney spent 55 percent (Fowler, Franz, and Ridout 2016). The 2018 race for one of Florida's Senate seats between incumbent Democrat Bill Nelson and Republican Rick Scott cost a record $207 million, and more than half of that money was spent on advertising (OpenSecrets.org n.d.).

Is paid media worth the enormous investment? Victorious candidates probably feel like its money well spent. Losing campaigns are more likely to join the chorus of skeptics who wonder whether paid media—particularly advertising—actually shapes voting behavior as intended. Academic research indicates that while advertising can be impactful, its effects fall short of the claims made by media strategists, whose financial compensation is usually tied to the amount of advertising aired by the campaign that hired them (Ball 2016). Or the effects are different than intended. That is because paid media by a single campaign is only one of many sources of information about the race. Opposing campaigns and their allied independent groups are also airing ads, perhaps an equal number of them (see box 5.1,

BOX 5.1 | Groups Do the Dirty Work

Campaigns are not the only source of political advertising. Outside groups and political parties air their own spots and have been doing so for decades. Since at least the 1990s, political groups have been exploiting loopholes in campaign finance law that allow them to spend unlimited funds to run ads *on behalf of* candidates they support (see chapter 8). These ads are subject to some restrictions on what they say, and the groups and parties that sponsor them are prevented from coordinating their efforts with the campaigns. But as additional loopholes have emerged, outside group ads now serve as a barely regulated outlet for paid media communication.

Outside advertising has taken various forms over the years. Political parties began spending unlimited "soft money" on ads supporting their candidates beginning in the 1990s. Advocacy groups were engaging in similar efforts. At the time, campaign finance law allowed groups and parties to spend unlimited funds on advertising and other forms of campaigning as long as they avoided explicitly advocating the election or defeat of a particular candidate. That meant an ad could not connect a candidate with words or phrases like "vote for," "vote against," "defeat," and "support." Instead, the messaging had to be about issue education, mobilization, or party building. In reality, these so-called "issue ads" looked and sounded like standard campaign spots in every other way. A typical attack "issue ad" would attack a candidate for objectionable policy positions without using a word like "defeat." The 2002 Bipartisan Campaign Reform Act was supposed to close this loophole, but the Supreme Court gutted much of the law in 2010 with *Citizens United v. Federal Election Commission*. The decision affirmed the notion that the First Amendment protected groups (as well as corporations and individuals) from most restrictions on political advertising and other forms of electioneering.

Today, outside groups can spend as much they can raise as long as they don't coordinate their efforts with the campaigns. They can even use "defeat" and other "magic words." The *Citizens United* decision triggered massive growth in ad expenditures by super PACs, raising immediate concerns about the scale of spending and the overwhelmingly negative tone of their messages. Even more insidious have been so-called dark money expenditures by political groups that mask themselves as nonpartisan, nonprofit organizations. Unlike super PACs, dark-money groups are not required to publicly disclose their donors to the Federal Election Commission.

BOX 5.1 | (*continued*)

Candidate-sponsored ads still outnumber spots aired by outside groups. Outside groups sponsored 22 percent of U.S. House races in 2018. That was a substantial increase over 2016, when outside group ads made up 15 percent of the total (Fowler, Franz, and Ridout 2018). Dark-money spending declined in 2018, but that is in part because they funneled huge sums through allied super PACs (Evers-Hillstrom 2019). Even if group spending is flat, concerns remain about the lack of transparency. Wealthy donors can anonymously pour millions of unregulated dollars into nonprofit organizations with sometimes mysterious origins, which then either spend unlimited funds on campaign ads or donate to super PACs who do the same.

Campaigns usually appreciate the outside help. Group and party spending can help close the gap between well-funded candidates and those who struggle to raise money. More importantly, outside groups can get away with the sort of aggressive attacks that would backfire if they came directly from the candidate. "Independent groups that are unaccountable to voters will do the dirty work of running these kinds of harsh attack ads that the candidates would rather not do themselves" (Brooks and Murov 2012). In 2012, attack ads made up 83.1 percent of group-sponsored ads aired in federal races compared with only 39 percent of candidate-sponsored ads (Fowler, Franz, and Ridout 2016). That is no coincidence. Whereas candidate-sponsored negative spots can backfire, attack ads sponsored by outside groups are more likely to have the desired persuasive effect (Brooks and Murov 2012; Dowling and Wichowsky 2015). That is mostly because voters do not connect the candidate with attacks made on their behalf by outside groups (Dowling and Wichowsky 2015).

REFERENCES

Brooks, Deborah Jordan, and Michael Murov. 2012. "Assessing Accountability in a Post-Citizens United Era: The Effects of Attack Ad Sponsorship by Unknown Independent Groups." *American Politics Research* 40, no. 3: 383–418.

Dowling, Conor M., and Amber Wichowsky. 2015. "Attacks without Consequence? Candidates, Parties, Groups, and the Changing Face of Negative Advertising." *American Journal of Political Science* 59, no. 1: 19–36.

Evers-Hillstrom, Karl. 2019. "'Dark Money' Groups Funneled Millions to Powerful Super PACs during 2018 Midterms." OpenSecrets.org, Center for Responsive Politics (Jan. 3): https://www.opensecrets.org/news/2019/01/dark-money/.

Fowler, Erika Franklin, Michael M. Franz, and Travis N. Ridout. 2016. *Political Advertising in the United States*. Boulder, CO: Westview.

"Groups Do the Dirty Work"). Family members and close friends also can be sources of information and influence, either interpersonally or through social media. For better or worse, the news media interfere with the paid message's impact when they fact-check the veracity of an ad's claim or cover the ad as a news story. Finally, as noted in chapter 2, voters are not empty vessels: most are partisans who process information in ways that are compatible with their "priors." A thirty-second spot probably won't budge a partisan one way or the other. Less committed undecided voters are more susceptible to influence, but they may not see the ad. There also might be backlash or other unintended consequences.

It may be true that paid media allow maximum control over the content and distribution of the message. But there is no way to control how the message will be received and acted upon by voters. That dynamic will be examined later in the chapter. Before turning to the research on the effects of advertising, it is worth examining the mechanics of its, content, production, and distribution.

WHERE TO AIR?

Most campaigns ads are aired on television. Television is the medium of choice for research on the effectiveness of advertising. It is true that online advertising (aka "digital") is where much of the growth and innovation are. And radio is an underappreciated—and understudied—medium for paid campaigns communication. But for campaigns, television is where the bulk of paid media communication happens. During the 2018 midterm elections, the number of TV ads aired for gubernatorial, Senate, and House races increased by 58 percent compared with the 2014 midterms. Online digital ads continued to make gains, but they still made up only 10 percent of ad spending by Senate candidates between May 31 and October 31, 2018 (Fowler, Franz, and Ridout 2018).

The typical campaign commercial on television lasts about thirty seconds. That's not much time to make a pitch to inattentive voters, but ad producers pack a lot in. Television ads combine both visual and audio. One TV spot might feature the candidate facing the camera telling their story and summarizing their platform, with uplifting music playing in the background. An attack ad might show dark images and slow-motion video, accented by menacing music, narrated by an actor using ominous tones to describe the horrible things that will happen if the candidate's opponent is elected. Text usually features prominently in both positive and negative spots, not only the candidates' names but also key words and phrases that emphasize the ad's message.

President Lyndon Johnson's infamous 1964 "Daisy" ad combined provocative audio and visual components. Johnson's opponent was Barry Goldwater, a Republican who once said he would consider using nuclear weapons to fight the Vietnam War. The Daisy ad was an attempt by the Johnson campaign to capitalize on Goldwater's controversial position. The black and white spot showed a three-year-old girl picking the petals of a daisy, counting as she tosses them aside, while birds chirp in the background. When her count reaches "nine," she looks up and the image of her face freezes. An adult male voice takes over, ominously counting down from ten as with a rocket launch, "ten . . . nine . . . eight . . ." At "zero," startling footage of a nuclear explosion fills the screen while Johnson's voice is heard saying, "These are the stakes: to make a world in which all of God's children can live, or to go into the dark. We must either love each other, or we must die." The ad closes with stark white text on a black background that says, "Vote for President Johnson on November 3," read aloud by a different male voiceover that concludes, "The stakes are too high for you to stay home."

Goldwater is not mentioned in the ad. It aired only once, but the spot was shown in its entirety in news stories by two broadcast networks (Iyengar 2011). That was free advertising for the Johnson campaign. Fifty-two years later, the Hillary Clinton campaign enlisted the actress who played the little girl to appear in an ad casting Donald Trump as too reckless to be in charge of the nation's nuclear arsenal. "The fear of nuclear war we had as children—I never thought our children would have to deal with that again," the former "Daisy Girl" said to the camera.

Traditionally, TV spots have been used *persuade* undecided voters to support the ad's sponsor. But that means there is a lot of waste, especially with broadcast television on the major networks. An ad aired on a major network during prime time will reach not only undecided voters but also people who have already made up their minds. These viewers are probably not persuadable. Such waste is inevitable, but it can be reduced through targeting. Recall from chapter 2 the differences between macrotargeting and microtargeting. *Macrotargeting* is targeting based on the aggregate characteristics and interests of particular groups of people. More precise is *microtargeting*, which is based on the known or predicted characteristics of individuals rather than a group of individuals. To some extent, television ads can be ma-crotargeted based on the audience leanings for a particular program.

Cable is more conducive to targeting than broadcast television. Many cable networks have niche audiences that may include a pre-ponderance of voters being targeted by a campaign. MSNBC is a good bet for Democratic candidates running in a primary race; like-wise for Republican candidates on Fox News. Audiences for enter-tainment programs on cable also exhibit patterns that are useful for targeting certain voters. In 2004, for example, the campaign to reelect George W. Bush determined that viewers of the Golf Channel leaned to the right, so they ran spots on the channel to reach uncom-mitted Republicans. The ads also reached already committed Bush supporters as well as supporters of their opponent, but presumably such waste was lower than if they had been aired on broadcast television.

Cable can also be more precisely targeted based on geography. Whereas ad buys on broadcast TV reach the entire media market, cable ads can be bought through local cable providers for zone areas within media markets (Fowler, Ridout, and Franz 2016). Local cable "spot" buys can help reduce the wasteful reach of voters who live out-side of the targeted population. Such waste is common with broadcast media markets such as Greater New York, Los Angeles, and Chicago, which include a number of congressional and state legislative districts. Broadcast television markets and legislative districts do not share the same boundary lines. For example, Georgia's Twelfth Congressional District is covered by four broadcast television markets. Reaching voters across the district requires advertising in all four, which means wastefully broadcasting ads to people in other congressional districts and the neighboring state of South Carolina (Willis 2014).

One problem with cable is that slots are limited because national advertisers buy up most of the available time. That is one reason that broadcast programs remain irresistible to campaigns. Local TV news programs are a staple for political ad buyers because viewers are already primed to pay attention to political content. Sporting events, especially NFL football, are appealing because they are so often watched live, making it less likely that the viewer will skip the commercials. CBS programs such as *60 Minutes* and the vari-ous *NCIS* and *CSI* shows are staples because their audiences tend to be older than shows on the other networks. Seniors are regular voters, which is why weeknight programs such as *Wheel of Fortune* and *Jeopardy!* are also campaign ad mainstays. A campaign targeting left-leaning women may want to buy time on the *Ellen DeGeneres Show* (Livingston 2014).

TV advertising is expensive, but candidates for federal office are eligible for a discount. The Federal Communications Commission (FCC) requires TV stations to charge the lowest possible advertising rate for candidates running for office. That means candidates enjoy the financial advantage of a volume discount without having to buy ads in volume. These *lowest unit rates* apply to ads run during the final sixty days of a general election and forty-five days before primaries. They do not apply to ads run by super PACs and other independent groups; only candidate-sponsored ads qualify for the discount. But space is limited. In competitive races, premium time slots get snatched up months in advance. Mitt Romney's 2012 presidential campaign bought late and paid more as a result. For the sake of flexibility, the campaign booked spots on a week-to-week basis rather than months in advance. Discounted time slots were sold out, forcing the campaign to spend more and actually reach fewer people (West 2018).

Delay may have helped Donald Trump in 2016. Because the campaign waited so long to advertise, television spots were scarce, forcing the campaign to turn to online outlets. Half of his campaign's media budget ended up going to digital ads. Despite spending far less on advertising than Clinton overall, the Trump campaign spent more advertising on Facebook than did the Clinton campaign. It spent half a million dollars to buy the banner ad viewable on YouTube on Election Day. The campaign "targeted 13.5 million persuadable voters in sixteen battleground states, discovering the hidden Trump voters, especially in the Midwest" (Persily 2017: 65). The Trump campaign swore by digital. What explains its relative appeal?

Digital

Spending on online digital advertising made up an estimated 22 percent of overall political advertising during the 2018 midterm elections. That was a massive increase over the previous midterm cycle just four years earlier, when digital ad spending made up only 1 percent of the total (Janetsky 2018). Texas Senate candidate Beto O'Rourke spent 34 percent of his advertising total on digital, including $8 million on Facebook and $2 million on Google (Fowler, Franz, and Ridout 2018).

The growth of digital is not surprising. Digital ads have many advantages over television spots. They tend to be much less expensive to air. It helps that online space is unlimited, whereas campaigns buy "time" on television and radio. Digital is also nimble. Whereas it can take days to produce a TV spot, paid digital messages can be created and launched in a matter of hours. It helps that digital formats can be remarkably simple. Widely used display or "banner" ads combine basic text with imagery, and their elements can be tweaked and interchanged as needed. Interactive versions show basic animations on demand. Online video ads are similar to TV spots in terms of format, but their length can be as short as six seconds.

The most obvious plus is that digital messages can be microtargeted to individual voters based on behavior associated with a particular device or social media account. That means less waste and more precision. For the most part, the best a campaign can do on television is macrotarget spots based on the demographic characteristics and assumed political tendencies of the audience for a program or network. TV ads reach a lot of nontargets. Although TV's massive reach can compensate for the inefficiency, campaigns are embracing digital's capacity to communicate specific messages to particular voters.

Anyone who uses their phone or computer to buy something or plan a trip has been on the receiving end of digital microtargeting. An online search for "laptop reviews" or "Costa Rica hotels" can result in a relentless stream of online ads from computer manufacturers and discount travel websites. That is because a digital tracker is stored on a person's device when they visit a website or buy a product online. Internet searches are linked with the account of the person who conducted the search. Facebook and other social media profiles provide rich data about an individuals' interests, likes and dislikes, and likely political orientations. All of this online activity feeds into the development of an individual profile that advertisers use to customize messages. Online data are matched with offline data such as what charities people support, the car they drive, the magazines they subscribe to, and their brand preferences. For political relevance, the profile is rounded out with public data about the individual's party registration and how often the person votes (Vega 2012). Campaigns use these profiles to "send" the appropriate message to an individual they guess will be receptive to it.

Presumably the ads hit their targets. On Facebook, clickable display ads or videos (labeled "sponsored") appear on the newsfeeds of individuals whose profiles suggest could be possible supporters. During the 2012 general election, people who Googled "immigration reform" saw a display ad for Obama. During the Republican primaries that year, people who searched for conservative talk radio host

"Rush Limbaugh" saw an ad for the GOP candidate Rick Santorum (Farnam 2012). Sometimes digital microtargeting is based the precise location of an individual's device. Digital display ads can be sent to voters' phones while they wait in line at the polls on Election Day. In 2010, people attending the Minnesota State Fair saw mobile ads from Michelle Bachmann's congressional campaign telling them that "while you're at the fair, you should know that [my opponent] voted to raise taxes on your corn dog and your deep-fried bacon and your beer" (West 2018: 8). The Michigan Republican Party sent attendees of a 2017 skilled-trades education convention digital advertising touting Republican support of funding for programs in their sector (Livengood 2018).

Of course, sometimes the data are misleading or wrong. A person who regularly watches Ben Shapiro's videos on YouTube probably leans to the right. A frequent visitor to Vox.com probably leans to the left. Both of these individuals can be counted on to vote regularly because they devote significant time to political content. But all of these assumptions could be off base. Although it is likely that someone who follows Donald Trump on Twitter also supports him, it's also possible that they are simply curious. Internet searches can certainly be misleading. Was a person who Googled "Hillary Clinton emails" in 2016 a likely Trump supporter, or just someone who wanted to catch up on the controversy? How about a person who searches for "Kamala Harris"? Can we assume that person is a Democrat seeking more information about a potential presidential nominee? Probably. But it also could be a Republican seeking damaging information about a possible future opponent. Errors like these are compensated for with more data that theoretically combine to create a reasonable profile of an individual's likes and dislikes. But sometimes a single Google search is enough to trigger a digital campaign spot that reflects clumsy assumptions about the person's political leanings.

Another advantage of digital is that regulation is minimal. As we will see, a TV ad must include a statement disclosing who paid for it. With online ads, disclosure is required only if the ad is placed on a website. That exempts spots appearing on social media. It means an attack ad can appear on YouTube and be widely shared on Facebook without clear information about who is responsible for it. The loophole partly explains why it was not until after the votes were counted in 2016 that officials determined that a company linked to the Russian government paid for a number of outrageously misleading campaign ads on Facebook.

Digital ads also benefit from their capacity for interaction. Whereas TV spots are passively viewed, people can click on a digital that intrigues them, taking them to a campaign website that invites the user to donate money, provide an email address and phone number, or simply gather more information. That click also tells the campaign something about the individual, especially if the person takes further online action. "Action rates" are just one of the metrics that advantage digital over other outlets. With digital, advertisers can measure not only clicks but also such indicators as "conversions"—whether the user took action such as donating money or providing an email address—and a "bounce rate"—the percentage of people who just leave the site. With video spots, advertisers can determine how often people watched 25, 50, 75, or 100 percent of the video—or none of it.

The line between television and digital advertising is blurring as people watch more and more programming on smart TVs and mobile devices. As early as 2012, the Optimizer tool allowed the Obama campaign to combine voter data with information collected through viewers' set-top boxes to more precisely determine what types of people were watching what and when (Laposky 2015). Smart TVs allow advertisers to target based on household characteristics. And as more and more people "watch TV" on their phones, advertisers can reach them in the same way they do on television, but with individualized data predicting viewers' political orientations and behavior.

Digital advertising appears in multiple forms. Online video ads are like television spots in their look and appearance; sometimes campaigns use variations of the same ad on both television and online formats. Campaigns pay more for "nonskippable" video ads that force the viewer to watch the entire spot. Display or "banner" ads combine text with imagery and can appear on social media feeds and websites.

Radio

Radio ads do not generate much attention, but they can be crucial to campaigns. Campaigns embrace them partly because they run under the radar. Compared with television, they don't attract much scrutiny from the news media. Campaigns and outside groups thus save their most inflammatory attacks for radio. That is in part "because there is no visual connection with a candidate and less chance of a backlash against the sponsor of such an ad" (Jasperson 2005: 275).

Campaigns also like radio because it is less expensive than television. For example, radio ads made up 20 percent of all ads aired in the Little Rock media market during the 2002 elections but consumed only 2.5 percent of ad spending (Overby and Barth 2006). Audiences tend to be small but loyal: people tend to stick with one or two stations, changing stations far less often than with television (Overby and Barth 2006). Some listeners tune in to a particular station for hours at a time, especially if tuning in at work or at home.

Audiences tend to fit politically relevant categories. That means radio is a natural medium for macrotargeting. Republican campaigns can use a variety of talk radio programs to reach regular voters who lean to the right. Talk radio programs aimed at African American audiences are a good bet for Democratic campaigns. Spanish-language radio can be used to target Latino voters.

WHAT TO SAY?

The content of campaign advertising fits two dimensions: tone and substance. The most familiar dimension is tone—that is, whether the ad can be classified as positive, negative, or comparative. Commonly called **attack** ads, negative spots focus on the opponent with no mention of the candidate who stands to benefit from the message. Comparative spots include information about both candidates. These are commonly referred to as **contrast** ads. **Positive** spots focus solely on the candidate being supported in the ad.

Purely negative **attack** ads typically make up about half of campaign advertising. But there is some variation over time and across races. Candidates with no serious challenger are free to air mostly positive spots touting their background, record, and policy platform—and that is what they do (Fowler, Franz, and Ridout 2016). The overwhelming majority of ads sponsored by parties or outside groups are negative, whereas candidate-sponsored ads tend to be evenly dispersed across all three categories (Fowler, Franz, and Ridout 2016). When Barack Obama first ran for president in 2008, he had raised so much money that his campaign could afford to spend millions on positive ad messaging on top of the negative ad advantage he had over his opponent, John McCain. Obama's **positive advertising** included a thirty-minute infomercial that ran during prime time. Relatively strapped for cash, McCain was limited to mostly "going negative" (West 2018).

Ads also vary in terms of substance. They tend to focus on candidates' policies, their personal qualities, or a combination of both. **Policy** ads center on one or more of the candidate's or the opponent's issue positions, whereas **personal** ads focus on image, biography, personality, or leadership style. With policy ads, a single issue that tops the public's agenda might be the focus of issue ads nationwide. For Democrats running in the 2018 midterm elections, that issue was health care. According to the Wesleyan Media Project, health care was mentioned in more than half of all pro-Democratic ads aired in federal and gubernatorial races (Fowler, Franz, and Ridout 2018). But sometimes a policy ad features a narrow issue that taps into a local priority. When Democrat Joe Cunningham ran for Congress in a Republican-leaning district, his campaign ran a contrast ad criticizing his opponent for supporting offshore drilling. Nationally, Republicans tend to favor measures that would boost the domestic supply of fossil fuels and create jobs in the energy sector. But South Carolina's First Congressional District covers most of the state's coastline, and even Republicans there were concerned about the threat of major oil spills to the tourist industry and the Port of Charleston. The ad showed Cunningham bobbing in the ocean, where he warned that "even a small leak can kill our economy and ruin our beaches."

Recent presidential candidates have aired more policy than image-centered ads with one exception: in 2016, 60 percent of ads supporting Hillary Clinton centered on personal qualities, mostly attacking Donald Trump's character. By comparison, over 70 percent of Trump advertising was focused on policy (Frankin Fowler, Ridout, and Franz 2016). One Clinton spot ("Mirrors") depicted a succession of clips showing young girls looking at themselves in the mirror interspersed with clips of Donald Trump insulting women's physical appearances. Trump is heard saying, "A person who is flat-chested is very hard to be a ten," and "Does she have a good body? No. Does she have a fat [beep]? Absolutely." The ad concludes with a black screen and the text, "Is this the president we want for our daughters?" In another ("Role Models"), a succession of wide-eyed young children are shown watching Trump on television making obscene and inflammatory statements such as "you can tell them to go [beep] themselves." This time, the question raised on the black screen is "Our children are watching. What example will we set for them?" The ads were memorable, widely aired, and shared far and wide; "Mirrors" had more than five million views on YouTube. But the focus on Trump's personality "[left] very little room for discussion in advertising of the reasons why Clinton herself was a better choice." Trump and allied groups ran far fewer ads, but their focus on policy differences may have better resonated with voters (Fowler, Ridout, and Franz 2016: 468).

Ads that emphasize personal qualities can also be positive in tone. New candidates commonly air "establishment" ads early in the race to introduce themselves to voters. Some campaigns are now launching their advertising campaigns with long-form narrative videos rather than thirty-second television spots (see box 5.2, "¡Ocasio!"). Democratic candidates embraced this format in 2018 (see chapter 6). But television remains the dominant medium for positive advertising. Incumbents and other well-known candidates use positive image spots to remind voters of their accomplishments and appealing personal qualities. When Norm Coleman first ran for Senate in 2002, his daughter Sarah was featured in an ad touting his record of fulfilling his promises—both as Minnesota lawmaker ("If he says we're bringing [a professional hockey team back to the state], he doesn't stop until stop until we get it") and as a dad ("If he says we're getting ice cream, he doesn't stop until we get it"). When Coleman ran for reelection six years later, Sarah reappeared in an ad plugging her dad's record of "bring[ing] people together to get things done" on rural health care, tax cuts, and job creation.

Box 5.2 | ¡OCASIO!

Did a campaign ad win the 2018 Democratic primary election for Alexandria Ocasio-Cortez? Probably not. But her two-minute video called "Courage to Change" certainly got people talking. And it exemplified a new type of video advertising: documentary-style productions that tell stories and run minutes long rather than the usual thirty seconds. Like establishment ads that run on television, they aim to introduce new candidates to voters. But these relatively lengthy videos are designed for social media sharing, not airing on television (Peters and Maheshwari 2018). Compelling videos go viral, attracting volunteers and campaign contributions. Congressional candidate M. J. Hegar's three-minute video, "Doors," got millions of views within days of posting and a tweet from *Hamilton* creator Lin-Manuel Miranda, who said, "MJ, you made the best political ad anyone's ever seen" (Rieger 2018).

Ocasio-Cortez used her establishment video to introduce herself to voters in New York's Fourteenth Congressional District. She narrated a script that she wrote herself. It was produced by a pair of fellow socialists for about $10,000 (Jilani 2018). In the video, Ocasio-Cortez tells her story as an "educator, an organizer, a working-class New Yorker" born to a mom from Puerto Rico and a dad from the Bronx. "Women like me aren't supposed to run for

(continued)

BOX 5.2 | (continued)

office," she says, as footage rolls of the candidate doing everyday activities: getting dressed and putting on makeup, riding the subway, chatting with neighbors. The most relatable shot views her from a distance as she changes into heels on a subway platform.

New York's Fourteenth Congressional District is a safe Democratic seat: winning it meant winning the Democratic primary. Her opponent was Joe Crowley, who had served the district for ten terms. Crowley was no obscure backbencher: he was a member of the Democratic leadership in the U.S. House. He raised $3 million compared with Ocasio-Cortez's $200,000. Crowley outspent her by eighteen to one (Zanger 2018).

Policy-based contrast would be difficult for Ocasio-Cortez. Crowley was no squishy centrist. His voting record fit the politics of the dark-blue district, making him among the chamber's most liberal members. He was a progressive Democrat who supported Medicaid for All and liberal immigration policies. But Ocasio-Cortez could credibly run to Crowley's left on a number of issues. She favored abolishing ICE and supported free college. More importantly, she could frame Crowley's strengths as weaknesses: a powerful party boss at the local as well as the national level, his millions in contributions included corporate money. The video is mostly about Ocasio-Cortez. But forty-two seconds in, slow-motion footage of a Crowley appearance on *Fox News Sunday* pops up while Ocasio-Cortez is heard saying, "after 20 years of the same representation, we have to ask: who has New York been changing for?" She describes various ways life had gotten harder for working families as affluent New Yorkers prospered during Crowley's tenure. She never utters Crowley's name, but the contrast is clear:

> This race is about people versus money—we've got people, they've got money. It's time we acknowledged that not all Democrats are the same. That a Democrat who takes corporate money, profits off foreclosure, doesn't live here, doesn't send his kids to our schools, doesn't drink our water or breathe our air, cannot possibly represent us.

Her campaign poster also stood apart. Its bold design and color scheme evokes Rosie the Riveter, the heroic female figure from the "We Can Do It" World War II posters. Its logo features an inverted exclamation point—*¡OCASIO!*—to accentuate the candidate's Latina heritage. The candidate's photo is "stylized and dramatically lighted," two graphic designers noted, identifying her "as a young woman of color, a defining element of her campaign against a fifty-six-year-old white male incumbent" (Strals and Willen 2018).

BOX 5.2 | (*continued*)

Ocasio-Cortez did not just win: she beat Crowley by a wide margin, 57 to 42 percent. She won big for a number of reasons. A local organizer for Bernie Sanders, Ocasio-Cortez was an ambitious canvasser who advocated for positions that connected with voters in a district where Sanders performed well in the 2016 New York primary. In addition, the district had been redrawn in ways that may have worked against Crowley. He was a middle-aged white man from Queens representing a district that included a larger chunk of the Bronx; its population was half-Hispanic, and its white population was increasingly young and hip. In other words, the landscape was less favorable to Crowley than it once was (see chapter 1). But shifting demographics were only part of the story. Ocasio-Cortez won across demographics in neighborhoods throughout the district, outperforming Crowley even in on his home turf. The ad highlighted that Crowley's family had moved away from the district to the Washington, D.C.area (Goldmacher 2018). At age twenty-eight, Ocasio-Cortez would become the youngest woman to be elected to Congress. Her youth, energy, and unapologetically progressive message—captured so vividly in the video—may have been a better fit for NY-14 in 2018.

REFERENCES

Goldmacher, Shane. 2018. "An Upset in the Making: Why Joe Crowley Never Saw Defeat Coming." *New York Times* (June 27): https://www.nytimes.com/2018/06/27/nyregion/ocasio-cortez-crowley-primary-upset.html.

Jilani, Zaid. 2018. "How a Ragtag Group of Socialist Filmmakers Produced One of the Most Viral Campaign Ads of 2018." *The Intercept* (June 5): https://theintercept.com/2018/06/05/ocasio-cortez-new-york-14th-district-democratic-primary-campaign-video/.

Peters, Jeremy W., and Sepna Maheshwari. 2018. "Viral Videos Are Replacing Pricey Political Ads: They're Cheaper, and They Work." *New York Times* (Sept. 10): https://www.nytimes.com/2018/09/10/us/politics/midterm-primaries-advertising.html.

Rieger, J. M. 2018. "A Texas Democrat Has One of the Best Ads—and Most Effective Opponent Attacks—You'll See in 2018." *Washington Post* (June 25): https://www.washingtonpost.com/news/the-fix/wp/2018/06/25/a-texas-democrat-has-one-the-best-ads-and-most-effective-opponent-attacks-youll-see-in-2018/?utm_term=.e6cb6b6d5a01.

Strals, Nolen, and Bruce Willen. 2018. "Ocasio-Cortez Scored a Victory—for Well-Designed Campaign Posters." *Washington Post* (June 28): https://www.washingtonpost.com/news/posteverything/wp/2018/06/28/ocasio-cortez-scored-a-victory-for-well-designed-campaign-posters/?utm_term=.bde042f5d234.

Zanger, Doug. 2018. "Alexandra Ocasio-Cortez Went DIY on Her Campaign Ad, and It's a Runaway Hit." *Adweek* (June 27): https://www.adweek.com/creativity/alexandria-ocasio-cortez-went-diy-on-her-campaign-ad-and-its-a-runaway-hit/.

Positive image spots tend to be loaded with clichés: the candidate reading to school kids in a classroom, walking in a park and shaking hands with factory workers, and throwing a football or Frisbee with family (the Coleman ad features both a football and a Frisbee). The family dog often makes an appearance. Some spots embrace the clichés. An ad for Florida Republican Ron DeSantis aimed at reinforcing his embrace of Donald Trump. The ad's format was standard family-centered testimonial: DeSantis is shown playing with blocks and reading to his kids while his wife, Casey, touts his parenting skills. But to underline the pro-Trump theme, the book he's reading to his infant son is Trump's *Art of the Deal*. The toy blocks are being used to help his toddler daughter "build the wall." A Trump campaign sign serves as a prop for a reading lesson: "Make. America. Great. Again," DeSantis says to his kid as he points to the words on the sign.

Some spots communicate both policy and image. When Republican Brian Kemp ran for Georgia governor in 2018, one of his spots depicted the candidate holding a shotgun while sitting next to a guy Kemp described as "Jake, a young man interested in one of my daughters." Nervously eyeing the shotgun, Jake ticks off a list of Kemp's policy priorities, then agrees to Kemp's demand that he show "a healthy appreciation for the 2nd Amendment . . . sir." In another ad, Kemp celebrated being a "politically incorrect conservative" by telling viewers that he proudly says "Merry Christmas" and "God bless you," and that he "stand[s] for the National Anthem." He also said he supported President Trump and "iron-clad borders," then conceded that "if any of this offends you, I am not your guy." Both ads accentuated Kemp's image as a Trump-brand conservative while communicating his policy priorities, at least in broad terms.

Democratic Senate candidate Jason Kander also combined policy with the personal in his campaign's "Background Checks" spot. A former army captain who served in Afghanistan, Kander is shown swiftly assembling an AR-15 assault rifle while wearing a blindfold. The objective was to convey authenticity on an issue that typically vexes Democratic candidates while explaining his support for strengthening background checks before gun purchases—a controversial position in the pro-gun state of Missouri, and one for which his opponent, Senator Roy Blount, had attacked him. After assembling the gun, Kander challenges his opponent to do the same, knowing that Blount could do no such thing.

In addition to the message, television and radio ads must include a disclaimer about the message's origin. By law, candidates for federal office must include a statement saying they approve of the ad's message. The statement must be delivered in the candidate's voice; on TV, it must be accompanied by the candidate's image, video or still. Known as the "stand by your ad" provision of campaign finance law, the rule forces candidates to visually associate themselves with the attacks they deliver. The candidate usually says something like "I approve this message," but sometimes the wording varies to make a political point. After Kander's blindfolded assembly of an AR-15, for example, he said, "I approve this message [pausing to remove to his blindfold] because I'd like to see Senator Blount do this."

WHAT IS THE MESSAGE?

Every campaign needs a clear message. That is a truism in politics. The message should be communicated in all aspects of the operation, not just through paid media. But a campaign's paid media serve as the primary mechanism for conveying the message. Paid media are where campaigns focus their strategic communication efforts. During the process of developing a message, strategists describe hypothetical ads to explain how the message would work. It thus makes sense to use this chapter to turn our attention to messaging.

In 1984, Ronald Reagan's official reelection message was "Leadership That's Working." But it was a famous sixty-second TV ad that sharpened its meaning and formed the campaign's de facto message. Titled "Stronger, Prouder, Better," the spot is better known as "Morning in America." The political landscape was promising for Reagan: the economy had improved after a crippling recession early in his first term. Yet there were signs of trouble: the budget deficit had doubled, and joblessness persisted in the industrial Midwest. Reagan had to remind voters of how much worse conditions were—economically and culturally—before he took office. The ad leads off with a dulcet-toned narrator saying, "It's morning again in America," before describing how conditions had improved, such as "inflation at less than half of what it was just four years ago." The point was to capture a sense of optimism while drawing upon nostalgia for the distant past:

> Set to the music of sentimental strings, images include a paperboy on his bicycle, a family taking a rolled rug into a house and campers raising an American flag. The subtext is that after 20 years of social tumult, assassinations, riots, scandal, an unpopular war and gas lines, Mr. Reagan returned the United States to the tranquility of the 1950s. (Beschloss 2016)

Reagan's opponent was Walter Mondale, who had served as vice president under Jimmy Carter, Reagan's predecessor in the White House. Carter's 1980 loss to Reagan after only one term was partly blamed on economic stagnation and a crisis of national confidence. It was no accident then that Reagan's ad closes with a question, "Why would we ever want to return to where we were less than four short years ago?" reminding viewers of Mondale's connection with the unpopular previous administration and its association with bleaker times.

What makes an effective message? Strategist Joel Bradshaw offers seven criteria—the "Six C's". Bradshaw uses the term "theme" instead of message, but his criteria apply to both. An effective message should be

- clear,
- concise,
- compelling,
- connected,
- credible, and
- contrasting.

The first three criteria are self-explanatory: it makes intuitive sense for a message to be clear, concise, and compelling. For a message to be *connected*, it must be match the priorities of targeted voters at that particular time. When Gretchen Whitmer successfully ran for Michigan governor in 2018, her message was "Fix the Damn Roads"—a theme that connected with voters so viscerally that she heard people shouting it to her when she marched in a Fourth of July parade. A *credible* message is one that makes sense given the candidate's biography, issue priorities, and strengths and weaknesses. "Change You Can Count On" was a credible message for Barack Obama in 2008 when he ran as an outsider aiming to be the first African American president. When he ran for reelection, however, he could no longer credibly run as a change candidate, so his campaign opted for an incumbent-friendly word that signaled a desire for continued progress: "Forward" was his message in 2012. A *contrasting* message is one that at least implies a sharp difference with the opponent. Hillary Clinton's "Stronger Together" message in 2016 highlighted what her campaign perceived to be contrast with her opponent, Donald Trump; she aimed to unite rather than divide.

A campaign's overall message can often be boiled down to a single statement or phrase. Ideally, the message is so catchy and simple that it can be used for television ads, bumper stickers, buttons, T-shirts, and yard signs. Perhaps no message is more famous than Donald Trump's "Make America Great Again" slogan, best known for its appearance on red baseball caps. An abbreviated version became a widely embraced hashtag, #MAGA. The advantage of a simple slogan is that it lends itself to repetition not only by the candidate but also by volunteers when they canvas or post onto social media.

One tool campaigns use when crafting a message is the Tully Message Box. The box was named after Democratic campaign strategist Paul Tully, a messaging expert, but it is widely used by campaigns from both parties. It entails a simple exercise: draw a square; divide it into four quadrants; and write a phrases or statements that respond to the prompts shown in figure 5.1.

Figure 5.1 Tully Message Box

What we say about ourselves	What our opponents say about themselves
What we say about our opponents	What our opponents say about us

Campaigns can use the Tully Message Box in a variety of ways. It can serve as a tool for brainstorming during the early stages of message development. It also can serve as a mechanism for testing the effectiveness of a particular message: it passes muster only if it lends itself to coherent responses to all four prompts. At minimum, the nature of the prompts centers message development on the need for contrast with one's opponents.

When a candidate is criticized for lacking "message discipline," that can mean one of two things. One is that the campaign adopted a message but didn't stick with it. The other possibility is that the campaign experimented with several messages but never settled on a single one. Hillary Clinton's 2016 campaign rejected eighty-four possible messages before narrowing the selection to two: "I'm With Her" and "Stronger Together" (MacManus and Cilluffo 2017). John Kerry's 2004 presidential campaign also never settled on a consistent message. Democratic strategist Paul Begala mocked the campaign for its message of "JHOS"—an acronym for jobs, health, oil, and security. "Those are four topics. Those are four interesting issues. But that's not a message," Begala said in an interview for the documentary, . . . *So Goes The Nation*. By contrast, Kerry's Republican opponent embraced his campaign's message from the start. George W. Bush's "Steady Leadership in a Time of Change" made sense because "steady" *contrasted* with the notion that Kerry frequently changed his mind—"flip-flopped"—most notably on funding for the war in Iraq. "Steady" also was a *credible* attribute for Bush who, even among his critics, was seen as someone who adhered to his principles. Four years earlier, Bush's message was "Restoring Integrity to the White House"—a theme that *connected* with voters' "Clinton fatigue" after years of scandal, and *contrasted* with Gore, who was inextricably linked to Clinton after serving as his vice president for two terms.

Doug Jones needed a message that appealed to at least a few Republicans as well as his fellow Democrats. Jones ran in a 2017 special election for a U.S. Senate seat for Alabama, a state that Trump had won by twenty-eight points just one year earlier. The race was tight partly because his Republican opponent, Roy Moore, had been accused by several women of making unwanted sexual advances toward them when they were teenagers. Even so, Jones had to win the support of non-Democrats to win a beet-red state like Alabama. His message: finding common ground. His campaign reasoned that one year into the Trump presidency, Democrats and Republicans alike were exhausted by divisive partisanship that had actually worsened under Trump. In other words, the message *connected* with voters' concerns at that time. Whereas electing Moore promised more Trump-like division, Jones had a reputation for decency and civility (Klein 2017). That made common ground a *credible* message that provided *contrast* with Moore.

The common ground message served as a central theme in a TV spot aimed at moderate white Republicans. Called "Honor," the ad tells a story about two Civil War officers—one from Alabama, the other from Maine—who clashed during the Battle of Gettysburg. "Those times are past, long ago, and our country is better for it.

But now we fight too often over other matters. It seems as if we're coming apart," Jones says to the camera, before promising to "go to Washington and meet the representatives from Maine and those from every other state not on a battlefield, but to find common ground, because there's honor in compromise and civility. To pull together as a people and get things done for Alabama." It would be a stretch to credit the message and the ad for Jones's 1.7-point victory. And Moore ended up winning 91 percent of Republicans. But according to exit polls, 74 percent of self-described moderates voted for the Democrat (*Washington Post* 2017).

WHEN TO AIR?

Campaigns think strategically about the timing of their spots. "The heart of a candidate's advertising strategy concerns decisions on when, where and how often to broadcast ads" (West 2014: 29). As we will see, a number of studies suggest that advertising effectiveness decays after a few weeks or even a few days (Bartels 2014; Gerber et al. 2011; Hill et al. 2013). Cash-strapped candidates may thus be better off waiting until end of the race to match or exceed their opponents' advertising efforts (Hill et al. 2013). That is when less partisan undecided voters are most likely to finally choose one candidate over the other. That is why Bill Clinton's 1992 presidential campaign saved its major ad buys for the final two weeks of the race (West 2018).

The risk of waiting is missing the opportunity to use early advertising to "define" the candidate and her opponents. The ad decay research casts doubt on the efficacy of such efforts, but campaigns are convinced that they matter. Lesser known candidates use positive establishment spots to introduce themselves to voters; familiar candidates use them to reintroduce themselves and remind voters of their positive attributes. Negative spots are employed to define opponents' in unfavorable terms before voters get to know them well. In 2012, the Obama campaign ran a slew of anti-Romney spots as soon as Romney won enough primaries to secure his party's nomination—well before he could formally reintroduce himself to general election voters at the party convention. The ads were aimed at defining Romney as a wealthy plutocrat who was disconnected from the concerns of regular Americans. One spot challenged Romney's reluctance to release his tax returns. Another charged Romney with shipping jobs overseas when he was governor of Massachusetts.

In 2016, Clinton may have waited too long to advertise in key states she ended up losing. In Wisconsin, pro-Clinton ads did not appear at all until the final week of the race, whereas Trump and his allies had started advertising there in mid-September. A similar pattern emerged in Michigan, a state Trump won by only twelve thousand votes (Fowler, Ridout, and Franz 2016).

WHAT IS THE IMPACT?

Do campaign ads influence voters? If a campaign spends more than half of its budget on paid media, is this money well spent? Early research on political communication suggested that advertising and other media had limited direct influence on the attitudes and behavior of voters. Interpersonal relationships were more important. Under one theory, campaign messages were communicated indirectly through a "two-step flow" process that started with influential "opinion leaders," who passed them on to less sophisticated citizens (Lazarsfeld, Berelson, and Gaudet 1944). This and other "minimal effects" models of mass communication (Klapper 1960) held sway until the 1980s. Then methodological advances and new theoretical models allowed researchers to isolate the impact of particular sources of influence. Focused primarily on the effects of negative advertising, some of the evidence was troubling. One set of studies reported that attack ads discourage people from voting (Ansolabehere and Iyengar 1995), suggesting that negative advertising was less about persuading voters to change their minds and more about demobilizing them from turning out. A meta-analysis of dozens of studies suggested that, although negative advertising and other forms of attack campaigning may not depress turnout, it may diminish citizens' trust in government, dampen the sense that their vote matters, and darken the public mood (Lau, Sigelman, and Rovner 2007). More recent research affirmed concerns about detrimental consequences of negative advertising (Stevens 2009).

But a number of studies have suggested that TV spots could have measurable positive consequences on the electorate. Some reported that exposure to negative campaigning and advertising in particular can actually boost political engagement and voter turnout (Brooks and Geer 2007; Freedman and Goldstein 1999; Goldstein and Freedman 2002; Wattenberg and Brians 1999). Others report that campaign advertising can be more informative than television news (Patterson and McClure 1976; Zhao and Chaffee 1995). Whereas television news tends to focus on trivial "game" or "horse race" aspects of elections (Patterson 1994), a typical TV spot contains at least some information about the candidates' issue positions (Patterson and McClure 1976). Policy-based contrast ads can be particularly useful because they provide information about the policy priorities of both candidates (Mattes and Redlawsk 2014). Research on the 2000 presidential and congressional races found evidence that campaign advertising improved people's interest in the election, their familiarity with the candidates, and their likelihood of voting (Freedman, Franz, and Goldstein 2004).

How could that be? A typical TV spots lasts only thirty seconds. Campaign advertising is notoriously clichéd and full of hyperbole and sometimes misleading insinuations—or, as the study's authors concede, "often petty, sometimes offensive, and infrequently uplifting or inspiring" (Freedman, Franz, and Goldstein 2004: 734). How could they also be informative and engaging? The authors explain:

> Campaign ads tend to be rich in informational content, and advertising conveys information in an efficient, easily digestible way. Like product advertising, political commercials are carefully tested and skillfully produced. Text, image, and music work to complement and reinforce each other. And an ad's basic message—its bottom line—is usually simple to identify. (Freedman, Franz, and Goldstein 2004: 725)

Negative ads in particular can have a "stimulation effect" on turnout because they convey what is at stake in the election (Goldstein and Freedman 2002). They clearly communicate sharp—albeit sometimes exaggerated—contrasts between the candidates. The implication is that failing to vote means giving in to the other side, and that doing so has consequential policy implications.

But what campaigns want to know is this: Does political advertising *persuade* voters to support one candidate over another? There are reasons to be skeptical about advertising's capacity to change voters' minds. The more political aware people are, the more likely they are to pay attention to various media surrounding the election. Yet highly engaged people tend to be more partisan and therefore more entrenched in their political views. Partisans tend to make up their minds months before ads pervade the airwaves. Campaign ads certainly interest them, and they are likely to see and pay attention to them; they might even share the ones they like or loathe on social media. But politically aware individuals are unlikely to change their minds about the candidates in response to an ad they see on television. A clever spot might make them feel better about a candidate they are inclined to support. But through the process of motivated reasoning (see chapter 2), politically aware individuals can explain away or simply forget any damaging information or imagery contained in an ad that attacks their preferred candidate. Not so for so-called persuadables. Naturally, persuadables—undecided voters—are the preferred recipients of campaign advertising. Their views are subject to change. But undecided voters also tend to be less engaged in politics and therefore less likely to pay close attention to what they see and hear (Zaller 1992). They might not see the ad.

Yet campaign ads are difficult to ignore. They are inescapable during competitive election campaigns. Brief, easily digestible, and simple to comprehend, TV ads provide an efficient mechanism for less engaged citizens to form basic impressions about the candidates. An array of recent studies suggests that ads can be quite persuasive, particularly among citizens with relatively low levels of political awareness. In one laboratory-type experiment set during the 2000 presidential election, Bush ads pushed "least aware" subjects toward Bush, and Gore ads pushed similar subjects toward Gore (Valentino, Hutchings, and Williams 2004). One experiment reported evidence of candidate spots influencing subjects' perceptions of the 1996 presidential candidates, Bill Clinton and Bob Dole (Kaid 1997). Another experiment centered on the 1998 Democratic primary for governor found that campaign ads are most effective when they appeal to the emotions of voters (Brader 2005). An experiment assessing the impact of advertising on viewers' impressions of an unknown candidate found that positive spots created more favorable images than negative ads, yet voters were responsive to negative ads if they focused on a specific issue and provided supporting evidence (Kahn and Geer 1994).

The capacity of campaign spots to persuade—which has been demonstrated in laboratory-type experiments—has also been confirmed by research conducted in the field. Ground-breaking research on the 2006 gubernatorial race in Texas reported strong short-term effects of television advertising on voter preference (Gerber et al. 2011). A comprehensive, book-length study of the 2004 presidential race reported that campaigns could use "wedge issues" like abortion, same-sex marriage, and immigration to persuade a surprisingly large number of voters to vote against their party (Hillygus and Shields 2009). A study of the 1996 Senate races concluded that campaign advertising had a persuasive effect on voting decisions (Goldstein and Freedman 2000). Another concluded that Obama's advertising advantage over McCain in 2008 yielded a small but measurable increase in votes, particularly in nonbattleground states, where field operations were relatively minimal. Outairing McCain on television may have helped Obama win both North Carolina and Florida, and perhaps even Indiana, in the Electoral College (Franz and Ridout 2010).

One reason it is difficult to isolate the impact of advertising is that voters are so often inundated with other potential sources of influence, especially during presidential elections. TV ads are just part of a mix that includes not only saturation news coverage but also door-to-door canvassing, direct mail, candidate visits, and phone calls. However, voters living in nonbattleground states are not quite as overwhelmed. Field operations in particular are kept to a minimum in geographic areas that are designated as either safe or out of reach. One innovative study exploited this phenomenon to conduct a natural experiment aimed at isolating the effects of advertising during the 2004 presidential election (Huber and Arceneaux 2007). The researchers determined that many of these noncompetitive areas border battleground states and therefore share the same television media market. Delaware, for example, was a safe Democratic state, which meant neither party spent much time or money there on field operations, candidate appearances, or special events. But Delaware is located in the Philadelphia media market, and Pennsylvania was a battleground state in 2004. That meant Delaware voters were inundated with TV ads intended for voters in their neighboring state but were otherwise ignored by the presidential campaigns. So when evidence emerged that voters in Delaware and similar noncompetitive states were impacted by campaign messaging, the researchers could attribute the attitude change to advertising since other sources of influence such as canvassing were less prevalent.

How do ads manage to encourage voters to support one candidate over the other? Researchers in this field point to two psychological processes that explain the effects of campaign communication. One perspective is known as **priming**. This theory suggests that ads simply "prime voters to invoke *different evaluative criteria* when assessing candidates" (Gerber et al. 2011). Rather than directly change voters' minds about a set of issues, ads are used to merely encourage viewers to base their voting decisions on an issue or characteristic that is advantageous to the candidate. When George W. Bush ran for reelection in 2004, many of his television spots centered on the threat of terrorism—perhaps the only major policy area where he had a clear advantage over his Democratic opponent, John Kerry. Only three years after 9/11, the campaign's objective was to prime viewers to prioritize this issue over all others when deciding which candidate to support. That explains why they produced ads like "Wolves," a TV spot that combined creepy footage of a pack of predatory wolves with criticisms of Kerry "and the liberals in Congress" slashing intelligence operations and therefore weakening "America's defenses." Hillary Clinton's "Mirrors" and "Role Models" spots, described earlier in the chapter, were aimed at priming viewers to prioritize Trump's character flaws when deciding which candidate to support. Most people had already made up their minds about Trump; the ads were aimed at reminding certain voters what they didn't like about him in the hope that they would act accordingly when casting their vote.

The other perspective centers on the information content of advertising (Gerber et al. 2011). Here, persuasion depends on the capacity of voters to learn from campaign communication. When voters make what are known as *memory-based* evaluations, they develop opinions based on what they can remember. They are not likely to remember much from an ad they watched in passing, without the expectation of having to act on it. By contrast, *online processing* is more enduring and impactful. Online processing is when "people evaluate persuasive communication as they receive it, updating an online tally of overall opinion after each message and storing the tally in memory" (Hill et al. 2013: 522). It requires effort, which means the receiver is more likely to remember its message and draw upon it when casting a vote.

The reality is, memory-based processing is much more common than effortful online processing. Lacking strong interest, most people engage in memory-based processing during the course of an election campaign. That helps explains a consistent research finding that has significant implications for campaign strategy: advertising effects tend to decay quickly. One study of the 2000 presidential election and the 2006 midterms confirmed that although ads can be persuasive, their impact can be strikingly short-lived. Especially notable was the finding that although advertising effects were large for nonpresidential elections, their impact decayed to almost nothing within days if not weeks (Hill et al. 2013). These findings were consistent with those of a study of the 2006 Texas governor's race, which reported a "rapid decay" in advertising effects (Gerber et al. 2011). Similarly, an online experiment conducted during the 2012 election reported a rapid decay in an ad-triggered boost in intentions to vote for Obama (Bartels 2014). This particular ad contrasted footage of Mitt Romney's awkward and off-key singing of "America the Beautiful" with images and narrative about his firm shipping jobs overseas to Mexico, China, and India. According to the experiment, the short-term effect was a 2.8-point increase in intentions of voting for Obama. But by Election Day, that effect had disappeared due to a "boomerang effect" among Romney supporters who were influenced by the ad during the short term, but returned to Romney within days. To author Larry Bartels, it wasn't that these Romney supporters forgot the ad. Rather, they engaged in a form of processing that operated over a period of days or weeks rather than immediately upon exposure to the ad.

In addition to persuading uncommitted voters to change their minds, ads are also aimed at mobilizing supporters to the polls. With mobilization-centered messaging, the objective is simply to *activate* the predispositions of likely supporters. As we will see in chapter 7, mobilization is the primary objective of a campaign's field operation. In some ways, it is easier to mobilize than persuade. It is also less risky (Panagopoulos 2016). Messages aimed at voters inclined to be supportive will encounter little resistance. Likely supporters just need reassurance that their candidate is worth supporting. Some of the studies discussed above confirm that ads are capable of mobilization (e.g., Brader 2005), although others find ads are more effective at persuasion (e.g., Huber and Arceneaux 2007).

The 2016 presidential election illustrates the potential impact of advertising, but also its limits. Trump won despite lagging behind Clinton in most television media markets. Pro-Clinton spots made up 72 percent of TV advertising. That is an unusual imbalance in presidential elections. Although it is common for one party to out-advertise the other, the gap has never neared three to one. The closest comparison was 2008, when the Obama campaign aired 60 percent of televised advertising. Like Obama, Clinton outraised her opponent by a wide margin, allowing her to invest heavily in television advertising. And according to a series of innovative field experiments by a group of political scientists, the ads helped Clinton and hurt Trump. In the experiments, watching an ad attacking Trump lowered his favorability rating by two points and boosted the likelihood of voting for Clinton. Trump ads attacking Clinton boosted his favorability but had no effect on attitude toward Clinton (Sides, Tesler, and Vavreck 2018). In the real world, Clinton performed better in counties where her campaign advertised more heavily, even when controlling for other factors that explain the results. Even so, the overall impact was small—typical for a presidential race. Only a massive increase in advertising would have helped her win Wisconsin and Pennsylvania, two of the three formerly "blue" states that swung against her (Sides, Tesler, and Vavreck 2018).

In the end, campaign advertising is nowhere near as impactful as campaigns hope it will be. Negative advertising produces particularly mixed outcomes. Attacks may be memorable and informative, but evidence is mixed on whether they actually help the candidate who stands to benefit. Candidates risk a backlash when they attack their opponent: "Although attacks probably do undermine evaluations of the candidates they target, they usually bring evaluations of the attackers down even more, and the net effect on vote choice is nil (Lau, Sigelman, and Rovner 2007: 1185). Such a backlash may have hurt Hillary Clinton, whose 2016 paid media effort relied mostly on TV and online ads attacking Trump's unfitness for the presidency (Fowler, Ridout, and Franz 2016). By contrast, positive advertising can help—but only if the candidates stay positive and outspend their opponent (Malloy and Merkowitz 2016). This "only if" caveat is typical. Campaign advertising can help a candidate win, but only if the timing is right. Only if the ad is seen as fair and relevant. Only if both sides don't saturate the airwaves. Only if persuadable voters are paying attention. Even when all of these conditions are met, advertising effects may be only slightly more than minimal.

CONCLUSION

Uncertainty about impact has not dampened paid media spending. Voters were inundated with ads campaign ads during the 2018 midterm election. It was a "do everything" race as campaigns invested heavily in both traditional TV and online advertising (Fowler, Franz, and Ridout 2018). For Democrats, the midterms were an opportunity to rebuke a historically unpopular president and retake the majority in the House of Representatives. For Republicans, the objective was to hold as many House seats as possible while defending their majority in the Senate. Nearly one hundred House races were rated competitive by the *Cook Political Report* compared with only sixty-eight races four years earlier. Contributions poured in to the campaigns themselves as well as the party committees and especially left-leaning outside groups. "Money was no object this cycle," said Steve Passwaiter, vice president of political advertising at Kantar media/CMAG, an ad measurement firm. And most of that money was spent on paid media as advertising expenditures broke records (Fisher 2018).

The scale of paid media should no longer surprise us. The possibility of even marginal effects compels campaigns to spend thousands and sometimes millions of dollars on advertising. Getting outspent by an opponent can result in a loss of a percentage point or two, and that can be decisive in a tight race. Why risk it? A campaign that has the money would rather pour money into paid media than wonder if their loss can be blamed on spending too little.

KEY TERMS

attack advertising (aka negative advertising): paid media that contains only negative messaging about an opponent with no messaging about the candidate who sponsored the message.

comparative advertising (aka contrast advertising): paid media that contrasts the sponsoring candidate with their opponent.

positive advertising: paid media solely about the candidate who is sponsoring the message.

priming: the communication process of shaping the criteria by which individuals assess candidates.

DISCUSSION QUESTIONS

1. What are the pros and cons of running ads online instead of on television?
2. Under what circumstances might we see measurable effects of campaign advertising on election results?
3. Research shows that voters learn as much, if not more, from a thirty-second TV spot than a typical TV news story. Why do you think that is?
4. Assess Donald Trump's 2016 message, "Make America Great Again," in terms of the Six C's. To what extent was Trump's message clear, concise, compelling, credible, connected, and contrasting?

RECOMMENDED READINGS

Fowler, Erika Franklin, Travis N. Ridout, and Michael M. Franz. 2016. "Political Advertising in 2016: The Presidential Election as Outlier?" *The Forum* 14, no. 4: 445–69.

From the authors of numerous studies of campaign advertising, this report presents a number of surprising findings about the 2016 race. Hillary Clinton spent far more on television advertising than Donald Trump, but her advertising overwhelmingly focused on Trump's personality and fitness for office, whereas Trump's advertising provided more policy-based contrasts.

Huber, Gregory A., and Kevin Arceneaux. 2007. "Identifying the Persuasive Effects of Presidential Advertising." *American Journal of Political Science* 51, no. 4: 957–77.

Employs an innovative research design to assess the capacity of television advertising to persuade voters. The authors exploit a natural experiment whereby voters in nonbattleground states are unintentionally exposed to advertising aired in adjacent battleground states.

West, Darrell. 2017. *Air Wars: Television Advertising and Social Media in Election Campaigns, 1952–2016*, 7th ed. Thousand Oaks, CA: Sage.

This classic provides a comprehensive analysis of campaign advertising since the beginning of television. Chock-full of data analysis and examples from recent elections. Includes useful overviews of production techniques and ad buying strategies.

REFERENCES

Ansolabehere, Stephen, and Shanto Iyengar. 1995. *Going Negative: How Political Advertisements Shrink & Polarize the Electorate*. New York: Free Press.

Ball, Molly. 2016. "There's Nothing Better Than a Scared, Rich Candidate." *The Atlantic* (Oct.): https://www.theatlantic.com/magazine/archive/2016/10/theres-nothing-better-than-a-scared-rich-candidate/497522/.

Bartels, Larry M. 2014. "Remembering to Forget: A Note on the Duration of Campaign Advertising Effects." *Political Communication* 31: 532–44.

Beschloss, Michael. "The Ad That Helped Reagan Sell Good Times to an Uncertain Nation." *New York Times* (May 7): https://www.nytimes.com/2016/05/08/business/the-ad-that-helped-reagan-sell-good-times-to-an-uncertain-nation.html.

Brader, Ted. 2005. "Striking a Responsive Chord: How Political Ads Motivate and Persuade Voters by Appealing to Emotions." *American Journal of Political Science* 49, no. 2: 388–405.

Broockman, David E., and Donald P. Green. 2014. "Do Online Advertisements Increase Political Candidates' Name Recognition or Favorability? Evidence from Randomized Field Experiments." *Political Behavior* 36: 263–89.

Brooks, Deborah Jordan, and John G. Geer. 2007. "Beyond Negativity: The Effects of Incivility on the Electorate." *American Journal of Political Science* 51, no. 1: 1–16.

Farnam, T. W. 2012. "Obama Has an Aggressive Internet Strategy to Woo Supporters." *Washington Post* (April 6): https://www.washingtonpost.com/politics/obama-has-aggressive-internet-strategy-to-woo-supporters/2012/04/06/gIQAavB2zS_story.html?noredirect=on&utm_term=.f8a358017ffb.

Fisher, Sara. 2018. "Political Ad Spending Hits New Record for 2018 Midterm Elections." *Axios* (Nov. 6): https://www.axios.com/record-midterm-ad-spend-explodes-money-was-no-object-1541450836-f92d1767-ad5f-4d85-99ee-96d9847e7691.html.

Fowler, Erika Franklin, Michael M. Franz, and Travis N. Ridout. 2016. *Political Advertising in the United States*. Boulder, CO: Westview.

———. 2018. "The Big Lessons of Political Advertising in 2018." *The Conversation* (Dec. 3): http://theconversation.com/the-big-lessons-of-political-advertising-in-2018-107673.

Fowler, Erika Franklin, and Travis N. Ridout. 2014. "Political Advertising in 2014: The Year of the Outside Group." *The Forum* 12, no. 4: 663–84.

Fowler, Erika Franklin, Travis N. Ridout, and Michael M. Franz. 2016. "Political Advertising in 2016: The Presidential Election as Outlier?" *The Forum* 14, no. 4: 445–69.

Franz, Michael M., and Travis N. Ridout. 2010. "Political Advertising and Persuasion in the 2004 and 2008 Presidential Elections." *American Politics Research* 38, no. 2: 303–29.

Freedman, Paul, Michael Franz, and Kenneth Goldstein. 2004. "Campaign Advertising and Democratic Citizenship." *American Journal of Political Science* 48, no. 4: 723–41.

Freedman, Paul, and Ken Goldstein. 1999. "Measuring Media Exposure and the Effects of Negative Campaign Ads." *American Journal of Political Science* 43, no. 4: 1189–208.

Gerber, Alan S., James G. Gimpel, Donald P. Green, and Daron R. Shaw. 2011. "How Large and Long-Lasting Are the Persuasive Effects of Televised Campaign Ads? Results from a Randomized Field Experiment." *American Political Science Review* 105, no. 1: 135–50.

Gold, Hadas. 2016. "Sanders Gives Trump a Run for His Money on Social Media." *Politico* (Jan. 23): https://www.politico.com/blogs/on-media/2016/01/social-index-218135#ixzz3y7Mya2BG.

Goldstein, Ken, and Paul Freedman. 2000. "New Evidence for New Arguments: Money and Advertising in the 1996 Senate Elections." *Journal of Politics* 62, no. 4: 1087–108.

———. 2002. "Campaign Advertising and Voter Turnout: New Evidence for a Stimulation Effect." *Journal of Politics* 64, no. 3: 721–40.

Hill, Seth J., James Lo, Lynn Vavreck, and John Zaller. 2013. "How Quickly We Forget: The Duration of Persuasion Effects from Mass Communication." *Political Communication* 30, no. 4: 521–47.

Hillygus, D. Sunshine, and Todd G. Shields. 2009. *The Persuadable Voter: Wedge Issues in Presidential Campaigns*. Princeton, NJ: Princeton University Press.

Huber, Gregory A., and Kevin Arceneaux. 2007. "Identifying the Persuasive Effects of Presidential Advertising." *American Journal of Political Science* 51, no. 4: 957–77.

Iyengar, Shanto. 2011. "The Media Game: New Moves, Old Strategies." *The Forum* 9, no. 1: Article 1.

Janetsky, Megan. 2018. "Low Transparency, Low Regulation Online Political Ads Skyrocket." OpenSecrets.org (Mar. 7): https://www.opensecrets.org/news/2018/03/low-transparency-low-regulation-online-political-ads-skyrocket/.

Jasperson, Amy E. 2005. "Campaign Communications." In *Guide to Political Campaigns in America*. Edited by Paul S. Herrnson, 270–88. Washington, DC: CQ Press.

Kahn, Kim Fridkin, and John G. Geer. 1994. "Creating Impressions: An Experimental Investigation of Political Advertising on Television." *Political Behavior* 16, no. 1: 93–116.

Kaid, Lynda Lee. 1997. "Effects of the Television Spots on Images of Dole and Clinton." *American Behavioral Scientist* 40, no. 8: 1085–94.

Klapper, Joseph T. 1960. *The Effects of Mass Communication*. New York: Free Press.

Klein, Ezra. 2017. "The Inside Story of Doug Jones's Win in Alabama." *Vox* (Dec. 27): https://www.vox.com/policy-and-politics/2017/12/26/16810116/doug-jones-alabama-polls-roy-moore.

Laposky, Issie. 2015. "The Tech That Got Obama Elected Will Now Fire Ads at You." *Wired* (Oct. 6): https://www.wired.com/2015/10/civis-media-optimizer/.

Lau, Richard R., Lee Sigelman, and Ivy Brown Rovner. 2007. "The Effects of Negative Political Campaigns: A Meta-Analytic Reassessment." *Journal of Politics* 69, no. 4: 1176–209.

Lazarsfeld, Paul F., Bernard Berelson, and Hazel Gaudet. 1944. *The People's Choice: How the Voter Makes Up His Mind in a Presidential Campaign*. New York: Duell, Sloan, and Pearce.

Livengood, Chad. 2018. "Reaching Voters Where They Are: Political Marking Uses New Tech to Get Personal with Voters." *Crains Detroit Business* (Nov. 4): https://www.crainsdetroit.com/politics/reaching-voters-where-they-are-political-marketing-uses-new-tech-get-personal-voters.

Livingston, Abby. 2014. "The Best TV Shows for Political Advertisements." *Roll Call* (Sept. 21): https://www.rollcall.com/news/elections-2014-the-best-tv-shows-for-political-advertisements.

MacManus, Susan A., and Anthony A. Cilluffo. 2017. "Ten Takeaways from Campaign 2016 and a Look Forward." *Trump: The 2016 Election That Broke All the Rules*, Edited by Larry J. Sabato, Kyle Kondik, and Geoffrey Skelley, 227–42. Lanham, MD: Rowman & Littlefield.

Malloy, Liam, and Shanna Pearson-Merkowitz. 2016. "Going Positive: The Effects of Negative and Positive Advertising on Candidate Success and Voter Turnout." *Research and Politics* (Jan.–Mar.): 1–15.

Mattes, Kyle, and David P. Redlawsk. 2014. *The Positive Case for Negative Campaigning*. Chicago: University of Chicago Press.

OpenSecrets.org. "Most Expensive Races." https://www.opensecrets.org/overview/toraces.php?cycle=2018&display=currcandsout.

Overby, Marvin L., and Jay Barth. 2006. "Radio Advertising in American Political Campaigns: The Persistence, Importance, and Effects of Narrowcasting." *American Politics Research* 34, no. 4: 451–78.

Panagopoulos, Costas. 2016. "All about That Based: Changing Campaign Strategies in U.S. Presidential Elections." *Party Politics* 22, no. 2: 179–90.

Patterson, Thomas E. 1994. *Out of Order*. New York: Vintage.

Patterson, Thomas, E., and Robert D. McClure. 1976. *The Unseeing Eye: The Myth of Television Power in National Elections*. New York: Putnam.

Persily, Nathaniel. 2017. "Can Democracy Survive the Internet?" *Journal of Democracy* 28, no. 2: 63–76.

Sides, John, Michael Tesler, and Lynn Vavreck. 2018. *Identity Crisis: The 2016 Presidential Campaign and the Battle for the Meaning of America*. Princeton, NJ: Princeton University Press.

Stevens, Daniel. 2009. "Elements of Negativity: Volume and Proportion in Exposure to Negative Advertising." *Political Behavior* 31: 429–54.

Valentino, Nicholas A., Vincent L. Hutchings, and Dmitri Williams. 2004. "The Impact of Political Advertising on Knowledge, Internet Information Seeking, and Candidate Preference." *Journal of Communication* (June): 337–54.

Vavreck, Lynn. 2016. "The Ad That Moved People the Most: Bernie Sanders's 'America.'" *New York Times* (Dec. 30): https://www.nytimes.com/2016/12/30/upshot/the-campaign-ads-that-moved-people-the-most.html.

Vega, Tanzina. 2012. "Online Data Helping Campaigns Customize Ads. *New York Times* (Feb. 20): https://www.nytimes.com/2012/02/21/us/politics/campaigns-use-microtargeting-to-attract-supporters.html.

Washington Post. 2017. "Exit Poll Results: How Different Groups Voted in Alabama." *Washington Post* (Dec. 13): https://www.washingtonpost.com/graphics/2017/politics/alabama-exit-polls/?utm_term=.080ca942a38f.

Wattenberg, Martin P., and Craig Leonard Brians. 1999. "Negative Campaign Advertising: Demobilizer or Mobilizer?" *American Political Science Review* 93, no, 4: 891–99.

West, Darrell. 2018. *Air Wars: Television Advertising and Social Media in Election Campaigns, 1952-2016*, 7th ed. Thousand Oaks, CA: Sage.

West, Darrell. 2014. *Air Wars: Television Advertising and Social Media in Election Campaigns, 1952-2012*, 6th edition. Thousand Oaks, CA: Sage.

Willis, Derek. 2014. "Political TV Ads Can Be Wasteful. But That's Changing." *New York Times* (Oct. 21): https://nyti.ms/1t9Dl3R.

Wong, Julia Carrie. 2019. "Trump Campaigns Facebook Ads Target Latinos in Texas Days after Shooting." Guardian (Aug. 9): https://www.theguardian.com/us-news/2019/aug/08/trump-facebook-ads-target-latinos-anti-immigrant.

Zaller, John R. 1992. *The Nature and Origins of Mass Opinions*. Cambridge: Cambridge University Press.

Zhao, Xinshu, and Steven H. Chaffee. 1995. "Campaign Advertisements versus Television News as Sources of Political Issue Information. *Public Opinion Quarterly* 59, no. 1: 41–65.

6

Social Media

★ ★ ★

A voter watches Hillary Clinton's April 2015 announcement on YouTube that she was running for president. *Source*: *Richard B. Levine/Newscom*

LEARNING OBJECTIVES

★ Contrast campaigns' use of social media with their use of other media outlets.

★ Comprehend the relevant differences between Facebook, Twitter, and other social media platforms.

- ★ Assess the possible effects of social media campaigning.
- ★ Develop a critical grasp of "fake news" and its possible consequences.

BECAUSE HE WON, we sometimes forget that Donald Trump's 2016 presidential campaign operation was a chaotic mess. As the fall general election campaign began, the Trump team was "woefully behind its . . . opponent in every conceivable metric that scholars study" (Kreiss and McGregor 2018: 173). Trump was skeptical about what he perceived as wasteful spending on ineffective measures, so his campaign spent little on television advertising until the final six weeks of the campaign (Pearce 2016). His campaign farmed out much of its field operations to the Republican party (Confessore and Shorey 2016). Trump attracted far more media coverage than his Republican rivals during the primaries—much of it favorable in tone—but during the general election the amount of news coverage evened out and its tone turned decidedly negative (Patterson 2016), thanks in part to Trump's countless gaffes and what at the time appeared to be strategic errors.

The haphazard state of Trump's campaign gave him at least one advantage: he was forced to rely more on social media than conventional modes of communication. Whereas buying spots on television requires at least some advance planning, posting digital spots on social media is conducive to last-minute decision-making and flexibility. The campaign ended up spending half of its media budget on digital advertising, primarily on social media platforms (Persily 2017). Short on time, it leaned heavily on Facebook staffers for input on how to use the platform to reach voters (Baldwin-Philippi 2017). That led to such decisions as using Facebook's Lookalike Audience feature, which allowed the campaign to target people similar to known supporters and undecided voters (Baldwin-Philippi 2017). An internal Facebook report concluded that "Trump's FB campaigns were more complex than Clinton's and better leveraged Facebook's ability to optimize for outcomes" (Frier 2018).

To make news, there was little need for Trump to employ conventional earned media tactics (although he did grant more interviews than Clinton). He could just hold a rally and make outrageous statements. Hours of "free media" coverage would follow. Or he could just tweet whatever was on his mind. Not only did his tweets reach his thirteen million Twitter followers directly, but they also received secondary exposure as media coverage when the press deemed them newsworthy, as they often did. Followers helped spread the word. Trump's tweets were retweeted six thousand times on average compared with fifteen hundred retweets for Clinton. Trump's Facebook page had double the number of "likes" as Clinton's Facebook page, which is partly why his Facebook posts were five times more likely to be shared than Clinton's (Pew Research Center 2016).

Fake news and other disinformation efforts on social media also favored Trump. The 2016 election triggered alarm about the spread of false or misleading stories on social media—stories that mimic factual news stories produced by mainstream media outlets. Although questions remain about the extent of fake news proliferation and its impact in 2016 (Guess, Nagler, and Tucker 2019), researchers have established that false stories on social media heavily tilted in favor of Trump over Clinton (Allcott and Gentzkow 2017). Trump also was the intended beneficiary of Russia-sponsored digital ads aired on Facebook and other social media outlets aimed at depressing turnout among likely Clinton supporters, particularly African American voters (DiRiesta et al. 2018). For example, Russia's Internet News Agency created a fake Facebook account called Blacktivist, whose posts included a plea for African Americans to vote for Green Party candidate Jill Stein. Another Blacktivist post declared that "NO LIVES MATTER TO HILLARY CLINTON. ONLY VOTES MATTER TO HILLARY CLINTON." A third declared that "NOT VOTING is a way to exercise our rights" (Hohmann 2018).

According to conventional wisdom, social media helped Trump win the election despite being pummeled by the press, outspent on television, and outorganized in the field. We will never know if that was true. It may be that Trump's overall social media operation was no more innovative than Clinton's (Baldwin-Philippi 2017). As we will see in this chapter, recent research casts doubt on the reach and impact of fake news (Grinberg et al. 2019; Guess, Nagler, and Tucker 2019). In any case, Clinton actually won more votes than Trump nationwide; his victory through the Electoral College could have been explained by any combination of factors. While it is true that Clinton ran far more ads on television, their relentless focus on attacking Trump's character rather than providing policy-related contrasts may have spurred backlash among some voters (Fowler, Ridout, and Franz 2016). Finally, the "Comey letter" may have been more consequential than any other factor: just a week and a half before the election, FBI director Jim Comey sent a letter to Congress announcing an expansion of the agency's investigation of Clinton's use of a private email server, which may have shifted the electorate by three or four points—enough to help Trump win Michigan, Pennsylvania, and Wisconsin and therefore the Electoral College (Silver 2017).

All of this said, even if social media's importance was overstated, a Twitter-less and Facebook-free Trump campaign is difficult to imagine. Trump's embrace of social media platforms embodies their promise as outlets for reaching voters. As with earned media, campaigns can use social media to communicate with voters at little or no cost. As with paid media, the campaign has almost complete control over the content and production of the message. But as we will see in this chapter, social media is more promising than either earned media or media as a mechanism for controlling the chaos that characterizes election campaigning. That is because of three distinguishing characteristics that set social media apart from both:

Direct voter contact. Donald Trump's Twitter feed is a reminder that candidates can use social media to reach voters directly with their own content at a time of their choosing. No need to pay thousands of dollars to run an ad on television that reaches the wrong voters. No need to hold a press conference or grant an interview that will be covered ways that reflect the media outlet's priorities, not the candidate's. Instead, the campaign can post its own content—text, video, imagery, or all of the above—onto any or all social media platforms. A video's duration can be thirty seconds or thirty minutes. The candidate can post multiple times a day at no additional cost. Each post can be seen by anyone with a social media account. At minimum, it will be viewed by people who "like" or follow the candidate on social media.

Supporter sharing. A campaign's social media posts can be amplified if followers share them with people in their social media network. Social media's sharing capacity is an example of how campaigns can use these platforms to empower supporters to engage in "digital circulation" of campaign content on behalf of their preferred candidate (Baldwin-Philippi 2015). Supporters can also create their own posts—a tweet, for example, that ridicules a gaffe committed by the opposing candidate. But "social sharing" is easier than creating original content: all a supporter needs to do is use the appropriate function ("share" on Facebook; "retweet" on Twitter) to spread the candidate's post or other content that helps the candidate's cause. Even clicking on the "like" button or heart icon can expose the post to people in the user's network. A particularly compelling post can go viral.

Supporters share campaign-generated content on social media "because they find it compelling, want to help a candidate or cause, or want to signal their identity" (Kreiss 2016: 220). "Opinion leaders"—influential people within a network—are seen by campaigns as particularly important sharers (Baldwin-Philippi 2015). Their efforts may bear fruit: social media users are more likely to read political content if it is shared by actual friends and family. That applies even among recipients who are "entertainment seekers," and even when the shared content comes from a partisan source they disagree with (Anspach 2017).

Microtargeting. As we saw in the previous chapter, social media outlets provide effective platforms for online advertising that is microtargeted to individual voters based on their estimated predispositions. People reveal a large amount of politically relevant information about themselves on their social media profiles. An individual's gender, age, geographic location, profession, and interests are easy to discern; all serve as predictors of a person's political orientation and voting behavior. Likes and follows are particularly revealing, especially when a person likes or follows individual candidates or political causes. Liking a particular celebrity also might reveal something useful about a person's politics. Digital ads are not limited to social media; Google rivals Facebook as a top site for online campaign advertising. But social media platforms are appealing to campaigns because users share so much that is politically relevant about themselves.

These three qualities do not assume the campaign has complete control over what happens on social media. Each platform's proprietary algorithms shape what people see on their feeds, which means a user might not see a candidate's post if the formula predicts a lack of interest. In addition, a clumsy social media post can become an unflattering news story. That happened to Republican presidential candidate Rand Paul when he misspelled the word "friendship" in a tweet mocking two of his potential GOP 2016 rivals for their shared support for unpopular "common core" education. A post can be humiliating when it goes viral as a target of ridicule. Critics can use the comment function to respond to the post in ways that undermine the post's intent. Users can ignore the comments, but sometimes they take on a life of their own. On Twitter, for example, a tweet can be "ratioed" when the number of replies exceeds the amount of retweets—an embarrassing indicator of a mostly negative reaction to the post.

An individual's social media behavior can also be misleading. Just because someone likes a candidate on Facebook does not mean she can be counted on as a supporter. Donald Trump has plenty of Twitter followers who have no intention of voting for him.

The campaign's digital team, usually led by the digital director, is typically responsible for social media outreach along with online advertising, email, and the web site (see box 6.1, "The Online Communication Hub.") Social media is a useful broad category for the sake of organizing campaign communication efforts, but each platform is quite different. What they have in common is a capacity to enable *users to create and share content with each other through online social networks*. They differ significantly in terms of their audiences and functionality. These differences are constantly changing as each platform adjusts to shifting preferences, technological advances, and policy constraints. Whereas the basic format of the traditional thirty-second television spot has remained the same for more than forty years, social media platforms make frequent adjustments—often without warning—every election cycle (Kreiss, Lawrence, and McGregor 2018), and sometimes in the middle of an election cycle (Kriess 2016). Understanding the differences between each platform is a must, with the caveat that the distinctions described below are highly subject to change.

BOX 6.1 | The Online Communication Hub

Websites are Internet 1.0. There is nothing groundbreaking about a candidate's decision to launch a web page. The website is where candidates first establish their serious online presence. For all the talk about social media's reach and capacity for interaction, the website actually serves as the campaign's online communication hub. All of the campaign's online content can be hosted there or linked from there. The website is where curious voters can go for biographical information about the candidate as well as summaries of their issue positions. It is where journalists go to familiarize themselves with candidates they don't know. And it is where supporters can go to donate money, volunteer, or inform themselves about upcoming campaign events.

The problem with websites is that voters must actively seek them out. Users "visit" a website; it is not delivered to them. Browsers rarely stumble upon a candidate's website while engaging in other online activity. That is not the case for advertising, which people encounter unintentionally as they consume other content—watching TV, for example. Social media posts and emails can help by linking to the website. So can *search engine optimization (SEO)*. For campaigns, SEO is the process of boosting the likelihood that the campaign's official website will top the list of

---

(continued)

BOX 6.1 | (continued)

nonsponsored results when curious voters search for the candidate's name or relevant terms.

The website is an essential tool for raising money and collecting
voter data. Visitors to a candidate's website may first encounter an
interactive "splash screen" before they get to the home page. That
screen typically asks the user to give money, provide their contact
information, or both. Neither is required, but the user might have
to click on a button that allows them to continue to the site or
scroll to the bottom of the page. The assumption is that many
people who bother to visit the website are inclined to help the
candidate in some way, even if they remain uncommitted.

Providing contact information is nearly as important as making a financial contribution. The website usually asks visitors to
provide their name, email address, cell phone number, and zip
code. By providing that information, people are signaling possible, or perhaps likely, support for the candidate and a willingness
to receive follow-up emails and text messages. (Anyone who has
provided this information to a campaign can attest to the large
number of emails that will follow.)

Candidate websites also can feature a "store" page, where supporters can buy T-shirts, bumper stickers, campaign buttons, and
other items. Early in his bid for the 2020 Democratic presidential
nomination, Pete Buttigieg sold "Boot Edge Edge" coffee mugs
and T-shirts partly aimed at helping voters master the tricky pro-
nunciation of his name. These products might be sold for a premium (say, $25 for a basic T-shirt), which means the purchaser has
made a small campaign contribution. The product they bought
may reveal something of interest to the campaign; somebody
who ordered a onesie for a baby may be flagged for messaging
targeted at parents (Turk 2017). More importantly, the purchaser
probably had to provide their email address and phone number.
They will hear from the campaign again.

SOURCE

Turk, Michael. 2017. "Social and New Media—The Digital Present and
Future." In *Campaigns on the Cutting Edge*, 3rd ed. Edited by Richard
J. Semiatin. Washington, DC: CQ Press.

FACEBOOK

Facebook remains the dominant social media outlet. Sixty-eight percent of U.S. adults reported using Facebook in 2018. Facebook may
have a reputation for appealing to older audiences, but 80 percent of

adults aged eighteen to twenty-four reported using it—pretty close to the number associated with this age group's Snapchat use in 2018 (Smith and Anderson 2018). As figure 6.1 shows, it was a much more important source for news than the other social media outlets: 43 percent of U.S. adults reported getting news from Facebook compared

Figure 6.1   Social Media Sites as Pathways to News. Percentage of U.S. Adults Who Get News on Each Social Media Site

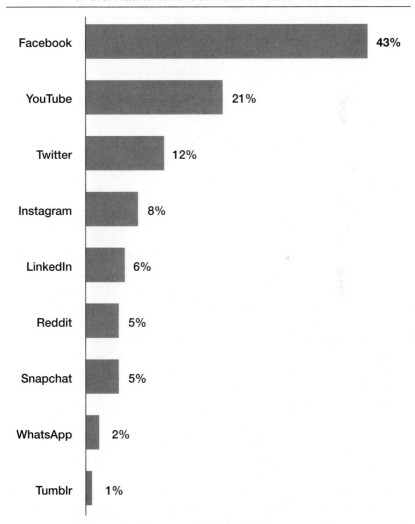

Source: Survey conducted July 30–August 12, 2018. "News Use Across Social Media Platforms 2018." Pew Research Center N = 4,581. Margin of error: ±2.5%.

with only 12 percent for Twitter, 8 percent for Instagram, and 5 percent for Snapchat (Shearer and Matsa 2018).

Facebook's massive reach across demographics makes it irresistible to campaigns. Social media strategists for 2016 presidential candidates, interviewed by a group of scholars, had this to say about the platform's audience (Kreiss, Lawrence, and McGregor 2018: 16):

> The majority of Americans are on Facebook so it was our biggest platform, our most diverse one. We could really try to get young Latinos, to older African-Americans of the South, to blue-collar workers in the Midwest. Really, the audience was everyone.
> Facebook is obviously the 800-pound gorilla of social platforms.... Facebook is going to provide you probably the broadest range of age groups that you can find.
> Facebook was our biggest source of traffic. It was our biggest source of engagement and so if we ever had something, Facebook always came first in my mind in terms of where to go with something. It was our most diverse audience.

Campaigns strategists also appreciate Facebook's capacity to collect and exploit highly specific data about individual users—not only their likes and dislikes but also their apparent political orientations and behavior. These data can be used to microtarget customized campaign ads. Leading up to the 2016 election, Facebook's sales pitch to political campaigns touted its ability to connect voter files with individual data collected through users' online activity—not only their social media behavior but also their online purchases (Bump 2014). That capacity came under scrutiny when Cambridge Analytica, a strategic communications firm hired by the Trump campaign in 2016, collected more data than people were comfortable with, forcing Facebook to adjust its data-sharing policies. But campaigns will take whatever individualized data they can get. A user's decision to like a dozen or so Democratic candidates—and no Republican candidates—tells a campaign where that person leans politically. A person who shares stories posted by a right-wing media outlet is a safe bet for Republican messaging. Consider Facebook's "I Voted" button. For years, Facebook has hosted programs aimed at boosting voter turnout, including the Election Day display of either an "I Voted" or "I'm a Voter" button that allowed users to boast to their friends about performing their civic duty. Users who clicked on that button are revealing useful data about themselves: not only did they vote, but they were also willing to encourage their friends to do the same.

Facebook's versatility is another plus (Kreiss, Lawrence, and MacGregor 2018). It hosts a dizzying array of features, many of them borrowed or influenced by other social media outlets. The Facebook "stories" feature resembles the Snapchat function of the same name. Like Twitter's Periscope and Instagram Live, Facebook Live allows users to stream live video. In 2016, the Trump campaign streamed its own Facebook Live broadcast of the third presidential debate for which Trump surrogates replaced journalists as pre- and postdebate analysts. Nine million people watched Trump's Facebook broadcast, and the campaign raised $9 million in contributions during and immediately after the event (Persily 2017).

As with most social media platforms, Facebook users see content through their newsfeeds. Facebook newsfeeds display a constantly updated series of posts by *friends* in users' networks and *pages* they like. On Facebook, friends can range from a lifelong pal to someone the user met in class yesterday. Users can "friend" a parent, professor, or coworker. Facebook friendship networks can include distant relatives and childhood classmates. As a result, Facebook networks can be more politically diverse than friendships based on interpersonal contact (Thorson, Vrega, and Kriger-Vilenchik 2015). People are more likely to encounter a wider range of political viewpoints on Facebook than they do elsewhere. For campaigns, that means users see posts about candidates and causes they both support and oppose. Uncommitted users can see posts not only by candidates vying for their vote but also by friends attempting to change their minds.

The most straightforward way for candidates to establish a Facebook presence is to launch a *page*. Ideally, a candidate's Facebook page is "liked" by existing and potential supporters (although opponents may also like the page for the sake of monitoring or merely curiosity). To build followers, a campaign can start by emailing the Facebook page link to existing supporters and uploading its email list to the "Suggest Page" function. Theoretically, users who like a candidate's page will see all of the candidate's posts as they go live. In reality, the Facebook algorithm prioritizes posts that it projects will lead to active engagement such as commenting and sharing. There is a good chance a post will get buried except for those users who have actively responded to the candidate's past posts.

What do candidates post? They can share their reactions to current events. They can post videos of rallies and speeches. They can share different versions of their television spots—longer versions, perhaps those with edgier content. Candidates can link to news articles and commentary they like. In practice, posts tend to "facilitate interpersonal connections rather than provide policy information"

(Baldwin-Philippi 2015: 9). Strategists for several of the 2016 presidential candidates said they used social media "in a way that fit with and conveyed the 'authentic' voice of their candidates" (Kreiss, Lawrence, and McGregor 2018: 13). For Jeb Bush, "that was everything from showing that he was a policy nerd and an introvert." Bernie Sanders also wanted to focus on issues, not photos of his meals or a cat (Kreiss, Lawrence, and McGregor 2018: 14). Younger, more tech-savvy candidates are more comfortable with posts that show their human side—if not photos of the candidate's cat or food, then perhaps a live video of the candidate interacting with neighbors or hanging out with the family.

TWITTER

Twitter's audience is much smaller than Facebook's; about one in four U.S. adults reported using Twitter in 2018 (Smith and Anderson 2018). But for campaigns, what is notable about Twitter is its importance as a news platform and the high level of political engagement of its audience. Three in four Twitter users rely on Twitter for news (Shearer and Matsa 2018). Twitter users tend to be more interested in politics and more likely to vote than the average person, and "wealthy enough to contribute to campaigns" (Bode and Dalrymple 2016: 326). Politically speaking, the audience is small but mighty. That makes Twitter a promising setting for *two-step flow* communication whereby candidates first influence highly engaged opinion leaders who are active on Twitter. These "influencers" then share what they know and think to their less engaged friends and family members (Kreiss 2016; Bode and Dalrymple 2016; Katz and Lazarsfeld 1955).

Originally a simple text-based platform, Twitter has gained features over time. A user's newsfeed displays a stream of text-based "tweets," which, until recently, appeared in chronological order as they were posted. Tweets are brief, capped at 280 characters (double the original 140-character limit). Originally text-only, users have been able to tweet images and video clips since 2010. Many users rarely post their own tweets—only half of users actually tweet—but they do actively engage with tweets posted by others: tweets can be liked, retweeted, and commented on.

For many users, Twitter serves as more of a new aggregator than a platform for interacting with friends and family. Users "follow" other Twitter accounts to see their tweets. People can follow their friends on Twitter, but they are more likely to follow celebrities and public figures—candidates, for example. The Twitter feed of a politically engaged individual will display a stream of tweets by politicians, media outlets, individual journalists, pundits, activists, and commentators (along with tweets related to their other interests).

A candidate can create a Twitter account in minutes. Another few minutes and the candidate is reaching potential voters directly through tweets of 240 characters or less. But a strong Twitter presence depends on followers. Attracting followers is easy if the candidate is a celebrity like Donald J. Trump, who already had more than four million followers when he declared his presidential candidacy in 2015. Lesser known first-time candidates face a significant challenge. A candidate can start by following other prominent people on Twitter: other public figures, journalists covering the race, as well as activists and other political "influencers." These tweeters will be notified that the candidate is following them and may return the favor (a journalist covering the race will be compelled to do so). They also will be notified if the candidates likes, retweets, or comments on their tweets, which also may attract additional followers.

Another challenge is getting followers to see a candidate's tweets. As with Facebook, a user's default time line is "curated" by an algorithm that shows top-ranked tweets first, above more recent tweets displayed in chronological order. Predictable tweets are likely to get buried. They also are less likely to result in active engagement by opinion leaders in the form of likes or retweets. Tweeting good news about polls and fundraising is a safe bet, but Twitter is conducive to spontaneity and unscripted commentary. Clever reactions to headlines are more likely to yield active engagement and news coverage, but controversial tweets can backfire. In 2016, the National Republican Senatorial Committee (NRSC) posted a tweet accusing Senate candidate Tammy Duckworth of having a "sad record of not standing up for our veterans." This was a gaffe: a veteran herself, Duckworth had lost both legs in combat during the Iraq War. The NRSC deleted the tweet (Kreig 2016).

For better or worse, candidates can make news on Twitter partly because the platform is so popular among journalists. That makes it a versatile earned media tool—the topic of chapter 4. In that chapter, we examined the strategies campaigns use to "manage the news" through their interactions with media outlets. For journalists covering campaigns, Twitter is an essential tool because they can follow their sources—candidates and pundits—as well as fellow journalists and competing news outlets. Election news breaks on Twitter. Candidates can tweet their reactions to events before they issue a statement. When news breaks, communication operatives can tweet their "spin" because they know journalists are constantly scanning their Twitter feeds for leads. Reporters are also monitoring each other's tweets, following their competition for scoops, sensitive to the possibility of missing something important. A *New York Times* reporter described Twitter's importance to journalists covering the 2012 election:

> It's the gathering spot, it's the filing center, it's the hotel bar, it's the press conference itself all in one. . . . It's the central gathering place now for the political class during campaigns but even after campaigns. It's even more than that. It's become the real-time political wire. That's where you see a lot of breaking news. That's where a lot of judgments are made about political events, good, bad or otherwise. (Hamby 2013: 24)

For many users, Twitter serves as a "second screen" during live events such as debates and conventions (Gil de Zúñiga, Garcia-Perdomo, and McGregor 2015; Kreiss, Lawrence, and McGregor 2018). Like many people, journalists watch live campaign events with one eye on the TV or computer screen and the other on their Twitter feed. That is because both their sources and fellow journalists "live-tweet" the event as it occurs. During a debate, for example, a journalist's Twitter feed acts as live focus group providing continuously streaming assessments of how the candidates are doing and which moments stand out as newsworthy (Schill and Kirk 2015). Twitter blows up when a candidate commits a gaffe or goes on the attack. Knowing that journalists are monitoring Twitter, members of the campaigns' communication teams and their surrogates post their own live tweets and encourage supporters to do the same (especially those with a large number of followers). Campaigns know the debate's media coverage will center on the horse race—who won and who lost (see chapter 4). They use Twitter to attempt to "spin" those assessments by providing live commentary as it happens and immediately after it occurs.

INSTAGRAM AND SNAPCHAT

Facebook and Twitter may grab headlines, but audiences are flat for both. Instagram, Snapchat, and other platforms have seen rapid growth in recent years, especially among younger audiences. Snapchat attracted 78 percent of U.S. adults aged eighteen to twenty-four in 2018; Instagram drew 71 percent of people in this age group (Smith and Anderson 2018). Neither were used much for news (Shearer and Matsa 2018). Even so, social media operatives for the 2016 presidential candidates viewed Instagram and Snapchat as "a way to reach younger audiences seeking backstage and behind-the-scenes looks at candidates and life on the campaign trail" (Kreiss, Lawrence, and McGregor 2018: 18).

Instagram shares key features with both Facebook and Twitter. As with both, it costs nothing for a candidate to create an Instagram account. Users follow other Instagram accounts to see their posts. Posts can be liked, commented on, and shared. But Instagram posts are limited to images and video. They can include text, but only if the text is embedded in an image or typed into the comments. It is common for campaigns to use Instagram to share photos and videos of the candidate interacting with voters on the campaign trail. Posts tend to be informal, intended to portray the candidate's human "non-politician" side. The live-video function allows candidates to interact with voters in real time. Sometimes these efforts fall flat. For example, Elizabeth Warren was ridiculed for awkwardly drinking a beer during a live video chat launching her 2020 presidential campaign.

Snapchat was once less useful to campaigns because of its original focus on person-to-person sharing of photos ("snaps") and brief videos that disappeared after ten seconds. But its "stories" function allows users to share content for up to twenty-four hours. And its "Discover" function hosts targeted advertising. In 2016, the platform launched programs aimed at reminding people to vote, streamed election results on Election Day, and shared election-related "geofilters." As with Instagram, Snapchat is used by campaigns as a platform for digital messages targeted at young voters. Bernie Sanders used Snapchat to reach the youth vote during his Democratic nomination race in 2016. Doug Jones used it to target young African American voters when he ran for U.S. Senate in Alabama in a special election in 2017. "The Snapchat geofilter option was a great solution for homing in on the younger African-American demographic, without advertising to the more conservative voters that surrounded them," said Andy Amsler, who helped lead Jones's digital strategy. "They took our message, personalized it, and then broadcasted it out to their friends and their networks" (Barrett 2018).

YOUTUBE

YouTube stretches the definition of social media. Users rarely build online YouTube identities in the way they do on other platforms. Most users treat it as a medium for watching videos on demand. But like the other social media platforms, users can create and post their own content. YouTube's original motto was "Broadcast yourself," an indicator of its early emphasis on original videos produced by amateur users. And YouTube makes it easy for users to share videos not only by email but also through their social media accounts. Videos "go viral" when they are shared by thousands if not millions of users on a social media platform like Facebook. Videos can be liked and commented on. Clearly there are social, user-centered aspects to YouTube.

YouTube's reach makes it irresistible to campaigns. According to Alexa's "Top Sites" service (https://www.alexa.com/topsites), YouTube was the second most popular website in the U.S. in 2018 behind Google, its parent company (Facebook was third). Three-quarters of U.S. adults said they used the site in 2018 (Smith and Anderson 2018). Thirty-eight percent of them used it for news (Shearer and Matsa 2018).

YouTube is owned by Google, which means users' search histories can be tapped for microtargeted video spots and display ads. Campaigns can pay to run particular ads for individuals who visit the site or watch a video. But it is the ability to post and share unlimited video content *at no cost* that makes YouTube essential even to campaigns with limited resources. Campaigns can post—and encourage their supporters to share—their standard thirty- and sixty-second spots produced for television on their YouTube account for free. They can also post longer spots that bend the creative norms of political advertising. For example, a 2016 Ted Cruz video depicted three kids playing with a Trump action figure and mocking it for being "too big to fail" and pretending to be a Republican. A satirical Cruz video depicted well-heeled lawyers, bankers, and journalists splashing through the Rio Grande River, which defines the U.S.–Mexico border, to dramatize the economic costs of illegal border crossings. When Carly Fiorina ran for the Senate in California in 2010, her campaign produced a lengthy video that came to be known as the "demon sheep" ad. The objective was to warn voters about the conservative bona fides of Fiorina's Republican primary opponent. The "demon sheep" appeared near the end of the spot: a man in a sheep's costume with glowing red eyes, hiding among innocent sheep grazing in a meadow—"a wolf in sheep's clothing," the narrator says, "Has He Fooled You?" the on-screen text asks. The ad was too long and too bizarre for television, but tens of thousands of people viewed it online.

YouTube also serves as a home for documentary-style videos that run minutes long. One example is the two-minute Ocasio-Cortez video analyzed as a case study in chapter 4. Another example was a three-and-a-half minute video introducing voters to M. J. Hegar, an Air Force helicopter pilot who challenged Rep. Joe Carter for Texas's Thirty-First Congressional District in 2018. Called "Doors," the cinematic video referenced a variety of momentous doors in Hegar's life: a door from her helicopter that crashed after being shot in Afghanistan; the glass door through which her abusive father pushed her mom; the Capitol Hill office doors slammed in her face when she lobbied Congress on women serving in combat; and her promise to "show the door" to her opponent. Hegar lost the deep-red district by only three points, but not before her video went viral, having been shared by the likes of *Hamilton* creator Lin-Manuel Miranda and actress Kristen Bell. Paying to air a video like this on television would be prohibitively expensive, but it streamed on YouTube for free. And because it was widely shared on social media, thousands of voters saw the ad (as did thousands of people outside of the district). So did donors and media outlets.

A campaign's YouTube page can host all of the campaign's videos: not only ads and minidocumentaries but also full candidate speeches, debate performances, rally footage, and testimonials. The site can also host campaign-approved amateur videos produced by supporters. When Bernie Sanders ran for president in 2016, his campaign posted a three-minute "Guide for Canvassing" video aimed at easing volunteers' concerns about knocking on doors. Similarly, Barack Obama's 2008 presidential campaign shared a video on "How to Canvass in Nevada," which offered advice on attire, demeanor, safety, how to use the script and walk list, what to say to voters, and—for out-of-state volunteers—how to pronounce the state's name correctly ("I hAd a blast in NevAda"). Sharing the video with volunteer canvassers was just a matter of providing the link to volunteers.

EMAIL

Email is old technology, and not widely seen as a form of social media. But like social media, email is often the responsibility of a campaign's digital team. And in some ways, it is a more important platform for campaigns than either Facebook or Twitter. Nearly all U.S. adults use email at least occasionally, and about 60 percent send and receive emails every day (Heimlich 2010). As with other forms of social media, users can create and share content with people in their networks. And email is a proven platform for fundraising (Green 2012). Most of the money raised online by the 2012 Obama campaign came in response to email messages. "People talk about Instagram and Snapchat and all these different digital platforms, but good ol' email remains the most crucial," said political scientist Ken Goldstein in an interview with National Public Radio (Anderson 2016). According to a digital staffer from the 2012 Obama campaign, "Social is good, social matters, but email is what rationalizes the existence of the [digital] program" due to its fundraising capacity (Kreiss 2016: 198).

As with other social media platforms, emails can be microtargeted. If a person is willing to share their email address with a campaign or any sort of political cause, that is enough for a campaign to make assumptions about that person's political leanings. It helps when the person also shares their zip code and answers a battery of political questions. The email address can be linked with that person's online identity, about which there will be data on various likely political orientations and behavior. That explains why one's email inbox can be filled with pleas for help, especially in the form of campaign contributions—even from candidates they did not sign up for. Campaigns also use their email lists to circulate online videos, information on volunteer recruitment efforts, and get-out-the-vote messaging. One objective is to encourage recipients to share the email with others in their network. That can happen organically, but campaigns can facilitate sharing by including a button or link labeled with something along the lines of "forward to a friend."

The subject lines of those emails are designed to be attention-grabbing so that people open them. "Hey" and "Are You Awake?" were subject lines for the Obama campaign in 2012. Sometimes the subject line is personalized to include the recipient's name. In 2016, the Clinton campaign sent a series of emails with subject lines like "I'm not kidding, David." The body of the email continued, "I'm not kidding, David. I'm asking you to donate $1 right this second." The subject line for an email sent on the evening of one of the Democratic primaries read, "We may not win tonight, David." That alarmist language is typical. During the general election, the Trump campaign sent an email with the subject line, "Breaking: Hillary to Be Indicted in November" (Anderson 2016).

Campaigns can assess the effectiveness of the wording of the subject line as well as other element of an email. They can collect data on whether an email was opened, what links were clicked, and whether the links were shared on other social media platforms (Baldwin-Philippi

2017). That makes email ideal for **A/B testing**—the practice of systematically comparing responses to one message (A) versus another (B). For example, a campaign can send the same email to two groups of people but vary the wording of the subject line. If subject line "A" has a higher open rate than subject line "B," the campaign can adapt A's subject line for future email messaging. The results of these tests inform not only future email efforts but also wording decisions for other aspects of the campaign.

IMPACT

Does it work? Does campaigning on social media influence voters as intended? The answer is complicated. Campaigns use social media in a variety of ways. Much of their social media activity falls under the category of paid media. When campaigns pay to run digital ads on Facebook and other social media platforms, assessing effectiveness is similar to measuring the impact of TV spots but with more metrics about engagement. Chapter 4 reviewed this rich literature and reported mixed results. Under some circumstances, campaign advertising can influence enough voters to decide a tight race. But sometimes the impact of campaign advertising is minimal, especially when the airwaves are saturated with political spots from both sides. In addition, the effects of advertising fade pretty quickly.

Why would effects be different when ads are streamed on social media rather aired than television? Perhaps the ability to microtarget customized ads to individual voters based on their likes and dislikes promises more opinion change. That is what Donald Trump's digital operation assumed. Half of the campaign's budget went to digital advertising in 2016 (Persily 2017), mostly on Facebook (Baldwin-Philippi 2017). It spent half a million dollars to buy YouTube's banner ad on Election Day. To gauge the effectiveness of its digital spots, the Republican National Committee claims it ran forty thousand to fifty thousand variants of its ads, making minor tweaks to format and content to see what worked best (Lapowsky 2016). Unfortunately, there is little academic research measuring the impact of digital advertising aired on social media. What little research exists casts doubt on the assumptions made by digital media strategists. One study suggests that Americans saw very little political advertising on Facebook during the 2018 midterms. Exposure was limited to regular Facebook users and those were very conservative or very liberal (Guess, Nagler, and Tucker 2019). A pair of studies assessed the effects of a high volume of targeted Facebook ads supporting candidates for legislative seats—one at the state level, the other for the U.S. Congress. In both cases, ad exposure was associated with a higher likelihood of recalling the candidate's name, but no apparent impact on how favorably the candidate was evaluated (Broockman and Green 2014). In other words, persuasion effects were minimal.

But campaigning on social media involves more than paying for online advertising. Social media allow candidates to use their own free posts to reach voters directly, sometimes avoiding the scrutiny of news media and minimizing the high costs associated with paid advertising. For all the money the Trump campaign spent on Facebook advertising, his unfiltered tweets reached millions of followers at no cost (albeit with plenty of media scrutiny). In addition, much of social media's promise as a campaign tool lies in its capacity for supporter engagement. Social media empower supporters to do their own campaigning on behalf of—and in opposition to—particular candidates and causes. What is the impact of the social media campaigning that does not entail paying for advertising?

Theoretically, social media messaging could be unusually effective. People may be more likely to let their guard down on social media than they do when consuming election news or encountering a campaign spot. Except for Twitter, social media are primarily used for maintaining social ties, not gathering political information. Rather than seek out political content, users encounter election-related posts incidentally as a byproduct of a nonpolitical social networking and entertainment. Users who are otherwise disengaged probably have social media friends who actively post about politics. These are people they know and trust. That matters because people are more likely to view information they receive from a trusted source as credible (Bode 2016a).

Research assessing social media's electoral impact suggests mixed results. Much of the research centers on how much people learn and whether social media boost voter turnout and other forms of participation. The results are mixed enough to raise doubts about whether social media deliver on their early promise to foster healthy democratic behavior. Although some studies report positive influences (Bode 2012, 2016a; Bond et al. 2012; Dimitrova et al. 2014; Skoric et al. 2016; Valenzuela, Park, and Kee 2009; Vitak et al. 2011), others call into question whether social media encourages either political learning (Baumgartner and Morris 2010; Conroy, Feezell, and Guerero 2012; Dimitrova et al. 2014; Towner and Dulio 2015) or political participation (Baumgartner and Morris 2010; Dimitrova and Bystrom 2017). The absence of consistent effects can be partly explained by users' contradictory preferences about politics on social media. According to one study, Facebook users dislike highly opinioned political posts (Thorson, Vrega, and Kliger-Vilenchik 2015). It is no secret that social media users can block, unfriend, or hide someone for political reasons, although such behavior is less common than people think (Bode 2016b). People seem to prefer neutral political content. But balanced posts are less likely to be read (Thorson, Vrega, and Kliger-Vilenchik 2015). Although people are exposed to a wide variety of political viewpoints on social media, they are selective about what they pay attention to and take seriously.

Of course, what campaigns want to know is whether their non-advertising social media activity yields more votes for their candidate. Here, what little research exists is revealing. In one study, actively sharing political content on Facebook or Twitter was associated with participating in the Iowa caucuses whereas passively following a candidate on social media was not (Dimitrova and Bystrom 2017). This finding is consistent with research showing that effects are limited unless the user actively engages with social media content (such as posting comments). Passively following a candidate on Facebook is not enough (Gil di Zúñiga et al. 2013).

"FAKE NEWS" ON SOCIAL MEDIA

Much of the conversation about social media has centered on the effects of the spread of "fake news." As president, Trump has used this term to discredit responsible media outlets and news stories that are critical of his behavior. But fake news once meant something else. The original conception of fake news refers to "fabricated information that mimics news media content in form but not in organizational process or intent" (Lazer et al. 2018: 1094). Concerns about this form of fake news escalated during the 2016 election, and Trump stood to benefit, not suffer. According to one analysis, the twenty most popular false news stories generated about 8.7 million shares, reactions, and comments on Facebook during the final three months of the election, outperforming the twenty most popular election stories produced by mainstream news outlets. All but three of the twenty false stories were overtly pro-Trump or anti-Clinton. These stories made absurd claims. One of the most popular stories claimed that Clinton sold weapons to ISIS when she served as secretary of state (Silverman 2016).

Some of the fake news was organically produced and shared by individual partisans in the U.S., especially those on the right. But much of it was traced to Russian efforts to disrupt the U.S. election (Lazer et al. 2018). A slew of false pro-Trump and anti-Clinton stories were posted on about 140 websites maintained by teenagers in the small Balkan town of Veldes, Macedonia. Locals there reportedly made as much as $3,000 per day from millions of page views of articles they copied and pasted from right-wing media in the U.S., then shared on Facebook. One of their most successful posts falsely claimed that the pope had endorsed Trump. Another reported that Clinton had once said, "I would like to see people like Donald Trump run for office; they're honest and can't be bought." During the primaries, the group experimented with posts promoting Bernie Sanders, but discovered that pro-Trump falsehoods performed far better (Silverman and Alexander 2016). The operation was reportedly launched by a Macedonian media attorney working with two American partners (Silverman et al. 2018), who themselves made so much money with their own fake news websites that they felt "uncomfortable talking about it because they don't want people to start asking for loans." Their website featured headlines like "BREAKING: Top Official Set to Testify Against Hillary Clinton Found DEAD" and "BREAKING: Michelle Obama Holds Feminist Rally at HER SLAVE HOUSE" (McCoy 2016).

Academic research confirmed the pro-Trump tilt of fake news during the 2016 election (Allcott and Gentzkow 2017). At least one study suggested that exposure to fake news had an impact on some voters' decisions in 2016. Specifically, voters who supported Obama in 2012 but defected to Trump in 2016 were unusually likely to believe three of the most popular false rumors circulating on social media: that the pope had endorsed Trump; that Clinton had sold weapons to ISIS; and that Clinton was in poor health due to serious illness (Gunther, Beck, and Nisbet n.d.).

How does fake news spread? Social bots play a role. Social bots are artificial intelligence systems that "are set to automatically produce content following a specific political agenda determined by their controllers, who are nearly impossible to identify" (Ferrara 2016). Bots not only generate their own posts but they can also be programmed to share, like, retweet, and even comment on other posts. According to one study of Twitter behavior, bots were responsible for about 3.8 million tweets during five weeks in September and October 2016, which amounted to about one-fifth of the conversation about the presidential election (Bessi and Ferrara 2016). That mattered because tweets posted by bots were retweeted at the same rate as tweets posted by humans. And they produced content automatically at breathtaking speed (Ferrara 2016).

Yet robots alone should not be blamed for spreading fake news. One groundbreaking study of Twitter activity from 2016 to 2017 found that humans spread false news at the same rate as bots. A false story is much more likely to go viral on Twitter than a true story, the authors concluded. Compared with stories based on accurate reporting, false stories reached more people, penetrated social networks more deeply, and spread much faster. False news about elections and other political topics was particularly susceptible to viral distribution compared with news about such topics as terrorism, science, and entertainment (Vosoughi, Roy, and Aral 2018).

In wake of the 2016 election, lawmakers intensified their scrutiny of social media's role in spreading misinformation. Facebook and Twitter responded to the pressure by undertaking a variety of measures to stem the flow: hiring more human monitors, upgrading machine-based monitoring, and detecting and closing down fake accounts (Harvey and Roth 2018; Mosseri 2017). One study indicated that Facebook's efforts had been successful as of summer 2018 (Allcott, Gentzkow, and Yu 2018). Yet reports of orchestrated efforts to spread fake news persist. A full year before the 2020 presidential primaries, several of the 2020 Democratic hopefuls were targeted on social media with misleading memes and hashtags aimed at sowing divisions within the party. For example, a widely shared grainy screenshot taken during Elizabeth Warren's Instagram Live candidacy announcement allegedly showed a blackface doll on top of her kitchen cabinet; a closer look revealed that the object in question was actually a vase. A tweet viewed by millions of people promised (but did not deliver) breaking news about Beto O'Rourke leaving a racist message on an answering machine in 1990s (Korecki 2019).

How widely do these stories circulate? Do they change people's minds? There are reasons to be skeptical about their reach and influence. Numerous studies have confirmed that conservatives or Trump supporters were more likely to consume and share fake news during the 2016 election than liberals or moderates (Grinberg et al. 2019; Guess, Nagler, and Tucker 2019; Guess, Nyhan, and Reifler 2018). Sharing fake news was far more common among people over the age of sixty-five than people in the youngest age groups (Guess, Nagler, and Tucker 2019). Mostly these were people who had already made up their minds about supporting Trump.

Overall, however, very few people engaged in any form of fake news dissemination (Guess, Nagler, and Tucker 2019). According to one study of Twitter use in the 2016 election, only 0.1 percent of individuals accounted for 80 percent of shares from fake new sources. These "supersharers"—probably "cyborgs," or "partially automated accounts controlled by humans"—tweeted an average of seventy-one times per day whereas a typical person tweeted a few days a week (Grinberg et al. 2019). It is also possible that relatively few people saw or remembered many fake stories in 2016 (Allcott and Gentzkow 2017). One study of web traffic data estimated that only 27 percent of Americans visited fake news websites during the final five weeks of the 2016 campaign. Visits to fake news sites may have actually dropped during the 2018 midterms (Guess et al. 2019). Even in 2016, most of the visits to fake news sites were among the 10 percent of people with the most right-leaning media diets (Guess, Nyhan, and Reifler 2018). These were not persuadable voters. Heavy fake news consumers already had highly skewed information diets. For them, fake news was comfort food that merely reinforced their predisposition to vote for Trump. For most voters in 2016, mainstream news outlets remained the most important sources of information (Grinberg et al. 2019).

CONCLUSION

Perhaps other fears about social media are also overblown. Social media's growth has intensified long-standing concerns about the enhanced ability of people to isolate themselves into like-minded media "filter bubbles" and "echo chambers" (Sunstein 2009; Pariser 2011). If true, that would challenge any campaign's effort to reach cross-pressured voters from the opposing party. But academic research provides mixed results here. Although people do seem to seek out information that supports their existing opinions—conservatives do gravitate toward Fox News and liberals to MSNBC—they do not necessarily avoid perspectives that challenge their predispositions. Most people who follow politics closely "have largely centrist information diets" despite the availability of partisan media outlets (Guess et al. 2018: 9). Political news websites tend to attract ideologically diverse audiences, calling into question the notion of a red/blue divide in internet use (Nelson and Webster 2017).

Social media may actually help, not hurt. On Twitter, people tend to follow media accounts on both ends of the political spectrum (Eady et al. 2019). Facebook users disagree with more of their Facebook friends than they think (Goel, Mason, and Watts 2010). People can "unfriend" users they object to, but only one in ten Facebook users does so (Bode 2016b). Their newsfeeds display perspectives they disagree with as well as news and information from sources they would not normally seek out (Messing and Westwood 2014; Bakshy, Messing, and Adamic 2015).

All of this means campaigns can enlist their supporters to use social media to connect with voters who might otherwise be difficult to reach. Political posts carry a lot of weight when they come from a credible opinion leader or friend who is trusted for their political judgment. Even so, campaigns can be remarkably cautious about empowering supporters to go beyond standard sharing and commenting. "In the end, digital and social media might largely constitute another set of channels and platforms for communication rather than a revolution in terms of overall campaign strategies" (Svensson, Kiousis, and Strömbäck 2015: 42). It could be that social media tools are just "extensions of traditional campaigns activities like fundraising, organizing volunteers, and identifying and turning out voters" (Towner and Dulio 2015: 73).

Donald Trump's "amateurish yet authentic style" may signal a trend toward spontaneity and "deprofessionalization." But even Trump "kept his followers at arm's length and limited his engagement to retweeting selected tweets" by his supporters (Enli 2017: 59). Clever social media posts can humanize candidates in ways that a thirty-second TV spot cannot. Livestreaming campaign events add a sense of spontaneity. Yet campaigns are risk-averse. Managing the chaos of social media electioneering may discourage the serious innovation required to meaningfully empower users.

KEY TERMS

A/B testing: the controlled comparison of responses to one message or format (A) versus another (B). Used to assess which message or format is more effective.

fake news: false information that deceptively mimics the style and format of truthful journalism.

DISCUSSION QUESTIONS

1. Why so you think campaigns tend to be risk averse in their social media outreach?
2. In what ways can candidates use social media platforms to empower supporters to campaign on their behalf?
3. Why is Facebook favored by campaigns over other social media platforms? How might campaigns more effectively use Snapchat or Instagram to reach young voters?
4. How concerned should we be about the spread of misinformation through social media? What is it about social media that is conducive to the distribution of "fake news"?

RECOMMENDED READINGS

Baldwin-Philippi, Jessica. 2017. "The Myths of Data-Driven Campaigning." *Political Communication* 34, no. 4: 627–33.

> The author of the book Using Technology, Building Democracy *concludes that counter to conventional wisdom, neither the Trump nor the Clinton campaign was particularly innovative in their use of social media in 2016.*

Guess, Andrew, Benjamin Lyons, Brendan Nyhan, and Jason Reifler. 2018. *Avoiding the Echo Chamber about Echo Chambers: Why Selective Exposure to Like-Minded Political News Is Less Prevalent Than You Think.* Report published by the Knight Foundation.

> *As the title suggests, this review of academic research may allay concerns about the extent to which citizens are limiting their exposure to news that supports their predispositions. People are more vulnerable to "echo chambers" in their offline social networks than online, the authors conclude. Many people pay too little attention to political news, and those who do tend to have diverse information diets.*

Kreiss, Daniel. 2016. *Prototype Politics: Technology-Intensive Campaigning and the Data of Democracy.* New York: Oxford University Press.

> *This book documents the Democratic Party's embrace of technological advances in the wake of John Kerry's loss to George W. Bush in 2004. Analyzes the work of 629 presidential campaign staffers from both parties from 2004 to 2012.*

REFERENCES

Allcott, Hunt, and Matthew Gentzkow. 2017. "Social Media and Fake News in the 2016 Election." *Journal of Economic Perspectives* 31, no. 2: 211–36.

Allcott, Hunt, Matthew Gentzkow, and Chuan Yu. 2018. "Trends in the Diffusion of Misinformation on Social Media." Unpublished manuscript.

Anderson, Meg. 2016. "Hey, [Insert Name Here], Check Out These Campaign Fundraising Emails." *National Public Radio* (July 3): https://www.npr.org/2016/07/03/484395568/hey-insert-name-here-check-out-these-campaign-fundraising-emails.

Anspach, Nicolas M. 2017. "The New Personal Influence: How Our Facebook Friends Influence the News We Read." *Political Communication* 34, no, 4: 590–606.

Bakshy, Eytan, Solomon Messing, and Lada A. Adamic. 2015. "Exposure to Ideologically Diverse News and Opinion on Facebook." *Science* 348 (June 5): 1130–32.

Baldwin-Philippi, Jessica. 2015. *Using Technology: Building Democracy*. New York: Oxford University Press.

———. 2017. "The Myths of Data-Driven Campaigning." *Political Communication* 34, no. 4: 627–33.

Barrett, Benjamin. 2018. "Where Does Snapchat Fit in 2018?" *Campaigns & Elections* (May 31): https://www.campaignsandelections.com/campaign-insider/where-does-snapchat-fit-in-2018.

Baumgartner, Jody C., and Jonathan S. Morris. 2010. "MyFaceTube Politics: Social Networking Web Sites and Political Engagement of Young Adults." *Social Science Computer Review* 28, no. 1: 24–44.

Bessi, Alessandro, and Emilio Ferrara. 2016. "Social Bots Distort the 2016 U.S. Presidential Election Online Discussion." *First Monday* 21 no. 11: ISSN 13960466. Available at: https://journals.uic.edu/ojs/index.php/fm/article/view/7090/5653. Date accessed: March 20, 2019. doi:https://doi.org/10.5210/fm.v21i11.7090.

Bode, Leticia. 2012. "Facebooking to the Polls: A Study of Online Social Networking and Political Behavior." *Journal of Information Technology & Politics* 9: 352–69.

———. 2016a. "Political News in the News Feed: Learning Politics from Social Media." *Mass Communication & Society* 19: 24–48.

———. 2016b. "Pruning the News Feed: Unfriending and Unfollowing Political Content on Social Media." *Research and Politics* (July–Sept.): 1–8.

Bode, Leticia, and Kajsa E. Dalrymple. 2016. "Politics in 140 Characters or Less: Campaign Communication, Network Interaction, and Political Participation on Twitter." *Journal of Political Marketing* 15: 311–32.

Bond, Robert M., Christopher J. Fariss, Jason J. Jones, Adam D. I. Kramer, Cameron Marlow, Jamie E. Settle, and James H. Fowler. 2012. "A 61-Million-Person Experiment in Social Influence and Political Mobilization." *Nature* 489: 295–98.

Broockman, David E., and Donald P. Green. 2014. "Do Online Advertisements Increase Political Candidates' Name Recognition or Favorability? Evidence from Randomized Field Experiments." *Political Behavior* 36: 263–89.

Bump, Philip. 2014. "How Facebook Plans to Become One of the Most Powerful Tools in olitics." *Washington Post* Nov. 26: https://www.theawl.com/2014/11/in-the-trenches-of-the-facebook-election/.

Confessore, Nicholas, and Rachel Shorey. 2016. "Donald Trump, with Bare-Bones Campaign, Relies on G.O.P. for Vital Tasks." *New York Times*

(Aug. 21): https://www.nytimes.com/2016/08/22/us/politics/donald-trump-fundraising.html?_r=0.

Conroy, Meredith, Jessica T. Feezell, and Mario Guerrero. 2012. "Facebook and Political Engagement: A Study of Online Political Group Membership and Offline Political Engagement." *Computers in Human Behavior* 28: 1535–46.

Dimitrova, Daniela V., and Dianne G. Bystrom. 2017. "The Role of Social Media in the 2016 Iowa Caucuses." *Journal of Political Marketing*, DOI: 10.1080/15377857.2017.1377141.

Dimitrova, Daniela V., Adam Shehata, Jesper Strömbäck, and Lars W. Nord. 2014. "The Effects of Digital Media on Political Knowledge and Participation in Election Campaigns: Evidence from Panel Data." *Communication Research* 41, no. 1: 95–118.

DiResta, Renee, Kris Shaffer, Becky Ruppel., David Sullivan, Robert Matney, Ryan Fox, Jonathan Albright, and Ben Johnson 2018. "The Tactics & Tropes of the Internet Research Agency." https://www.newknowledge.com/articles/the-disinformation-report/.

Eady, Gregory, Jonathan Nagler, Andy Guess, Jan Zilinksy, and Joshua A. Tucker. 2019. "How Many People Live in Political Bubbles on Social Media? Evidence From Linked Survey and Twitter Data." *SAGE Open* (Jan.–Mar.): 1–21.

Enli, Gunn. 2017. "Twitter as Arena for the Authentic Outsider: The Social Media Campaigns of Trump and Clinton in the 2016 US Presidential Election." *European Journal of Communication* 32, no. 1: 50–61.

Ferrara, Emilio. 2016. "How Twitter Bots Affected the US Presidential Campaign." *The Conversation* (June 21): http://theconversation.com/how-twitter-bots-affected-the-us-presidential-campaign-68406.

Flaxman, Seth, Sharad Goel, and Justin M. Rao. 2016. "Filter Bubbles, Echo Chambers, and Online News Consumption." *Public Opinion Quarterly* 80: 298–320.

Fowler, Erika Franklin, Travis N. Ridout, and Michael M. Franz. 2016. "Political Advertising in 2016: The Presidential Election as Outlier?" *The Forum* 14, no. 4: 445–69.

Frier, Sarah. 2018. "Trump's Campaign Said It Was Better at Facebook. Facebook Agrees." *Bloomberg* (Apr. 3): https://www.bloomberg.com/news/articles/2018-04-03/trump-s-campaign-said-it-was-better-at-facebook-facebook-agrees.

Gil de Zúñiga, Homero, Victor Garcia-Perdomo, and Shannon McGregor. 2015. "What Is Second Screening? Exploring Motivations of Second Screen Use and Its Effect on Online Political Participation." *Journal of Communication* (July): 1–25.

Gil de Zúñiga, Homero, Ingrid Bachmann, Shih-Hsien Hsu, and Jennifer Brundidge. 2013. "Expressive Versus Consumptive Blog Use: Implications for Interpersonal Discussion and Political Participation." *International Journal of Communication* 7: 1538–59.

Goel, Sharad, Winter Mason, and Duncan J. Watts. 2010. "Real and Perceived Attitude Agreement in Social Networks." *Journal of Personality and Social Psychology* 99, no. 4: 611–21.

Green, Joshua. 2012. "The Science behind Those Obama Campaign Emails." *Bloomberg* (Nov. 29): https://www.bloomberg.com/news/articles/2012-11-29/the-science-behind-those-obama-campaign-e-mails.

Grinberg, Nir, Kenneth Joseph, Lisa Friedland, Briony Swire-Thompson, and David Lazer. 2019. "Fake News on Twitter during the 2016 Presidential Election." *Science* 363 (Jan. 25): 374–78.

Guess, Andrew, Benjamin Lyons, Brendan Nyhan, and Jason Reifler. 2018. *Avoiding the Echo Chamber about Echo Chambers: Why Selective Exposure to Like-Minded Political News Is Less Prevalent Than You Think.* Report published by the Knight Foundation.

Guess, Andrew, Jonathan Nagler, and Joshua Tucker. 2019. "Less Than You Think: Prevalence and Predictors of Fake News Dissemination on Facebook." *Science Advances* 5 (Jan. 9): 1–8.

Guess, Andrew, Brendan Nyhan, and Jason Reifler. 2018. "Selective Exposure to Misinformation: Evidence from the Consumption of Fake News during the 2016 U.S. Presidential Campaign." Unpublished manuscript.

Gunther, Richard, Paul A. Beck, and Erik C. Nisbet. n.d. "Fake News May Have Contributed to Trump's 2016 Victory." Unpublished manuscript.

Hamby, Peter. 2013. "Did Twitter Kill the Boys on the Bus? Searching for a Better Way to Cover a Campaign." Discussion Paper #D-80. Joan Shorenstein Center on the Press, Politics and Public Policy.

Harvey, Del, and Yoel Roth. 2018. "An Update on Our Elections Integrity Work." Oct. 1: https://blog.twitter.com/official/en_us/topics/company/2018/an-update-on-our-elections-integrity-work.html.

Heimlich, Russell. 2010. "Email vs. Social Networks." Pew Research Center (Sept. 13): https://www.pewresearch.org/fact-tank/2010/09/13/email-vs-social-networks/.

Hohmann, James. 2018. "The Daily 202: Russian Efforts to Manipulate African Americans Show Sophistication of Disinformation Campaigns." *Washington Post* (Dec. 17): https://www.washingtonpost.com/news/powerpost/paloma/daily-202/2018/12/17/daily-202-russian-efforts-to-manipulate-african-americans-show-sophistication-of-disinformation-campaign/5c1739291b326b2d6629d4c6/.

Katz, Elihu, and Paul F. Lazarsfeld. 1955. *Personal Influence.* Glencoe, IL: Free Press.

Kim, Young Mie, Jordan Hsu, David Neiman, Colin Kou, Levi Bankston, Soo Yun Kim, Richard Heinrich, Robyn Baragwanath, and Garvesh Raskutti. 2018. "The Stealth Media? Groups and Targets behind Divisive Issue Campaigns on Facebook." *Political Communication* 35, no. 4: 515–41.

Korecki, Natasha. 2019. "'Sustained and Ongoing' Disinformation Assault Targets Dem Presidential Candidates." *Politico* (Feb. 20): https://www.politico.com/story/2019/02/20/2020-candidates-social-media-attack-1176018?fbclid=IwAR169iVYwr62UHsI6XWkL-SBPhgEcZpA8SSR97WPpDbr-gn1gULfE_igJSA.

Kreiss, Daniel. 2016. *Prototype Politics: Technology-Intensive Campaigning and the Data of Democracy.* New York: Oxford University Press.

Kreiss, Daniel, Regina G. Lawrence, and Shannon C. McGregor. 2018. "In Their Own Words: Political Practitioner Accounts of Candidates, Audiences, Affordances, Genres, and Timing in Strategic Social Media Use." *Political Communication* 35: 8–31.

Kreiss, Daniel, and Shannon C. McGregor. 2018. "Technology Firms Shape Political Communication: The Work of Microsoft, Facebook, Twitter, and

Google with Campaigns during the 2016 U.S. Presidential Cycle." *Political Communication* 35, no. 2: 155–77.Krieg, Gregory. 2016. "GOP Senate Group Deletes Tweet about Double Amputee Pol 'Not Standing Up for Our Veterans'." *CNN* (Mar. 8): https://www.cnn.com/2016/03/08/politics/tammy-duckworth-nrsc-tweet-deleted-veterans/.

Lapowsky, Issie. 2016. "Here's How Facebook *Actually* Won Trump the Presidency." *Wired* (Nov. 15): https://www.wired.com/2016/11/facebook-won-trump-election-not-just-fake-news/.

Lazer, David M. J., Matthew A. Baum, Yochai Benkler, Adam J. Berinsky, Kelly M. Greenhill, Filippo Menczer, Miriam J. Metzger, Brendan Nyhan, Gordon Pennycook, David Rothschild, Michael Schudson, Steven A. Sloman, Cass R. Sunstein, Emily A. Thorson, Duncan J. Watts, and Jonathan L. Zittrain. 2018. "The Science of Fake News." *Science* 359, no. 6380: 1094–96.

McCoy, Terrence. 2016. "For the 'New Yellow Journalists,' Opportunity Comes in Clicks and Bucks." *Washington Post* (Nov. 20): https://www.washingtonpost.com/national/for-the-new-yellow-journalists-opportunity-comes-in-clicks-and-bucks/2016/11/20/d58d036c-adbf-11e6-8b45-f8e493f06fcd_story.html?utm_term=.73210f389c2f.

Messing, Solomon, and Sean J. Westwood. 2014. "Selective Exposure in the Age of Social Media: Endorsements Trump Partisan Source Affiliation When Selecting News Online." *Communication Research* 41, no. 8: 1042–63.

Mosseri, Adam. 2017. "Working to Stop Misinformation and False News." Apr. 7: https://www.facebook.com/facebookmedia/blog/working-to-stop-misinformation-and-false-news.

Nelson, Jacob L., and James G. Webster. 2017. "The Myth of Partisan Selective Exposure: A Portrait of the Online Political News Audience." *Social Media + Society* (July-Sept.): 1–13.

Pariser, Eli. 2011. *The Filter Bubble: How the New Personalized Web Is Changing What We Read and How We Think*. New York: Penguin Books.

Patterson, Thomas. 2016. *News Coverage of the 2016 General Election: How the Press Failed the Voters*. A report published by the Shorenstein Center on Media, Politics, and Public Policy in conjunction with Media Tenor (December).

Pearce, Adam. 2016. "Trump Has Spent a Fraction of What Clinton Has on Ads." *New York Times* (Oct. 21): https://www.nytimes.com/interactive/2016/10/21/us/elections/television-ads.html.

Persily, Nathaniel. 2017. "Can Democracy Survive the Internet?" *Journal of Democracy* 28, no. 2: 63–76.

Pew Research Center. 2016. "Election 2016: Campaigns as a Direct Source of News." July 18: http://www.journalism.org/2016/07/18/election-2016-campaigns-as-a-direct-source-of-news/.

Schill, Dan, and Rita Kirk. 2015. "Issue Debates in 140 Characters: Online Talk Surrounding the 2012 Debates." In *Presidential Campaigning and Social Media: An Analysis of the 2012 Campaign*. Edited by John Allen Hendricks and Dan Schill, 198–218. New York: Oxford University Press.

Shearer, Elisa, and Katerina Eva Matsa. 2018. "News Use across Social Media Platforms 2018." *Pew Research Center*, Sept. 10.

Silver, Nate. 2017. "The Comey Letter Probably Cost Clinton the Election." *FiveThirtyEight* (May 3): https://fivethirtyeight.com/features/the-comey-letter-probably-cost-clinton-the-election/.

Silverman, Craig. 2016. "This Analysis Shows How Viral Fake Election News Outperformed Real News on Facebook." *Buzzfeed* (Nov. 16): https://www.buzzfeednews.com/article/craigsilverman/viral-fake-election-news-outperformed-real-news-on-facebook#.va37DQajn.

Silverman, Craig, and Lawrence Alexander. 2016. "How Teens in the Balkans Are Duping Trump Supporters with Fake News." *Buzzfeed* (Nov. 3): https://www.buzzfeednews.com/article/craigsilverman/how-macedonia-became-a-global-hub-for-pro-trump-misinfo#.hcRNEk6Ox.

Silverman, Craig, J. Lester Feder, Saska Cvetkovska, and Aubrey Belford. 2018. "Macedonia's Pro-Trump Fake News Industry Had American Links, and Is Under Investigation for Possible Russia Ties." *Buzzfeed* (July 18): https://www.buzzfeednews.com/article/craigsilverman/american-conservatives-fake-news-macedonia-paris-wade-libert.

Skoric, Marko M., Qinfeng Zhu, Debbie Goh, and Natalie Pang. 2016. "Social Media and Citizen Engagement: A Meta-analytic Review." *New Media & Society* 18, no. 9: 1817–39.

Smith, Aaron, and Monica Anderson. 2018. "Social Media Use in 2018." *Pew Research Center*, Mar. 1.

Sunstein, Cass. 2009. *Republic.com 2.0*. Princeton, NJ: Princeton University Press.

Svensson, Emma, Spiro Kiousis, and Jesper Strömbäck. 2015. "Creating a Win-Win Situation? Relationship Cultivation and the Use of Social Media in the 2012 Election." In *Presidential Campaigning and Social Media: An Analysis of the 2012 Campaign*. Edited by John Allen Hendricks and Dan Schill, 28–43. New York: Oxford University Press.

Thorson, Kjerstin, Emily K. Vrega, and Neta Kliger-Vilenchik. 2015. "Don't Push Your Opinions on Me: Young Citizens and Political Etiquette on Facebook." In *Presidential Campaigning and Social Media: An Analysis of the 2012 Campaign*. Edited by John Allen Hendricks and Dan Schill, 74–93. New York: Oxford University Press.

Towner, Terri L., and David A. Dulio. 2015. "Technology Takeover? Campaign Learning during the 2012 Presidential Election." In *Presidential Campaigning and Social Media: An Analysis of the 2012 Campaign*. Edited by John Allen Hendricks and Dan Schill, 58–73. New York: Oxford University Press.

Valenzuela, Sebastián, Namsu Park, and Kerk F. Kee. 2009. "Is There Social Capital in a Social Network Site?: Facebook Use and College Students' Life Satisfaction, Trust, and Participation." *Journal of Computer-Mediated Communication* 14, no. 4: 875–901.

Vitak, Jessica, Paul Zube, Andrew Smock, Caleb T. Carr, Nicole Ellison, and Cliff Lampe. 2011. "It's Complicated: Facebook Users' Political Participation in the 2008 Election." *Cyberpsychology, Behavior, and Social Networking* 14, no. 3: 1–17.

Vosoughi, Soroush, Deb Roy, and Sinan Aral. 2018. "The Spread of True and False News Online." *Science* 359 (Mar. 9): 1146–51.

7

The Ground Game

Democrat Stacey Abrams talks to canvassers during her 2018 bid for governor of Georgia. *Source*: *Michael A. McCoy/ZUMA Wire/Alamy Live News*

LEARNING OBJECTIVES

★ Grasp the differences between door-to-door canvassing and other types of direct voter contact.

★ Analyze why canvassing may be the most effective way to mobilize voters.

★ Assess the limitations of the ground game.

★ See the influence of social science on campaign practice.

AT ONE POINT in the 2016 election, it looked like Ted Cruz might best Donald Trump for the Republican nomination. Although Trump was leading in national polls, the first nominating contest would be held in Iowa, home of the state's famous caucuses. Caucuses are not like primaries. A primary is simply an election with party nominees on the ballot. As with any election, voters simply show up on Election Day and cast their votes. By contrast, caucuses require a serious time commitment. Caucus participants must attend an evening meeting and listen to speeches by supporters of each candidate. Nobody casts a vote until the speeches are over. The 2016 Iowa caucuses were held in February, and Iowa is one of the coldest states in the nation. It is no small feat to identify, persuade, and mobilize a sufficient number of supporters to show up on a freezing cold night and participate.

Iowa was a promising state for Cruz. More than half of Iowa Republicans are evangelical Christians, a population that had shown strong support for this conservative son of a preacher. Unlike Trump, Cruz had built a sophisticated data analytics team and ambitious field operation. Rather than pour money into expensive television advertising, Cruz turned to outside groups that invested in data-driven canvassing efforts aimed at mobilizing evangelical voters. Thousands of volunteers and paid canvassers blanketed the state, many of them armed with tablets and phones with an app loaded with data about prospective Cruz supporters. Meanwhile, Cruz, his wife, and father personally made motivational calls to caucus trainers, who were charged with guiding supporters through the process of caucus participation (Tau 2016).

Cruz came in first in a crowded field of twelve candidates, besting Trump by more than six thousand votes. Evangelical Christians made up 64 percent of the Republican caucus goers, an increase of seven points over 2012. Cruz outdid Trump among these voters by twelve points (Bump and Clement 2016). How much of Cruz's success in Iowa can be attributed to his ambitious investment in the "ground game"? Cruz fell short in every other state. Trump won the nomination despite a minimal field operation. Cruz's failure is a reminder that a strong operation cannot compensate for factors outside of the campaign's control.

Cruz and the outside groups supporting him invested in the ground game because there is plenty of evidence showing that it can work. Campaigns and parties know that the single most effective way to boost turnout is to mobilize voters in person, face-to-face. As we will see later in this chapter, the power of an interpersonal pitch is supported by academic research. Studies confirming the effectiveness of canvassing and other forms of what campaigns call *direct voter contact* have prompted campaigns and parties to invest more resources in this area. Nothing a campaign does is more "old school" than knocking on doors, shaking hands, and talking to voters face-to-face. Yet this is where much of campaigning innovation is taking place.

This chapter will focus on the ground game, the center of a campaign's voter contact efforts. It is on the ground—or in the field—where campaigns interact with voters on an individual, interpersonal level. But voter contact also includes direct mail along with other forms of paid media, the topic of chapter 5. As with television advertising, campaigns work with outside vendors for direct mail outreach. Even social media campaigning, covered in chapter 6, can be seen as a form of voter contact because, like direct mail, it entails individualized, microtargeted messaging. But social media efforts are typically managed by a campaign's digital team, not its field operation. This chapter centers on the ground game carried out by the campaign's field team.

As with direct mail and social media, part of the ground game's promise lies in its capacity for precise microtargeting. Recall from chapter 2 that microtargeting is targeting based on the known or estimated characteristics of individual voters. As we know by now, campaigns target persuasion efforts at either undecided voters or cross-pressured partisans who might defect, and mobilization messages at supporters to ensure they cast their vote. A field operation's primary responsibility is to personally contact individual voters and deliver the appropriate message. Field efforts tend to focus more on mobilizing supporters, but they also attempt at least some persuasion. In addition, they are tasked with updating information the campaign possesses about individual voters if it turns out the information is incorrect—if, for example, a volunteer canvasser sees an opponent's yard sign in front of the home of a voter incorrectly identified as a likely supporter in the voter database.

Voter contact also entails macrotargeting—that is, targeting voters based on the TV shows people watch, where they live, or other broad characteristics. Canvassers might knock on all of the doors in a neighborhood if the campaign estimates that at a large majority of its households are likely supporters (the traditional rule of thumb is 65 percent). A voter registration drive might be held at an event or in a location where likely supporters cluster (which is why Democratic campaigns set up voter registration tables on college campuses). Micro or macro, the objective is to interpersonally interact with as many potential and likely supporters and undecided likely voters as possible. Preferably, the interaction takes place in person, face-to-face, but **phone canvassing** also can help.

FIELD OFFICES

Most of a campaign's ground game is headquartered in **field offices**, each usually overseen by at least one field organizer. Field offices lead efforts to personally contact individual voters either through door-to-door canvassing, phone canvassing, or at local events. They also help the campaign build, maintain, and update the voter database used by the campaign to identify potential supporters, volunteers, and donors (see chapter 3). In other words, field offices serve as "points of coordination for volunteer activities, where the data possessed by national campaigns is translated into walk packets and call lists for local volunteers, who in turn talk to voters and collect more data at the doors and on the phones" (Darr 2017).

Field offices are bare-bones operations housed in temporary, low-rent office space equipped with cheap furniture. Empty pizza boxes outnumber desks. Yet between the field organizer's salary and equipment and technology, their costs add up. According to one estimate, a field office for a presidential campaign cost an average of $21,000 in 2012, which translates to about $50 per additional vote (Darr and Levendusky 2014). Their work is labor-intensive.

Presidential campaigns will open field offices in every state, concentrating them in or near competitive "battleground" states. Democratic presidential candidates tend to operate more field offices than their Republican counterparts; in 2012, the Obama campaign opened 786 field offices compared with Romney's 284 (Kreiss 2016). Clinton opened only 537 field offices in 2016 (see box 7.1, "Hillary Clinton's 2016 Uneven Ground Game"), but that dwarfed Trump's minimal ground game. Some presidential campaigns tend to open field offices in counties where their supporters are concentrated, whereas others will favor locations in tightly contested "swing" counties (Darr and Levendusky 2014).

BOX 7.1 | Hillary Clinton's 2016 Uneven Ground Game

Explaining Hillary Clinton's 2016 loss to Donald Trump will puzzle students of electoral politics for decades to come. One straightforward theory centers on the fact that the Clinton campaign opened far fewer field offices than Barack Obama's campaign did in 2008 and 2012. Whereas Obama opened 947 field offices in 2008 and 786 in 2012, Clinton had only 537 nationwide in 2016. Certain battleground states appeared particularly underresourced. The Clinton campaign opened only 40 offices in Wisconsin compared with 69 by Obama in 2012. In Ohio, there were only 81 field offices statewide compared with Obama's 132 (Darr 2017).

Clinton lost both states. In Wisconsin's Milwaukee County, a Democratic stronghold where Clinton opened only four offices compared with Obama's ten, Democratic turnout declined by 44,000 compared with 2012. She lost Wisconsin by half that number of voters (Darr 2017). The Clinton campaign's decision-making on where to deploy resources was guided by Ada, a sophisticated computer algorithm that combined polling data with individual voter information collected on the ground. Ada pegged Pennsylvania as an important state early in the race. That explains the candidate's frequent appearances there, as well as the campaign's decision to hold its closing rally in Philadelphia on the night before the election—a rally that featured both Michelle and Barack Obama as well as performances by Bruce Springsteen and Jon Bon Jovi. Ada also shaped the placement and location of field offices (Wagner 2016). Apparently it did not identify Wisconsin as vulnerable.

Would a stronger field presence have helped Clinton win Wisconsin and Ohio? Could she have won more states by opening more field offices nationwide? It is impossible to say. She lost Pennsylvania anyway. And the Trump campaign opened far fewer field offices overall than Clinton did as it delegated most of its ground game to the Republican National Committee. But as this chapter shows, canvassing can yield significantly higher turnout, especially when enthusiastic volunteers interact face-to-face with potential supporters. And the coordination of canvassing operations and volunteer outreach is a field office's primary function.

In any case, Democrats' advantage in the ground game dates back to their strengths among union organizers and residents of urban areas, where population density makes door-to-door canvassing more feasible than it is in Republican-rich rural areas. According to one study, the Obama campaign's advantage over McCain in the number of field offices helped him flip

BOX 7.1 | (continued)

three battleground states from Republican to Democratic in 2008 (Masket 2009). Field offices yielded 275,000 additional votes for Obama, helping him win Indiana and providing the margin of victory in North Carolina (Darr and Levendusky 2014). In 2012, Obama's field advantage translated into a slight but measurable turnout advantage over his Republican opponent Mitt Romney (Sides and Vavreck 2013; Weinschenk 2015).

Not only do field offices serve as coordination points, but also their staffers and volunteers can warn national campaign about emerging weaknesses. What is more, opening a local field office signals to volunteers that the national campaign prioritizes voters in that area (Darr 2017). Their absence can have the opposite effect—no small thing in 2016, when Democratic enthusiasm for their nominee was already lackluster.

SOURCES

Darr, Joshua P. 2017. "The Incredible Shrinking Democratic Ground Game." *Vox*, Nov. 16: https://www.vox.com/mischiefs-of-faction/2017/11/16/16665756/shrinking-democratic-ground-game.

Darr, Joshua P., and Matthew S. Levendusky. 2013. "Relying on the Ground Game: The Placement and Effect of Campaign Field Offices." *American Politics Research* 42, no. 3: 529–48.

Masket, Seth E. 2009. "Did Obama's Ground Game Matter? The Influence of Local Field Offices during the 2008 Presidential Election." *Public Opinion Quarterly* 73, no. 5: 1023–39.

Sides, John, and Lynn Vavreck. 2013. *The Gamble: Choice and Chance in the 2012 Presidential Election*. Princeton, NJ: Princeton University Press.

Wagner, John. 2016. "Clinton's Data-Driven Campaign Relied Heavily on an Algorithm Named Ada. What Didn't She See?" *Washington Post*, Nov. 9: https://www.washingtonpost.com/news/post-politics/wp/2016/11/09/clintons-data-driven-campaign-relied-heavily-on-an-algorithm-named-ada-what-didnt-she-see/?utm_term=.dc94d9be9f43.

Weinschenk, Aaron. 2015. "Campaign Field Operations and Voter Mobilization in 2012. *Presidential Studies Quarterly* 45, no. 3: 573–80.

Statewide races will center their field offices in or near densely populated areas. For local races, field operations might be run out of headquarters of the campaign or local party.

Paid staffers usually run the field office, but volunteers do most of the door knocking and phone canvassing. That said, it is not unusual for campaigns, parties, and outside groups to farm out the legwork to paid canvassers and commercial phone banks. Campaigns and groups prefer volunteers, but sometimes there are not enough of them.

DOOR-TO-DOOR CANVASSING

Also known as "door knocking," canvassing is the process of walking door to door in residential areas and talking to voters in person, usually at their homes. Canvassers are trained by field staffers, who provide maps and "walk lists" to track their interaction with voters. Walk lists show relevant information about the households being assigned to the canvasser, and the maps show exactly where they are located. Canvassers also are given a script to guide their conversation with the voter. The script is usually very specific, but sometimes canvassers depart from the precise wording and engage in informal give-and-take. Beginning with the 2008 campaign, Obama canvassers were encouraged to improvise by sharing their personal story about where they came from and why they supported the candidate. A Missouri college student described how the murder of his cousin spurred him into political action. An Obama volunteer from Illinois described being motivated to get involved by the closing of steel mills, the rise of teen pregnancy, and the death of a friend who drove drunk (Slevin 2008).

The primary objectives of canvassing are to persuade nonsupporters and mobilize supporters, mostly the latter. But canvassers also assist the campaign with **voter identification** ("voter ID")—that is, the process of collecting or updating vital information about each voter they contact. The script will include a set of questions. The canvassers will use answers to these question to gauge voters' level of support for the candidate and their likelihood of voting. The voter also might be asked to single out the policy issue or problem that concerns them the most. At the end of the conversation, the canvasser records the information they gathered so that the campaign can confirm or update the database to include (or change) the voter's level of support, likelihood of voting, and issue priorities. The updated information is then used to shape subsequent interactions. For example, a voter identified as a committed supporter with irregular voting habits will be flagged as someone who should be targeted for mobilization efforts as Election Day approaches. An undecided voter whose top issue priority is gun rights can be targeted for subsequent persuasion messaging that emphasizes the candidate's support for the Second Amendment.

Although hard copies of walk sheets and other materials are still common, campaigns are turning to mobile apps. These apps provide canvassers with phone access to interactive maps, scripts, walk lists, and—most importantly—the capacity to directly enter updated information collected about each voter, which is synced with the campaign's database in real time. This eliminates the step of returning hard copies of walk lists or tally sheets to the field office for manual entry by the field staff. It also automates "turf cutting"—the process of dividing a map into navigable plots to be assigned to each canvasser. Turf cutting is a time-consuming process for field organizers, as is the process of preparing packets of hard-copy canvassing materials.

PHONE CALLS

Although door knocking is considered the most effective form of interacting with voters, it is impossible to contact every voter through **face-to-face canvassing**. Most campaigns lack the volunteer workforce to knock on the doors of every targeted voter. Phone calls are much more time efficient. Calling a single voter takes no more than five minutes, and the conversation can be just as interactive as a doorstep exchange, albeit without the face-to-face contact.

Phone canvassing can be handled in a variety of ways. The most efficient approach is to hire a commercial telemarketing firm for either live phone calls by trained and paid employees at a remote call center or prerecorded phone messages. But academic research casts doubt on either method's ability to significantly boost turnout (Gerber and Green 2000; Shaw et al. 2012). That is why campaigns turn to live phone calls made by volunteers. Volunteers might rely on the same script as a paid caller, but they should be able to convey more enthusiasm and sincerity (although, as we will see, problems emerge due to uneven training and a tendency to depart from the script).

Traditionally, field staffers recruit volunteers to make phone calls at established times from a centralized "phone bank." Physical landline phones have been replaced by volunteers' own mobile phones, but the key ingredients remain the same: the campaign provides training, a script, call sheets listing targeted voters and their vital information, along with food and the occasional pep talk and gentle coaching. As with canvassing, however, mobile apps allow volunteers to make phone calls from any location they choose. The app provides a list of voters, their phone numbers, and a basic script. It also allows the volunteer to update campaigns on the voter's level of support and likelihood of voting. This advancement lets volunteers make calls from anywhere in the country. An activist living in a state or district with a noncompetitive election can make calls in support of a candidate facing a tough race in a swing district or state hundreds of miles away. Firsthand knowledge of the candidate's state or district may be lacking, but the convenience is undeniable.

ENTHUSIASM

Field offices and walk lists are tangible elements of voter contact, but energy and enthusiasm may be just as important. Canvassing is most effective when energetic volunteers convey sincere excitement about their candidate. Lackluster candidates can dampen morale and thus diminish the ability of volunteers to convey the campaign's message. An opponent who inspires intense hostility can help compensate. It might even make sense for volunteers to focus their conversations on the dangers of the opponent rather than the virtues of the candidate they support. Research on "negative partisanship" demonstrates that voters favor a party not because they like it, but because they loathe the opposing party, its candidates, and its members (Ladd 2017). Likewise, canvassers who are motivated by antipathy toward the opposing candidate are in a good position to convey the perils of losing the election. Voters identified as likely supporters will be receptive to that message. But problems emerge when alarmist messages are conveyed to voters who do not share those fears. Voters who have been targeted for persuasion might want to hear more about why volunteers favor the candidate they support rather than why they loathe the opponent.

Field staffers spur enthusiasm and morale—both positive and negative—through their interaction with volunteers. As part of their training, volunteers might get a pep talk that emphasizes the importance of their work. Candidates, their spouses, and other family members will sometimes visit field offices to "rally the troops" and boost morale during the arduous closing days of the campaign, sometimes making phone calls themselves and knocking on doors alongside the volunteers.

Voter enthusiasm matters most of all. When voters are excited about the candidate they support—or passionate about voting against the candidate they oppose—they are more likely to turn out to vote. They are more likely to open the door when a canvasser knocks and to answer the phone when a canvasser calls. Enthusiastic supporters are more likely to give money, volunteer to help the campaign, and talk to others about the candidates and the election. Rallies are more raucous when attendees are excited about the candidate (see box 7.2, "Do Appearances Matter?").

Democrat Doug Jones benefited from an enthusiasm gap when he faced Republican Roy Moore in a special election for one of Alabama's U.S. Senate seats in December 2017. Moore was accused of sexual misconduct with teenage girls and had a record of unseemly behavior.

Although he had a core of devoted followers, a sufficient number of Republicans stayed home due to their misgivings about their party's nominee. Democrats, by contrast, were energized both by their affinity toward their candidate as well as their antipathy toward Moore. Jones won the race by 1.5 percentage points in a state that Trump had won by 27.7 points only thirteen months earlier. Turnout among African American voters was disproportionately strong, buoyed by Jones's successful prosecution of two Ku Klux Klansman for their roles in the infamous 1963 bombing of the 16th Street Baptist Church in Birmingham, in which four black girls were murdered. According to exit polls, 30 percent of the electorate was African American, and 96 percent of them voted for Jones. Remarkably, the black share of the Alabama electorate was higher than it was in 2008 and 2012, when Barack Obama was on the ballot (Fausset and Robertson 2017).

BOX 7.2 | Do Appearances Matter?

Are voters positively affected by rallies, stump speeches, town hall meetings, and other candidate appearances? Campaigns certainly think so. The opportunity to see and hear a candidate in person can attract hundreds of potential voters—thousands for presidential candidates. A well-executed candidate appearance can yield volunteers, new supporters, and financial contributions. An inspirational speech delivered by the candidate can motivate existing supporters and volunteers to work harder and donate money. Or so campaigns think. What does the research say?

A candidate's travel schedule is carefully planned to optimize each event's location, timing, visuals, audience, and accompanying local media coverage. Often tied to the campaign's field operation, the *advance* team is responsible for setting up and executing events featuring the candidate and major surrogates. As the name suggests, advance staffers arrive early to scout the location and choreograph the visual aspects of the event. Their job is to make sure the stage is ready, the backdrop is camera-friendly, the microphones are working, and the room is full. One objective is to "earn" news coverage, so visuals matter. Cameras will be rolling, and the resulting imagery will fall flat when there is a half-empty room or a distracting stage backdrop. Presidential candidate John McCain once delivered a speech in front of a lime-green backdrop that attracted more attention than the substance of his remarks. Today, backdrops to speeches and rallies often consist of supporters waving flags or signs behind the candidate.

(continued)

BOX 7.2 | (continued)

What do the signs say? Is it a diverse crowd in terms of gender, race, and age? Does everybody look excited? These are challenges the advance team must tackle.

Do candidate appearances actually achieve their objectives? One study of 1980–1992 presidential elections reported a connection between candidate appearances and both turnout and support for the candidate (Jones 1998). Another study of the 1988, 1992, and 1996 presidential elections also showed a positive impact (Shaw 1999). Other findings are more ambiguous. In 1996, Bill Clinton's late-campaign appearances yielded additional support, but his opponent Bob Dole's did not (Herr 2002). According to an innovative set of field experiments from the 2006 Texas gubernatorial race, Governor Rick Perry's appearances coincided with slightly more favorable local news coverage. His appearances also accompanied a slight increase in donations and volunteers. However, in terms of candidate support, appearances corresponded with increased support for both Perry and his opponent—in other words, a wash (Shaw and Gimpel 2012). Overall, as with so much of the research reported in this book, the effects are modest and sometimes neutralized by other sources of influence.

SOURCES

Herr, J. Paul. 2002. "The Impact of Campaign Appearances in the 1996 Election." *Journal of Politics* 64, no. 3: 904–13.

Jones, Jeffrey M. 1998. "Does Bringing Out the Candidate Bring Out the Votes? The Effects of Nominee Campaigning in Presidential Elections." *American Politics Quarterly* 26, no. 4: 395–419.

Shaw, Daron. 1999. "The Effect of Candidate Appearances on Statewide Presidential Votes, 1988–96." *American Political Science Review* 93, no. 2: 345–61.

Shaw, Daron, and James G. Gimpel. 2012. "What If We Randomize the Governor's Schedule? Evidence on Candidate Appearance Effects from a Texas Field Experiment." *Political Communication* 29: 137–59.

GOTV

In the end, the success of a campaign's field operation is measured in terms of voter turnout. The **get out the vote** operation—GOTV for short—refers to efforts by campaigns, parties, unions, and groups to mobilize supporters to the polls. GOTV targets voters who have been identified as likely supporters, especially those who have shown a pattern of irregular voting. For example, a voter who has committed to supporting a candidate but failed to vote in the most recent election will be a prime target for GOTV efforts. GOTV entails recruiting volunteers to make phone calls, knock on doors, place door hangers on door knobs, drop off fliers, and sometimes literally drive identified supporters to the polls. GOTV can be a massive—and thrilling—volunteer enterprise.

If GOTV is a race, the finish line is usually Election Day, the first Tuesday after November 1—the date set by law for the general election of federal candidates. Most state and local elections are also held on the same day in November for the sake efficiency and convenience. Primary elections—the mechanism through which most state and local parties choose their nominees—are typically held in the spring or summer before the general election. During presidential election years, some states schedule their primaries as early as possible—the "first in the nation" New Hampshire primary is held in February—in an effort to garner attention from presidential candidates and the throngs of media following them from event to event.

GOTV efforts are more complex in states that allow voters to cast their ballots early or by mail. All states allow registered voters to cast an *absentee* ballot if they cannot vote in person on Election Day. But some states are more lenient than others. Particularly in states that allow *no-excuse absentee* voting, GOTV operations thus include an effort to encourage absentee voters to request their ballot in time, then mail their ballot or submit them in person before Election Day. Most states also allow some form of *early voting*, whereby voters cast their ballot in person either at a local election official's office or, in some states, other satellite voting locations. Some states even allow early voting on weekends. In three states—Colorado, Oregon, and Washington—elections are conducted entirely by mail. All eligible voters are automatically mailed a ballot, which may be returned by mail or delivered in person. In these states, GOTV entails encouraging supporters to complete and return their ballots before the deadline.

One way to get out the vote is to encourage supporters to make a specific **voting plan**. The "make a plan" tactic acknowledges that people are more likely to act on their intentions if they are asked to articulate the when, where, and how of following through. Simply asking logistic questions can help: What time to you plan to vote? Will you drive, walk, or take public transit? Will you travel to your precinct from home, work, or someplace else? Supporters who struggle to answer these questions can be offered a ride to the polls, but the questions alone can prompt the advance planning necessary for voters to overcome logistic challenges that keep them from participating.

According to one study, asking people about their voting plan raised turnout rates by 9 percent among households with only one eligible voter (Nickerson and Rogers 2010).

EFFECTIVENESS

Do these tactics actually work? How effective is the ground game at mobilizing turnout? Campaigns have invested a great deal of time and money into sophisticated field operations informed by good data. They are doing so partly because dozens of studies suggest so much promise. Investing in the ground game appears to be money well spent. But as we will see, not all field efforts yield the desired outcomes.

Modern campaigns did not always invest so much in mobilization. Traditionally, voter turnout was the responsibility of political parties, labor unions, and outside groups. Turnout declined significantly between the early 1960s and 1980s, and political scientists were eager to explain why. One influential study blamed the decline in mobilization efforts that accompanied the weakening of political parties (Rosenstone and Hanson 1993). Elections had become less party-centered and more candidate-centered, diminishing the capacity of parties to perform one of their more important functions: mobilizing voters to the polls. Democrats had also leaned on labor unions to rally their members to the polls, yet union membership and political clout had declined significantly. Campaigns were not yet picking up the slack, instead focusing their resources on paid and earned media. That changed in the early 2000s, when political scientists began reporting results of field experiments testing the effectiveness of voter turnout efforts. In their landmark study of the 1998 elections, Alan Gerber and Donald Green reported sharp increases in turnout among voters who were canvassed in person (Gerber and Green 2000). The study triggered dozens of similar experiments that also assessed the effectiveness of real-world mobilization tactics and messages (Green, McGrath, and Aronow 2013). By 2012, there were more than one hundred studies in this vein (García Bedolla and Michelson 2012). Today, voters are far more likely to report being contacted by a campaign than they were in 1980s and 1990s (see figure 7.1).

Much of the early research assessed the effectiveness of mobilization efforts by civic organizations and advocacy groups, but campaigns learned the lesson: canvassing can mobilize voters to the polls. Not only did campaigns step up their investments in the ground game,

Figure 7.1   The Ground Game

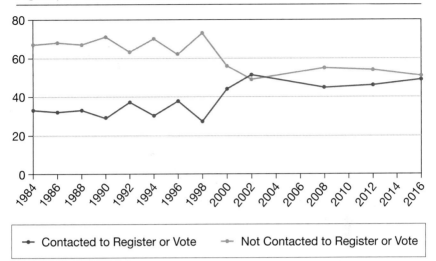

Source: American National Election Study (ANES) question text: "During the campaign this year, did anyone talk to you about registering to vote or getting out to vote (1984, 1986: or about voting)?"

they also began conducting their own field experiments to test the effectiveness of their own tactics and particular messages. Some presidential campaigns even hired political scientists and behavioral psychologists as consultants (Issenberg 2012). Now armed with reams of academic research, much of it conducted in the field using real-world tactics and messages, we are in a good position to assess what works and what may not.

Door-to-Door Canvassing

Academic research confirms that the single most effective way to get a supporter to vote is to ask them to do so through face-to-face interaction. The power of interpersonal canvassing was confirmed in the Gerber and Green paper and supported by numerous subsequent studies. In one study analyzing results of six experiments, for example, door-to-door canvassing boosted an individual's probability of voting by about 7 percent. Such an increase is notable since all six experiments involved local elections, which tend to experience turnout of less than 30 percent of the eligible electorate. The most dramatic effect was seen in Bridgeport, Connecticut, where candidates for city council and school board appeared on the ballot. Bridgeport citizens who were contacted by a volunteer were 14.4 percent more likely to vote than citizens who were not contacted (Green, Gerber, and Nickerson 2003).

Door-to-door canvassing can even mobilize low-propensity voters with low levels of socioeconomic resources to vote in midterm elections (Sinclair, McConnell, and Michelson 2013). The canvassing effect may be contagious: it can boost the likelihood that both members of a two-voter household will vote, including the individual who did not answer the door (Nickerson 2008).

Phone

Face-to-face canvassing is labor and time intensive, which is why campaigns turn to phones. But the evidence is mixed on whether campaigns can boost turnout by calling potential voters. Call centers staffed by professionals do not seem effective (Gerber and Green 2000). But when campaigns use phone banks staffed by volunteers, phone canvassing can boost turnout. For example, volunteer phone calls made by the Michigan Democratic Party's Youth Coordinated Campaign increased turnout by 3.2 percent for the state's 2002 gubernatorial election (Nickerson 2005). In another study, Democrats in Pasadena, California, also were mobilized effectively by phone calls made by volunteers (Alvarez, Hopkins, and Sinclair 2010). The success of volunteer phone calls lies in the nature of the conversations. Whereas professional callers are trained to adhere strictly to a script, volunteer callers are more likely to engage in a chatty, informal conversation and respond to questions. Volunteers manually dial the numbers themselves rather than rely on automatic dialers, which are distinguishable by the familiar brief pause after the recipient picks up the phone, and after which the recipient might hang up (Nickerson 2006).

The weak effects associated with professional callers suggest that interpersonal connections are crucial to the success of mobilization efforts. It is thus surprising that impersonal text messages reminding people to vote can also yield slight increases in turnout (Malhotra et al. 2011). A nationwide experiment conducted during the 2006 midterm elections found that texted reminders yielded a three percentage-point increase in the likelihood of voting. That is lower than the typical impact of traditional canvassing, but text messaging is much less expensive and labor intensive. Texting also reaches more people per attempt: 80 percent of the targeted population in this study received the intended text, whereas traditional canvassing reaches only 30 percent of intended recipients (Dale and Strauss 2009).

Social Pressure

What types of GOTV messages motivate people to vote? It may not matter much. According to one study, voters responded to messages that appealed to their sense of civic duty in the same way they reacted to other motivational messages such as one emphasizing the closeness of the election (Green, McGrath, and Aronow 2013). But messages that apply social pressure and scold nonvoters seem to yield noticeable effects. In one study, turnout increased dramatically among people who received a mailer that listed their name along with the names of their neighbors and whether they voted in recent elections. Under the heading of "WHAT IF YOUR NEIGHBORS KNEW WHETHER YOU VOTED?," the piece also promised a follow-up mailer after the next election showing who voted and who did not. Recipients seemed to respond to the shameful prospect of their neighbors learning about the failure to carry out one's civic duty (Gerber, Green, and Larimer 2008). Similarly, turnout rose among voters who received a "shame" mailer indicating that the names of nonvoters would be published in the local newspaper—more so than voters who received a "pride" mailer promising that the list would consist of voters (Panagopoulos 2010).

LIMITS

So, there is plenty of empirical support for the notion that a campaign's ground game can successfully mobilize voters to the polls. Much depends on the tactic (canvassing versus phone) and especially the messenger (volunteers are best). As we saw in chapter 3, the data used to distinguish between persuadable voters, committed supporters, and likely opponents, are sometimes fraught with inaccuracies. But what is clear is that "field" *can* matter. That said, it is worth considering important caveats.

Volunteer canvassers and phone callers may be particularly adept at mobilizing voters, but there are limits. Political scientists Ryan Enos and Eitan Hersh have documented the pitfalls of relying on volunteers to communicate directly with voters. Volunteer canvassers tend to be party activists and therefore ideologically extreme and demographically unrepresentative. They are very different from the people they are targeting, who are often politically moderate. For example, campaign workers for Obama's 2012 reelection were extremely liberal and very different demographically from the voters they contacted. Compared with undecided voters and even other Democrats, Obama volunteers were far more likely to be white, college educated, and think of themselves as "very liberal." The campaign targeted battleground states such as Ohio, yet many of the volunteers traveled from safe Democratic seats such as California, New York, and Massachusetts. Theoretically, a white farmer in Iowa who had not made up his mind could have been on the receiving end of a vote-for-Obama pitch from a black college student from Chicago.

This is important because there is plenty of evidence that the effectiveness of canvassing depends on the connection between the surrogate and the targeted voter. Enos and Hersh (2014) point to the abundance of evidence that mobilization efforts are more effective when canvassers and targeted voters share demographic characteristics. For example, mobilization efforts aimed at Latinos worked best when voters were contacted by fellow Latinos (Michelson 2003; Michelson 2006; Shaw, de la Garza, and Lee 2000); ditto for African American voters (Leighley 2001). The more local the better: voters are most effectively mobilized by canvassers they recognize as neighbors than by locals from other neighborhoods (Sinclair, McConnell, and Michelson 2013). Campaigns try to mitigate through "peer-to-peer" and "neighbor-to-neighbor" matching. That is, supporters are encouraged to reach out to others who share their interests, professional background, and place of residence. And they routinely provide scripts and train their volunteers to ask questions about the voters' concerns rather than push persuasion messages. But campaigns have limited leverage with unpaid volunteers, who are rarely "fired." And it is difficult to monitor canvassers except with centralized phone banks.

It is also worth noting that although mobilization efforts can boost turnout, they are most successful among high-propensity voters—that is, people who are already inclined to vote and just need an extra nudge. Among low-propensity voters, the effects of face-to-face mobilization are limited to prominent, high-turnout elections (Arceneaux and Nickerson 2009). Individuals classified as low-propensity voters but who have voted in past elections also seem responsive, as are newly registered voters (Alvarez, Hopkins, and Sinclair 2010). Canvassers will find that chronic nonvoters are less likely to come to the door and answer the phone. Campaigns that are counting on these voters to respond to their GOTV efforts face an uphill climb. What is more, the likelihood that mobilization efforts are exacerbating the gap between high- and low-propensity voters raises a serious ethical dilemma: practitioners who assume their turnout practices foster a healthy democracy need to realize that they may be unintentionally aggravating political inequalities between regular voters and chronic nonvoters (Enos, Fowler, and Vavreck 2014).

Other findings also raise concerns about the limits of the strategic effectiveness of a ground game. Asking voters to verbalize their "voting plan" yielded a dramatic increase in turnout among individuals who live alone, but no effect among those who live with others (Nickerson and Rogers 2010). Most significantly, although *mobilization* effects are well documented, *persuasion* effects may be non-existent (Kalla and Broockman 2018). In other words, canvassers can nudge reluctant voters to the polls, but they will have a hard time using a doorstep conversation to convince an uncommitted or cross-pressured voter to support their candidate. That is important because campaigns use their ground game to do both. Mobilization is typically the primary objective, but persuasion also is a key objective of a typical field operation. Such efforts may be futile during a general election, according to an ambitious "meta-analysis" that combines data from forty field experiments with data from nine original experiments conducted by the authors of the study. Campaigns can sometimes persuade voters to change their minds—during primaries, for example, when party cues dissipate, or when a candidate flip-flops on a controversial issue. But during general elections, effective persuasion depends on unusually heavy investment in identifying persuadable voters (Kalla and Broockman 2018).

CONCLUSION

A competent ground game can move certain voters to the polls. The impact of door-to-door canvassing can be dramatic. That is why campaigns, parties, and independent groups are investing more in fieldwork, even at the expense of paid media and other means of communicating with voters. That said, although voters can be mobilized through the ground game, few will be persuaded. Volunteers are crucial, but they must be well trained and relatable to the voter being canvassed. Campaigns need a lot of volunteers to handle the sometimes massive workload of executing a comprehensive ground game. The rest is outside of the campaign's control. The political landscape may make a win impossible, even with an ambitious field operation. A weak candidate—or even a strong candidate running at the wrong time or in the wrong place—may dampen the enthusiasm of volunteers, thereby diminishing their ability to motivate supporters to cast a ballot. Voters, even likely supporters, might also be lukewarm about the candidate or discouraged by the landscape, making them less responsive to the blandishments of canvassers. Some voters are simply out of reach, no matter how many times a volunteer knocks on their door.

KEY TERMS

face-to-face canvassing: interacting with individual voters in person to gather information and/or communicate campaign messages.

field office: a local headquarters for a campaign's ground game.

get out the vote (GOTV): campaigning that is centered on mobilizing supporters to cast their ballot.

phone canvassing: calling voters to gather information and/or communicate campaign messages.

voter identification (voter ID): the process of gathering information about individuals' intended voting behavior.

voting plan: the steps a voter must take to successfully cast a ballot.

DISCUSSION QUESTIONS

1. Field operations lean heavily on volunteers to contact voters in part because they are proven effective. But there are limits. What are those limits?
2. Why do you think canvassers are more effective at mobilizing voters to the polls than persuading them to support a particular candidate?
3. Let's say a "door-knocking" canvasser discovers that a voter identified as a likely supporter actually supports the opposing candidate. What should the canvasser do?
4. What can be done to improve mobilization efforts so that they are more successful with chronic nonvoters?

RECOMMENDED READINGS

García Bedolla, Lisa, and Melissa R. Michelson. 2012. *Mobilizing Inclusion: Transforming the Electorate through Get-out-the-Vote Campaigns.* New Haven, CT: Yale University Press.

Building on the work of Green and Gerber (below), this book reports the results of dozens of experiments testing the effectiveness of efforts to boost turnout among ethnic and racial minorities. Presents a theory— the Social Cognition Model of voting—to explain why some methods are more impactful than others. The most effective methods tap voters' sense of civic identity.

Gerber, Alan S., and Donald P. Green. 2000. "The Effects of Canvassing, Telephone Calls, and Direct Mail on Voter Turnout: A Field Experiment." *American Political Science Review* 94, no. 3: 653–63.

One of the first field experiments that assessed the impact of the ground game. Evidence that door-to-door canvassing efforts can boost turnout partly inspired campaigns to invest more resources in field operations starting in the early 2000s.

Rosenstone, Steven J., and John Mark Hansen. 1993. *Mobilization, Participation, and Democracy in America.* New York: Macmillan.

Why do some people vote and others do not? In grappling with this question, this influential book explains why voter turnout steadily declined in the twentieth century. One key reason was the decline in efforts to mobilize people to the polls. This finding spurred hundreds of studies testing the effectiveness of mobilization efforts, including both of the works described above.

REFERENCES

Alvarez, R. Michael, Asa Hopkins, and Betsy Sinclair. 2010. "Mobilizing Pasadena Democrats: Measure the Effects of Partisan Campaign Contacts." *Journal of Politics* 72, no. 1: 31–44.

Arceneaux, Kevin, and David W. Nickerson. 2009. "Who Is Mobilized to Vote? A Re-Analysis of 11 Field Experiments." *American Journal of Political Science* 53, no. 1: 1–16.

Bump, Philip, and Scott Clement. 2016. "How Ted Cruz Won Iowa." *Washington Post*, Feb. 1: https://www.washingtonpost.com/news/the-fix/wp/2016/02/01/what-we-can-learn-from-the-iowa-republican-entrance-poll/?utm_term=.3e1dd9cc501a.

Dale, Allison, and Aaron Strauss. 2009. "Don't Forget to Vote: Text Message Reminders as a Mobilization Tool." *American Journal of Political Science* 53, no. 4: 787–804.

Darr, Joshua. 2017. "The Incredible Shrinking Democratic Ground Game." *Vox*, Nov. 17: https://www.vox.com/mischiefs-of-faction/2017/11/16/16665756/shrinking-democratic-ground-game.

Darr, Joshua P., and Matthew S. Levendusky. 2014. "Relying on the Ground Game: The Placement and Effect of Campaign Field Offices. *American Political Research* 42, no. 3: 529–48.

Enos, Ryan D., and Eitan D. Hersh. "Party Activists as Campaign Advertisers: The Ground Game as a Principal-Agent Problem." *American Political Science Review* 109, no. 2: 252–78.

Enos, Ryan D., Anthony Fowler, and Lynn Vavreck. 2014. "Increasing Inequality: The Effect of GOTV Mobilization on the Composition of the Electorate." *Journal of Politics* 76, no. 1: 273–88.

Fausset, Richard, and Campbell Robertson. 2017. "Black Voters in Alabama Pushed Back against the Past," Dec. 13: https://www.nytimes.com/2017/12/13/us/doug-jones-alabama-black-voters.html.

García Bedolla, Lisa, and Melissa R. Michelson. 2012. *Mobilizing Inclusion: Transforming the Electorate through Get-Out-the-Vote Campaigns*. New Haven, CT: Yale University Press.

Gerber, Alan S., and Donald P. Green. 2000. "The Effects of Canvassing, Telephone Calls, and Direct Mail on Voter Turnout: A Field Experiment." *American Political Science Review* 94: 653–63.

Gerber, Alan S., Donald P. Green, and Christopher W. Larimer. 2008. "Social Pressure and Voter Turnout: Evidence from a Large-Scale Field Experiment. *American Political Science Review* 102, no. 1: 33–48.

Green, Donald P., Alan S. Gerber, and David W. Nickerson. 2003. "Getting Out the Vote in Local Elections: Results from Six Door-to-Door Canvassing Experiments." *Journal of Politics* 65, no. 4: 1083–96.

Green, Donald P., Mary C. McGrath, and Peter M. Aronow. 2013. "Field Experiments and the Study of Turnout." *Journal of Elections, Public Opinion and Parties* 23, no. 1: 27–48.

Issenberg, Sasha. 2012. *The Victory Lab: The Secret Science of Winning Campaigns*. New York: Crown.

Kalla, Joshua L., and David E. Broockman. 2018. "The Minimal Persuasive Effects of Campaign Contact in General Elections: Evidence from 49 Field Experiments." *American Political Science Review* 112, no. 1: 148–66.

Kreiss, Daniel. 2016. *Prototype Politics: Technology-Intensive Campaigning and the Data of Democracy*. New York: Oxford University Press.

Ladd, Jonathan M. 2017. "Negative Partisanship May Be the Most Toxic Form of Polarization." *Vox*, June 2: https://www.vox.com/mischiefs-of-faction/2017/6/2/15730524/negative-partisanship-toxic-polarization.

Leighly, Jan. E. 2001. *Strength in Numbers? The Political Mobilization of Racial and Ethnic Minorities*. Princeton, NJ: Princeton University Press.

Malhotra, Neil, Melissa R. Michelson, Todd Rogers, and Ali Adam Valenzuela. 2011. "Text Messages as Mobilization Tools: The Conditional Effect of Habitual Voting and Election Salience." *American Politics Research* 39, no. 4: 664–81.

Michelson, Melissa R. 2003. "Getting Out the Latino Vote: How Door-to-Door Canvassing Influences Voter Turnout in Rural Central California." *Political Behavior* 25, no. 3: 247–63.

———. 2006. "Mobilizing the Latino Youth Vote: Some Experimental Results." *Social Science Quarterly* 87, no. 5: 1188–206.

Nickerson, David W. 2005. "Partisan Mobilization Using Volunteer Phone Banks and Door Hangers." *Annals of the American Academy of Political and Social Science* 601: 10–27.

———. 2006. "Volunteer Phone Calls Can Increase Turnout: Evidence From Eight Field Experiments." *American Politics Research* 34, no. 3: 271–92.

———. 2008. "Is Voting Contagious? Evidence from Two Field Experiments." *American Political Science Review* 102, no. 1: 49–57.

Nickerson, David W., and Todd Rogers. 2010. "Do You Have a Voting Plan? Implementation Intentions, Voter Turnout, and Organic Plan Making." *Psychological Science* 21, no. 2: 194–99.

Panagopoulos, Costas. 2010. "Affect, Social Pressure and Prosocial Motivation: Field Experimental Evidence of the Mobilizing Effects of Pride, Shame and Publicizing Voting Behavior." *Political Behavior* 32, no. 3: 369–86.

Rosenstone, Steven J., and John Mark Hansen. 1993. *Mobilization, Participation, and Democracy in America.* New York: Macmillan.

Shaw, Daron, Rodolfo O. de la Garza, and Jongho Lee. 2000. "Examining Latino Turnout in 1996: A Three-State Validated Survey Approach." *American Journal of Political Science* 44, no. 2: 338–46.

Shaw, Daron R., Donald P. Green, and James G. Gimpel. 2012. "Do Robotic Calls from Credible Sources Influence Voter Turnout or Vote Choice: Evidence from a Randomized Field Experiment." *Journal of Political Marketing* 11, no. 4: 231–45.

Sinclair, Betsy, and Melissa R. Michelson. 2013. "Local Canvassing: The Efficacy of Grassroots Voter Mobilization." *Political Communication* 30: 42–57.

Slevin, Peter. 2008. "Obama Volunteers Share the Power of Personal Stories." *Washington Post,* July 26: http://www.washingtonpost.com/wp-dyn/content/article/2008/07/25/AR2008072503118.html.

Tau, Byron. 2016. "Ted Cruz's Super PACs Embrace Ground Game in Republican Campaign." *Wall Street Journal,* Feb. 18: https://www.wsj.com/articles/ted-cruzs-super-pacs-bet-on-ground-game-in-republican-campaign-1455830955.

Weinschenk, Aaron C. "Campaign Field Offices and Voter Mobilization in 2012." *Presidential Studies Quarterly* 45, no. 3: 573–80.

8

Fundraising

★ ★ ★

Donors who contributed $50,000 to Mitt Romney's presidential campaign were honored with the title of "Founding Member" of the campaign's victory fund. *Source*: *wonderlandstock/Alamy Stock Photo*

LEARNING OBJECTIVES

★ Comprehend the basic tenets of campaign finance regulations and how they have changed.

★ Grasp the intended and unintended consequences of lawmakers' efforts to limit the corruptive influence of campaign contributions.

★ Critically analyze the role of outside groups in elections.

★ Understand the practices candidates engage in to raise money for their campaigns.

HOW DO CAMPAIGNS PAY for all of this—the staff, the consultants, the data, the polling, the opposition research, and, the most expensive part, the advertising? They raise funds internally to pay for their own expenses. They also get external support from two sources: their political party and allied outside groups. Parties and outside groups can only give so much directly to the campaign, but they can—and do—*spend* money *on behalf of* the candidates they support. In fact, *independent expenditures* by outside groups and political parties make up a significant proportion of overall campaign spending. That matters because this area of campaign finance is less regulated than the money raised and spent by the campaigns.

This chapter provides an overview of the campaign finance system and the methods candidates use to fund the operations discussed in this book so far. Readers will be introduced to where the money comes from, how it gets raised, and how it is regulated.

Raising money is one of the first things a candidate will do—sometimes even before they officially declare their candidacy. An undeclared candidate might test the waters for a possible run by seeing how many donors they can attract and how much "early money" they can raise. An impressive early haul can scare off potential opponents. Early money can fund feasibility polls and opposition and counteropposition research—information that can inform whether a prospective candidate will decide to run at all. The need to raise early money explains why a typical elections textbook will cover this topic at the beginning of the book. With the book you are reading, however, campaign finance is saved for the end to reflect the book's focus on other aspects of the campaign. "How do campaigns pay for all of this?" is the right question to ask at this point in the analysis.

REGULATING CAMPAIGN FINANCE

The ways in which federal candidates now raise and spend money reflect nearly five decades of evolving campaign finance regulations. Congress has passed two major pieces of legislation since 1971 aimed at limiting the influence of wealthy donors. Yet Supreme Court decisions weakened the first and gutted the second. As a result, individuals and groups can spend as much money as they want to support—or oppose—any candidate running for federal office. Candidates spend far more time than they'd like raising money to directly fund their campaign operations. Their fundraising activities are tightly regulated. But the big money resides with independent groups, who face relatively few legal constraints on how much money they raise and spend to influence the outcome of elections.

Modern campaign finance reform escalated in the early 1970s. Federal legislation passed during this time placed strict controls on funding candidates running for federal office—that is, the presidency, the House, and the Senate. The Federal Election and Campaign Act of 1971 and its 1974 amendments included four major provisions:

1. Strengthening disclosure requirements so that candidates would have to report the name, address, occupation, and amount contributed of individuals and groups who gave more than $200.
2. Limiting the amount of money an individual could contribute to each candidate. At the time, the cap was $1,000 per election, which meant an individual donor could contribute no more than $1,000 to the candidate during the primaries and—if the candidate secured the nomination—$1,000 during the general election.
3. Providing for public financing of presidential elections. The presidential public funding program used federal tax dollars to fully fund each major party nominee's general election campaign. It also matched the first $250 of each individual contribution during the primaries. In return, the candidates had to agree to cap spending and refuse private donations.
4. Creating the **Federal Election Commission** (FEC), the agency charged with administering these new regulations.

The law also imposed spending limits on House and Senate campaigns, but that provision was ruled unconstitutional in 1976 with the Supreme Court's landmark *Buckley v. Valeo* decision. The decision also overturned a provision limiting independent spending by individuals or groups. In doing so, it established the notion that campaign *spending* is a form of political speech protected by the First Amendment. With *Buckley*, the Court upheld the law's contribution limits and disclosure requirements as well as the public financing of presidential elections. By the Court's logic, spending caps were permissible for presidential elections because participation in the public financing system was voluntary.

By contrast, House and Senate candidates could spend as much money as they could raise. So could groups and individuals as long as their spending was done independently *on behalf of* a candidate and did not explicitly advocate the election or defeat of a particular candidate. Independent spending on advertising and other campaign materials had to avoid what came to be known as "magic words" such as "vote for," "vote against," "elect," "support," "reject," or "defeat."

Subsequent Supreme Court decisions further weakened federal campaign finance regulations. In 2002, President George W. Bush signed the Bipartisan Campaign and Reform Act (BCRA), a law aimed at fixing two problems that had emerged since the original round of reforms in the 1970s. One problem had been the massive growth of **soft money** fundraising and spending by political parties. Although individuals could contribute no more than $1,000 in **hard money** directly to the candidate's campaign, the FEC had ruled that donors could contribute unlimited funds to political parties as long as the party used that money for "party-building activities" such as get-out-the-vote efforts. By the late 1990s, both parties were raising millions of dollars in soft money from wealthy donors who were willing to contribute far more than the hard-money limits permitted. But rather than invest in "party building," the parties spent most of that money on television ads aimed at helping their candidates. Party ads funded by soft money looked and sounded like regular campaign spots, but passed muster because they avoided using the magic words.

The second problem BCRA was supposed to fix involved outside group spending on advertising. The *Buckley* decision freed groups and individuals to spend unlimited funds on behalf of candidates as long as they avoided the magic words. Most of that money was spent on independent "issue ads," so called because they supposedly advocated for or against policy positions rather than supporting or opposing particular candidates. Independent issue ads had proliferated by the 1990s, raising additional concerns about major donors bypassing the hard-money system to spend millions on election-related advertising. To close this loophole, BCRA prohibited corporations, groups, and unions from airing "electioneering communications" advertising within thirty days of a primary or caucus, or sixty days of a general election.

With bipartisan support in Congress, BCRA was supported by advocates seeking to reduce the influence of major donors. But it was opposed by an assortment of groups from across the political spectrum. Their objections eventually made their way to the

Supreme Court, which overturned many of its key provisions. With *FEC v. Wisconsin Right to Life* (2007), the court struck down the law's restrictions on electioneering communications. *Davis v. FEC* (2008) overturned a provision aimed at leveling the playing field for candidates challenging wealthy self-financed candidates. But the most important case was *Citizens United v. FEC (2010)*, which affirmed and expanded upon the rationale of the *Buckley* opinion thirty-four years earlier: campaign spending was a form of political speech, so any restrictions on spending violated free speech protections guaranteed by the First Amendment. Congress could not inhibit the ability of anyone—an individual citizen, a corporation, an advocacy group, a union, a candidate—to campaign on behalf of a candidate or a cause.

As a result, groups may now spend unlimited funds to support the candidates they support and oppose the candidates they oppose. They may now use the "magic words" in their paid media. The only major constraint is that groups cannot coordinate their activities with the candidates' campaigns. These are supposed to be independent expenditures on behalf of a candidate, not directly for a candidate.

BCRA's major provisions may have been deemed unconstitutional, but one consequential change remains intact. The law doubled the maximum individual contribution to $2,000 per election and made it adjustable to inflation. As of the 2019–20 cycle, the maximum was up to $2,800. That was an important increase. $1,000 was a lot of money when the amended **Federal Election Campaign Act (FECA)** was passed in 1974. But when BCRA was passed in 2002, the price tag for a typical congressional campaign had more than doubled. By 2002, $1,000 was a modest sum for wealthy donors who were capable and eager to contribute far more, which explains why donors who had maxed out their hard-money contributions then turned to soft money. Doubling the cap and adjusting it to inflation made it possible to fund a campaign primarily through hard money.

Public funding of presidential campaigns also remains intact, but only in theory. Presidential candidates are still eligible for taxpayer-funded matching funds during the primaries and full public funding during the general election. But they must agree to spend no more than the government grant provides, which would have been only $96 million in 2016. Hillary Clinton raised nearly $1.2 billion to fund her presidential campaign; Donald Trump raised about $650 million. Both candidates could afford to opt out, and they did. So did both Barack Obama and Mitt Romney in 2012. By then, the public fund was no match for what candidates from both major parties could raise and spend on their own.

Each state has its own campaign finance system. About half of states have their own optional public financing systems, each with its own required minimums, spending caps, and pledges to refuse private contributions. Maine and five other states have full public funding. Most states also limit individual and PAC contributions, although the amounts vary. At the local level, a number of major cities have enacted or implemented new public finance systems that include matching funds to encourage small donors, vouchers, and other features.

OUTSIDE GROUP SPENDING

Not surprisingly, group spending increased sharply in the wake of *Citizens United*. Outside groups support and oppose candidates in a variety of ways. Groups funded by Charles and David Koch (the "Koch brothers") have supported libertarian and conservative candidates and causes through voter database maintenance, among many other projects. Before he ran for president, Billionaire Tom Steyer launched NextGen America in 2013 to promote candidates who support combating climate change largely through registering and turning out younger voters. But it remains the case that most outside group money is spent on advertising. During the 2008 presidential primaries, group-funded ads made up only 3 percent of advertising activity despite competitive nomination contests for both parties. Four years later, ads from outside groups made up about 60 percent of advertising aired during the Republican primaries (Franz 2013). In 2016, outside groups were responsible for more than half of Republican primary ads (Franz 2017). In U.S. Senate races, groups sponsored over one of three ads in both 2014 and 2016 compared with only 5 percent in 2000 and 2006. Group investment in U.S. House races doubled as a percentage of ads aired between 2006 and 2014 (Franz 2017). Groups have also increased their spending in state elections, especially single-issue groups funded by megadonors. Republicans have garnered more group support than Democrats, especially during presidential elections. Group-sponsored advertising was practically nonexistent during the 2016 nomination contest between Hillary Clinton and Bernie Sanders (Franz 2017).

The expansion of group activity is notable because donors can give them unlimited amounts of money. That was not always the case. Concerns about group influence once centered on the role of traditional **political action committees (PACs)**—FEC-registered organizations created for the sole purpose of raising and spending campaign funds. Traditional PACs raised concerns because so many of them were formed by corporations or interest groups that represented business interests. By the 1980s, candidates relied heavily on PAC contributions to fund their campaigns. For all the concerns about undue influence, however, traditional PACs were and are tightly regulated. Under the FECA, a traditional PAC is allowed to contribute no more than $5,000 directly to a candidate per election.

A new breed of groups face no such constraints. So-called **super PACs** cannot give directly to a candidate's campaign, but they can spend unlimited amounts of the money they raise as long as they do not coordinate their activities with thecampaign. There are no individual contribution limits; donors may give as much as they like. The amounts can be staggering. In 2018, Michael Bloomberg donated $63.2 million to Independence USA PAC, a super PAC he created to support candidates who back his progressive positions on firearms, climate change, education, and same-sex marriage (Center for Responsive Politics n.d.). Las Vegas casino developer Sheldon Adelson and his physician wife, Miriam, dropped $55 million on three conservative super PACs in a single month during the 2018 midterms (Kopp 2018).

A different type of group faced even fewer restrictions, at least until recently. In 2012, wealthy donors began pouring some of their campaign contributions into so-called **dark money** groups. These groups claimed to be nonprofit organizations because their primary purpose was something like "social welfare" rather than electoral politics—even if they sponsored campaign advertising. The distinction initially allowed these groups to avoid registering with the FEC and disclosing their donors. As with super PACs, donors to dark money groups could contribute as much as they liked. The difference was that the groups were not required to disclose who their donors were and how much they gave. We did know how much the groups spent on campaigning. Dark-money group spending on federal elections rose from $139 million in 2010 to $312 million in 2012, and then dropped off to $180 million in 2014 and $183 million in 2016 (Center for Responsive Politics n.d.). In 2018, the Supreme Court let stand a lower court decision that required nonprofits that campaign for or against political candidates to disclose the identities of their donors. Dark money activity may have faded. Super PACs appear to be the outside group of choice, but that could shift again.

Outside groups are not supposed to be coordinate their efforts with the candidates' campaigns. That is why their support is called independent expenditures. But opinions vary on how much coordination is too much. Groups and campaigns cannot share voter data with each other. A campaign cannot have a two-way conversation with a group about ad buys and messaging strategy. Yet there are ways around these restrictions. Either the campaign or the group can simply go public with their strategy or make materials available for anyone to use. That is why campaigns sometimes post online stock video footage showing their candidates doing the sorts of things candidate are seen doing in television spots: shaking hands with voters, speaking to groups, hanging out with their family, reading to children. They make the footage public so that groups can use clips in their ads without violating coordination restrictions. For example, Senate Majority Leader Mitch McConnell's 2014 reelection campaign uploaded a video onto its YouTube channel that had no narration or dialogue: just two minutes of video footage showing McConnell sitting on a coach with his wife, signing papers at his desk, speaking to groups of voters, and running meetings. Ten days after the video was posted, a pro-McConnell super PAC ran a spot using several of the clips. Coordination was unnecessary, but the group's ad clearly included materials produced by McConnell's campaign (National Public Radio 2014).

The post–*Citizens United* growth in outside group spending matters for a number of reasons. Groups are now in a better position to set the election's issue agenda, forcing candidates to respond to the policy priorities of well-financed groups. Coordination restrictions mean candidates sometimes lose control of their messaging or their messaging is undercut, especially if outside groups spend more than they do on advertising. On the other hand, outside groups are free to be more aggressive in attacking opponents, providing cover to candidates who are reluctant to do so themselves. "Instead of the campaign attacking the opponent directly, outside groups can do this, allowing the candidate to deny 'going negative' while still reaping the advantage that the attack may generate" (Francia, Joe, and Wilcox 2017: 152). Not surprisingly, outside groups tend to run more negative ads than the campaigns do (Chand 2017; Gold 2014).

More importantly, wealthy donors can now spend millions of dollars attempting to influence election outcomes. They may be disappointed in their investment. As we have seen throughout this book, campaign advertising and other electioneering activities rarely deliver on their promises. In one study of U.S. Senate races in 2010, 2012, and 2014, outside group spending only slightly increased the intended beneficiary's vote share (Chaturvedi and Holloway 2017). That said, even marginal effects can be consequential. A one-point impact can swing an election.

Group spending has attracted intense scrutiny, but it would be a mistake to overlook the activities of various party groups. Both parties have committees for each of their governing bodies. The Democratic National Committee and the Republican National Committee are the central committees for their respective parties, although their primary purpose is to focus on their presidential candidates. That is because both parties have separate committees to support their House and Senate candidates. There also are separate party committees for guber-natorial and other state-level candidates. The committees were cre-ated primarily to raise and spend money. But as with outside groups, much of their activity entails independent spending on behalf of their candidates in various ways. The party committees are a significant source of opposition research and candidate training. They also air party-sponsored ads to support their candidates running in competi-tive races. But party spending is no longer limited to the committees. Party leaders have created their own super PACs, freeing them to raise huge amounts from large donors and spending that money on adver-tising. By far the top group spender in U.S. House races in 2018 was the Congressional Leadership Fund (see box 8.1, "Inside Groups"), a super PAC closely associated with Republican House Speaker Paul Ryan (Campaign Finance Institute 2018).

BOX 8.1 | Inside Groups

Its name does not reveal much. The Congressional Leadership Fund (CLF) sounds like an organization that might sponsor train-ing for emerging leaders on Capitol Hill. Actually, CLF is a super PAC with close ties to the Republican Party. It was launched in 2011 for the sole purpose of retaining and expanding the Republican majority in the U.S. House. Its Democratic equivalent is the House Majority PAC, also created in 2011. Its goal was to regain control of the House for Democrats.

Technically, both groups are super PACs, which means they can raise and spend unlimited funds on behalf of the candidates they support and against the candidates they oppose. But these are

BOX 8.1 | *(continued)*

not "outside groups," despite their generic nonpartisan names and their legal status as independent organizations. These are party groups led by party insiders with strong ties to congressional leadership. They raise huge sums of money from major donors. For example, Las Vegas casino developer Sheldon Adelson and his physician wife, Miriam, donated $15 million each to the CLF in 2019 alone and a total of $20 million in 2016 (Washburn 2018).

In 2018, the CLF spent tens of millions in a desperate attempt to stave off GOP losses and hold the House majority. It fell short of this goal despite spending nearly twice as much in **independent expenditures** as the House Majority PAC (Center for Responsive Politics 2018). Like most super PACs, it spend most of its money on ads attacking the opposing party's candidates. One example was a spot linking a Democratic House candidate with Libyan dictator Mu'ammar al-Gaddhafi. The Democratic target was Aftab Pureval, a local public official who was challenging Republican incumbent Steve Chabot for Ohio's First Congressional District. With images of terrorist acts and Pureval's face on the screen, the narrator says, "Pureval's lobbying firm made millions helping Libya reduce payments owed to families of Americans killed by Libyan terrorism." Although Pureval did practice law at a firm that settled terrorism-related lawsuits against Libya, he did not work on those cases (Herndon 2018). Pureval lost to Chabot 52 to 46 percent.

For Democrats, the top independent spender was the CLF's equivalent on the Senate side. In 2018, the Senate Majority PAC spent $111.6 million in independent expenditures in its failed effort to take Democratic control of the Senate (Center for Responsive Politics 2018). By far its top donor was Michael Bloomberg, who alone contributed $20 million one month before Election Day. The group spent $18 million in an effort to defeat Josh Hawley, the Republican candidate for one of Missouri's U.S. Senate seats. Hawley defeated incumbent Democrat Claire McCaskill by nearly 6 percentage points.

SOURCES
Center for Responsive Politics. 2018. "Super PACs." https://www.opensecrets.org/pacs/superpacs.php?cycle=2018.

Herndon, Astead W. 2018. "The Most Inflammatory Ads of the Midterms." *New York Times* (Oct. 22): https://www.nytimes.com/2018/10/22/us/politics/election-ads-immigration-racism.html.

Washburn, Kaitlin. 2018. "What Is the Congressional Leadership Fund?" Center for Responsive Politics (Aug. 29): https://www.opensecrets.org/news/2018/08/what-is-the-congressional-leadership-fund/.

CANDIDATE FUNDRAISING

Even with group and party spending, candidates must raise a great deal of money to fund their own campaigns. For all the talk about outside group money, candidates must focus their own fundraising efforts on "hard money"—tightly regulated funds donated directly to the candidate's campaign. Hard money includes contributions from individual Americans, no matter the amount (but capped at $2,800 per election as of 2020). It also includes contributions from traditional PACs, which are capped at $5,000 per election. Disclosure is required: candidates must report to the FEC the name, address, occupation, and amount contributed of individuals and groups who gave more than $200. The FEC shares this information with the public by posting it to its website.

How do candidates raise hard money? They ask for it. The single most effective way for a candidate to raise money is to make personal pleas directly to individual donors. That is why candidates spend so much of their time calling prospective donors and attending fundraising events. Meanwhile, technological advances enable the candidate's campaign finance team to raise impressive sums from small-dollar donors.

"DIALING FOR DOLLARS"

When a candidate first decides to run for office, they might think they're going to spend most of their time interacting with voters. They would be wrong. They will probably spend more time talking to donors than any other group of people. It takes a lot of money to fund a campaign, and the candidate is the campaign's most effective fundraiser. That can mean several hours per day on the phone making calls to donors.

They call it "dialing for dollars" because that is exactly what it is. The candidate picks up a phone and calls individual donors and asks them for money to help fund the campaign. Of course, anyone can make fundraising calls: family members, staffers, volunteers. But donors are much more likely to give if the candidate is doing the asking. If the campaign's finance team has conducted thorough donor research, the caller knows quite a lot about the prospective contributor: their personal background, giving history, and their "capacity"—that is, how much they can afford to give based on available information. Using that information, the donor might be asked about their spouse or children (by name). They might be asked about their own policy priorities or given an update on how the campaign is progressing. The call typically ends with "the ask" for a specific amount. The amount varies depending on past giving history and estimated capacity.

"Call time" can range from a spare twenty minutes riding in a car between events to four hours in a quiet office with the door closed. For lawmakers on Capitol Hill, the location can be tricky. Federal lawmakers are not allowed to make calls from their offices or on the grounds of the U.S. Capitol. They can call from their car. But they can also walk a block or two to one of the national party committees' offices and make calls from there. For example, the National Republican Congressional Committee's offices are located a half a block from the nearest U.S. House office building. The Democratic Senatorial Campaign Committee's offices are located in a cozy townhouse directly across from the Capitol building. Both have office space and staff available to support call time by lawmakers.

Most candidates hate asking for money. "You might as well be putting bamboo shoots under my fingernails," said U.S. Rep. John Larson (D-Conn.) when asked about the experience of making calls to potential donors. "An hour and a half is about as much as I can tolerate. There's no way to make it enjoyable," said Rep. Reid Ribble (R-Wis.). When told that professional fundraisers recommend four hours of call time a day, he replied: "I've never had four hours a day. Not even close to it. I've got work to do. I don't know how anybody could put that much time to it. That'll burn everybody out. Why would you want this stupid job if you had to do that?" (Grim and Siddiqui 2017). When elected officials retire, they often cite the burden of having to spend so much time raising money. For example, when U.S. Rep. Rodney Alexander announced his retirement in 2013, he partly blamed the rigors of fundraising. "It's just a grueling business and I'm ready for another part of my life" (Kroll 2013).

FUNDRAISING EVENTS

Candidates also complain about the number of fundraisers they are expected to host or attend. Fundraisers are appealing nonetheless because the candidate can interact with many prospective donors at once. Do the math: if fifty attendees contribute the $2,800 maximum, the fundraiser will net at least $140,000. It helps when a fundraiser featuring a candidate appearance can specify a high "suggested minimum donation" on the invitation.

For donors, fundraisers provide an opportunity to interact with the candidate face-to-face, not over the phone. That is why fundraisers often feature a "photo line" for large donors, who are rewarded with a grip-and-grin photo with the candidate. Donors also will hear a candidate's speech that is aimed at "insiders" like them. The candidate might give them an update on campaign strategy and an assessment of where things stand. Sometimes candidates are too candid. When Hillary Clinton famously dismissed half of Trump's supporters as belonging in a "basket of deplorables," she was trying to fire up a crowd at a fundraiser. When Mitt Romney appeared to write off nearly half of the electorate with his infamous "47 percent" gaffe, he was speaking to a group of major donors in a closed-door fundraiser. He was trying to reassure nervous donors by explaining why it was proving so difficult to gain majority support: 47 percent of the public would vote for President Obama "no matter what" because they were "dependent upon government, who believe that they are victims, who believe the government has a responsibility to care for them, who believe that they are entitled to health care, to food, to housing, to you-name-it." This frank assessment was intended for major donors, not the general public. Unfortunately for Romney, a bartender filmed the remarks on his phone and shared it with *Mother Jones* magazine.

A major fundraising event often features a sit-down dinner and remarks by the candidate. Donors are there for the chance to see and even meet the candidate, not to eat mediocre food. But some fundraisers are more creative. A fundraiser for U.S. Rep. Derek Kilmer—a known *Star Wars* fan—featured a "galactic trivia battle." Other novelty fundraisers include concerts, ski trips, and beach parties (Levinthal 2013).

BUNDLING

Like hosting fundraising events, **bundling** is an efficient way to collect individual contributions. Bundling is the practice of combining several individual donations into one larger contribution. Bundling can help a campaign raise a lot of funds through hard money. It serves as a loophole for individuals and groups seeking to give more than the maximum hard-money contribution. A donor who has already reached the $2,800 cap can stretch their financial support by bundling individual contributions from family, friends, and associates, and delivering them to the campaign. It is common for lobbyists and PACs to bundle individual contributions as a means of magnifying their influence. EMILY's List, a PAC that aims to elect prochoice women candidates, was a pioneer in the practice of bundling.

Major bundlers tend to be wealthy, well-connected insiders who are strong supporters of a particular candidate. They can be incentivized to raise serious cash. George W. Bush's 2004 presidential campaign bestowed the title of "Ranger" to individuals who bundled $200,000 or more and "Super Ranger" to those responsible for at least $300,000. A "Pioneer" was someone who bundled at least $100,000 (Drinkard and McQuillan 2003). Hillary Clinton's 2008 presidential campaign awarded the title of "HillRaiser" to anyone who bundled more than $100,000. Hundreds of bundlers met or exceeded these minimums.

Regulation is minimal. There is no cap on bundled contributions. It is true that lobbyists and PACs must report their bundled contributions to the FEC. And some presidential campaigns have voluntarily revealed at least some of their major bundlers. But campaigns are not required to disclose their names. A donation that is part of a bundle is treated like any other individual contribution reported to and disclosed by the FEC.

SMALL-DOLLAR DONATIONS

Candidates tend to keep their bundling under wraps because the practice evokes voters' concerns about the influence of big money. Not so for their efforts to raise small-dollar donations—contributions of less than $200. These contributions tend to come from rank-and-file supporters, not wealthy donors. A successful small-dollar donation effort is seen as an indicator of grassroots strength. It can be a proxy for widespread voter enthusiasm. When Bernie Sanders ran for president in 2016, he boasted that the average contribution to his campaign was only $27. He made this claim so often that *Saturday Night Live* spoofed it in a skit. Like other candidates who attract small-dollar contributions, Sanders could claim that most of his contributions were less than $200. Trump could say the same about his first presidential bid in 2016 as well as the early stages of his reelection campaign.

Technology makes it easy to give in small amounts. Anyone who googles a candidate's name will be directed to the campaign's website, where a "contribute" button will be featured prominently. Suggested amounts might be as low as $1 (in 2016, $27 was one of the options for Sanders). Making a contribution requires only a credit card and a few mouse clicks or phone taps. Impulse giving is easy. And once a person provides their contact information to a candidate, party, or political organization, they will receive countless texts and emails asking for contributions of any amount. Online solicitations intensify shortly before the FEC's filing deadline, after which a campaign's fundraising totals are made public and therefore scrutinized for signs of success or failure. Both major parties have ties with technology platforms that their candidates can use for online fundraising—ActBlue for Democrats and the recently launched WinRed for Republicans.

Sometimes small contributions turn into larger ones. That is in part because any contribution under the $2,800 cap will yield follow-up asks for additional funds. It also matters that online giving is conducive to repeat donations in small increments. It is now routine to let donors set up recurring automatic monthly payments from a credit card. Obama was particularly effective at attracting "mid-range repeaters"—donors who started off with a small contribution but then kept giving to the point that their total contributions added up to $200 or more, crossing the small-dollar threshold (Campaign Finance Institute 2008). The campaign discovered that people who signed up for its repeat giving program—which allowed quick contributions without reentering credit card information—gave about four times as much as other donors (Scherer 2012).

POLITICAL ACTION COMMITTEES

Candidates also lean on traditional political action committees (PACs) for hard money. PACs exist because corporations and labor unions cannot give directly to candidate's campaigns. Neither can political advocacy groups, trade associations, and membership organizations. As we have seen, a groups can form a super PAC to spend unlimited funds on behalf of a candidate. But to make direct contributions, it must form a traditional PAC. PACs are organizations created for the sole purpose of raising money and distributing funds to candidates and other political causes. At the federal level, they must register with the FEC and disclose their donors. A PAC can give up to $5,000 to a candidate per election cycle.

There are several types of PACs. Super PACs were discussed earlier in this chapter. A corporation such as AT&T can form a traditional PAC and raise money from managers and shareholders. A union such as the International Brotherhood of Electrical Workers can create a PAC and raise funds from members. A PAC launched by a trade group such as the National Beer Wholesalers Association may raise funds from members and employees. An issue advocacy group such as the National Rifle Association can form a "nonconnected" PAC, which allows them to raise money from the general public (not only their members or staffers). PACs created by elected officials are called leadership PACs because they tend to be formed by congressional leaders. In reality, any politician can launch a leadership PAC, and it is common for aspiring leaders who are effective fundraisers to form one to support political allies (and therefore build influence) through campaign contributions. During the 2018 midterm elections, one of the top hard-money contributors to Republican House candidates was Mark Meadows, a congressman with close ties to President Trump.

PACs are selective about the candidates they support. Business PACs favor likely winners, regardless of party. Single-issue and ideological PACs will only fund candidates who support their positions. But even politically aligned candidates need to demonstrate they can win. To strengthen its case, a campaign's finance team might prepare a "PAC Kit"—a packet that includes biographical information about the candidate, policy papers, favorable news clips, and a list of endorsements. Poder PAC—an organization for prochoice Latina Democrats—states on its website that it supports "viable federal candidates who are committed to winning by putting together a campaign plan that reflects an effective fundraising program and a campaign organization." Like many PACs, the group requires campaigns to complete a lengthy candidate questionnaire with questions aimed at gauging both issue compatibility and electoral viability.

A growing number of Democratic candidates have made public pledges to refuse donations from corporate PACs. Democratic presidential candidate Elizabeth Warren was one of them. In a speech during a January 2019 campaign stop in Des Moines, Iowa, she said: "I don't believe democracy should be for sale to billionaires and giant corporations. I don't take corporate PAC money." The truth is, hard-money contributions by corporate PACs are dwarfed by independent spending by super PACs. And business PACs err on the side of caution when making direct contributions. Incumbents attract the lion's share of corporate PAC contributions because they are usually favored to win. Even though Republicans are seen as more probusiness, corporate and trade PACs give to both parties. For example, the National Association of Realtors—the top PAC contributor in 2017–2018—made 51 percent of its contributions to Democratic candidates and 48 percent to Republicans. The defense contractor Northrup Grumman gave most of its funds to Republican candidates, but not by much: Democrats got 43 percent of its direct contributions in 2017–2018 (Center for Responsive Politics 2018).

CONCLUSION

It is difficult to raise enough money to fund a competitive campaign. Candidates must spend far more time than they'd like calling donors and attending fundraisers. They would rather be talking to voters. Most would rather not accept money from PACs. Although the financial burden can be eased by independent expenditures made by the party and outside groups, the campaign cannot control what either says and does. In any case, getting help from outside groups carries a negative stigma, at least among progressive candidates.

Few candidates are happy with the status quo. For the foreseeable future, however, fundraising will consume an inordinate amount of a candidate's time and energy. The success of campaigns' small-dollar donation programs is encouraging, but their yields cannot keep up with the need for more funds. Meanwhile, the Supreme Court has affirmed the notion that campaign spending is protected by the First Amendment, which means the "millionaires and billionaires" decried by Bernie Sanders remain free to spend unlimited sums to attempt to influence elections.

Are wealthy donors wasting their millions? Most of their money is spent on television advertising, whose effects are measurable yet nowhere near as powerful as their price tag suggests (see chapter 5). The fact that they cannot coordinate their efforts with the candidates they support inhibits clear and consistent messaging. As with so many of the communication efforts described in this book, the impact of group-sponsored campaigning is tough to discern.

KEY TERMS

bundling: the practice of combining several contributions into one larger contribution.

dark money: campaign spending by political groups that disguise themselves as non-partisan nonprofit organizations.

Federal Election Campaign Act (FECA): the primary law regulating campaign finance for federal elections in the U.S.

Federal Election Commission: independent regulatory agency that enforces federal campaign finance law in the U.S.

hard money: regulated campaign contributions that are given directly to the candidate's campaign and reported to the FEC.

independent expenditure: campaign communication *on behalf of a* candidate but uncoordinated with the candidate's campaign.

political action committee (PAC): an organization created for the sole purpose of raising money and distributing funds to candidates and other political causes.

soft money: campaign contributions made to a political party or group with no cap on the amount given.

super PAC: a political action committee that can raise unlimited contributions from donors but cannot coordinate its activities with the campaigns it supports.

DISCUSSION QUESTIONS

1. Discuss the *unintended* consequences of lawmakers' efforts to limit the influence of wealthy donors.
2. In what ways is *bundling* a loophole around individual and PAC contribution limits?
3. Are you concerned about the amount of campaign spending by outside groups? Why or why not?
4. Some advocates of campaign finance reform support public financing of elections. As with the now-dormant presidential public financing system, candidates would receive taxpayer funds to cover the cost of campaigning if they agree to a spending cap. Would you support such a measure? Why or why not?

RECOMMENDED READING

La Raja, Raymond, and Brian F. Schaffner. 2015. *Campaign Finance and Political Polarization: When Purists Prevail.* Ann Arbor: University of Michigan Press.

The authors of this book are sympathetic to the notion that private financing of campaigns seems rigged to favor wealthy interests, but their findings raise doubts about the effects of tighter restrictions. Reforms aimed at curtailing the corruptive impact of money on politics have had the unintended consequence of magnifying the influence of ideological wealthy donors and interest groups.

Perry, Paul. 2018. "What It's Like to Be Rolodexed: One Candidate's Journey into the Reality of Political Fundraising." *The Intercept* (Jan. 31): https://theintercept.com/2018/01/31/democratic-party-political-fundraising-dccc/.

First-person account by a candidate who ran for the Democratic nomination for Pennsylvania's Seventh Congressional District. The essay focuses on the candidate's time spent courting donors and interacting with party leaders on the subject of raising money.

REFERENCES

Campaign Finance Institute. 2008. "Reality Check: Obama Received About the Same Percentage from Small Donors in 2008 as Bush in 2004." Nov. 24: http://www.cfinst.org/press/releases_tags/08-11-24/Realty_Check_-_Obama_Small_Donors.aspx.

———. 2018. "Independent Spending Continues Record Pace; Party Groups Lead The Way." *Campaign Finance Institute* (Oct. 23): http://www.cfinst.org/press/PReleases/18-10-23/INDEPENDENT_SPENDING_CONTINUES_RECORD_PACE_PARTY_GROUPS_LEAD_THE_WAY.aspx.

Center for Responsive Politics. 2018. "Top PAC Contributors to Candidates, 2017–2018" https://www.opensecrets.org/pacs/toppacs.php?Type=C&pac=A&cycle=2018.

———. n.d. "Dark Money Basics." https://www.opensecrets.org/dark-money/basics.

———. n.d. "Top Individual Contributors to Super PACs." https://www.opensecrets.org/overview/topindivs.php?view=sp&cycle=2018.

Chand, Daniel E. 2017. "'Dark Money' and 'Dirty Politics': Are Anonymous Ads More Negative?" *Business and Politics* 19, no. 3: 454–81.

Chaturvedi, Neilan S., and Coleen Holloway. 2017. "Postdiluvian? The Effects of Outside Group Spending on Senate Elections after *Citizens United* and *Speechnow.org v. FEC*." *The Forum* 15, no. 2: 251–67.

Drinkard, Jim, and Laurence McQuillan. 2003. "'Bundling' Contributions Pays for Bush Campaign." *USA Today* (Oct. 16): https://usatoday30.usatoday.com/news/politicselections/nation/2003-10-15-cover-bundlers_x.htm.

Francia, Peter L., Wesley Joe, and Clyde Wilcox. 2017. "Campaign Finance— New Realities Beyond *Citizens United*." In *Campaigns on the Cutting Edge*, 3rd ed. Edited by Richard J. Semiatin. Los Angeles: SAGE.

Franz, Michael M. 2013. "Interest Groups in Electoral Politics: 2012 in Context," *The Forum* 10, no. 4: 62–79.

———. 2017. "Considering the Expanding Role of Interest Groups in American Presidential Elections." *Interest Groups & Advocacy* 6, no. 1: 112–20.

Gold, Matea. 2014. "Big Spending by Parties, Independent Groups Drowns Airwaves in Negative Ads." *Washington Post* (Oct. 22): https://www.washingtonpost.com/politics/big-spending-by-parties-independent-groups-drowns-airwaves-in-negative-attacks/2014/10/21/b4447f66-593c-11e4-b812-38518ae74c67_story.html?noredirect=on.

Grim, Ryan, and Sabrina Siddiqui. 2017. "Call Time for Congress Shows How Fundraising Dominates Bleak Work Life." *HuffPost* (Dec. 6): https://www.huffpost.com/entry/call-time-congressional-fundraising_n_2427291?guccounter=1.

Kopp, Emily. 2018. "Sheldon Adelson Breaks Spending Record on Midterm Elections, Surpassing $100M." *Roll Call* (Oct. 22): https://www.rollcall.com/news/politics/sheldon-adelson-breaks-all-time-spending-records-on-the-midterm-elections-surpassing-100-million.

Kroll, Andy. 2013. "Retiring GOP Congressman: Fundraising Is 'The Main Business' of Congress." *Mother Jones* (Aug. 8): https://www.motherjones.com/politics/2013/08/retiring-rodney-alexander-congressman-fundraising-congress/.

La Raja, Raymond, and Brian F. Schaffner. 2015. *Campaign Finance and Political Polarization: When Purists Prevail.* Ann Arbor: University of Michigan Press.

Levinthal, Dave. 2013. "Need Political Cash? Use the Force." *Center for Public Integrity* (May 12): https://publicintegrity.org/federal-politics/need-political-cash-use-the-force/.

National Public Radio. 2014. "What's with This Video of McConnell Doing Stuff?" Mar. 29: https://www.npr.org/sections/itsallpolitics/2014/03/29/295927924/whats-with-this-video-of-mcconnell-doing-stuff.

Perry, Paul. 2018. "What It's Like to Be Rolodexed: One Candidate's Journey into the Reality of Political Fundraising." *The Intercept* (Jan. 31): https://theintercept.com/2018/01/31/democratic-party-political-fundraising-dccc/.

Scherer, Michael. 2012. "Inside the Secret World of the Data Crunchers Who Helped Obama Win." *Time* (Nov. 7): http://swampland.time.com/2012/11/07/inside-the-secret-world-of-quants-and-data-crunchers-who-helped-obama-win/.

Conclusion

An ordinary president would be favored to win reelection in 2020. The political landscape should give the incumbent an edge. Only three presidents since World War II have failed to win a second term— Gerald Ford in 1976, Jimmy Carter in 1980, and George H. W. Bush in 1988. Both Carter and Bush were blamed for a weak economy.[1] That does not appear to be Donald Trump's problem. He inherited a steadily recovering economy from his predecessor, then presided over three additional years of job growth and low unemployment. An incumbent president should easily win reelection under these circumstances. That is what happened to Bill Clinton in 1996, Ronald Reagan in 1984, Richard Nixon in 1972, and Lyndon Johnson in 1964—all of whom secured Electoral College landslides. There was little their opponents could do to overcome the advantages incumbents enjoy when the national economy is in good shape. Even if their challengers had run well-resourced, smart campaigns, the odds of winning were slim to none.

---

[1] Ford did not technically run for reelection. As Richard Nixon's vice president, he became president in 1974 when Nixon resigned in the midst of the Watergate scandal. Similar circumstances applied to Lyndon Johnson, who became president when John F. Kennedy was assassinated in 1963. But whereas Johnson had served as Kennedy's running mate during the 1960 election, Ford was not on the ballot with Nixon in 1972; he had been appointed vice president after Spiro Agnew was forced to resign after being charged with tax evasion. Ford lost to Carter by only two percentage points despite a weak economy and the cloud of scandal surrounding the Nixon administration he briefly served on.

Of course, Donald Trump is no ordinary president. Another element of the landscape works against him: he is extraordinarily unpopular for a president governing during a strong economy. Trump's unpopularity matters because a president's approval rating—along with the state of the economy—is an important predictor of reelection odds. Barack Obama won a second term despite lingering economic insecurity partly because he was revered by Democrats and popular enough among a sufficient number of independents. Republicans have been similarly devoted to Trump. But among independents, less than 40 percent approved of his handling of his job as president throughout the first half of his term (Gallup 2019).

All of this reminds us that the 2020 presidential election could be largely determined by two factors: the economy and the president's approval rating. Both are out of the hands of the candidates' campaign operations. As president, Trump could make policy decisions aimed at heading off an economic downturn—by easing or eliminating his tariffs on China, for example. He could also adjust his behavior in ways that would boost his approval rating. He could tone down his tweets, for example. But that seems unlikely, and the stability of his low approval ratings throughout his presidency suggests that people's attitudes toward Trump would be difficult to budge.

All the Trump campaign can do is adapt to his unpopularity among non-Republicans. Trump seems most comfortable firing up his base on Twitter and at public rallies; mobilizing his supporters to vote should be a cinch. A strong economy would make it easier for the campaign to limit defections from weak Republicans and GOP-leaning independents. They might even persuade a sufficient number of independents who don't like Trump but also don't want to risk the dramatic change that might come with a Democratic president. Meanwhile, Trump's Democratic opponent's campaign can't do anything about the economy, nor can it do much, if anything, to influence the president's approval ratings. They can prime voters to base their vote on Trump's weaknesses: his unfitness for public office and policy failures such as health care. But the fundamentals are out of their control.

Such is the plight of the modern campaign operation. A campaign can raise gobs of money to fund a sophisticated data-driven field effort and outspend its opponent with clever spots on the airwaves, and then lose because the landscape overwhelmingly favored their opponent. A dynamic House candidate can hire a crack campaign team, and then fall short because too many voters in the district identify with the opponent's party. This sort of thing happens to candidates at the federal, state, and local levels. A campaign cannot change or control the political landscape. They can only adapt to it and hope their efforts make a difference at the margins.

Adapting to the landscape is what campaigns do. This book has introduced readers to the strategies and tactics that campaigns can employ to influence the outcome of the election *at the margins*. Many voters will vote for their party's nominee no matter what. These tend to be reliable voters. But some likely supporters' predispositions need to be reinforced. Campaigns target them with *mobilization* messages to make sure they are on board and they cast a ballot. *Persuasion* messages are aimed at the likely voters who have not made up their minds. If more votes are needed, the campaign will target different persuasion messages at opposite partisans who are out of sync with their party's nominee on an issue that matters to them. How do campaigns know who needs to be mobilized and who needs to be persuaded? They start with a database of voters. The core of the database is a public voter file, which may be added to and updated through *voter identification* and supplemented with commercial data. Polls can help the campaign identify strengths and weaknesses among various groups of voters and how much people know about the candidates and their issue positions.

Things get chaotic from here. Campaigns are short-term operations housed in temporary office space. They must gear up quickly, build a team and basic infrastructure, and then react to ever-changing events. A major party candidate will have access to a voter database containing a lot of useful information, but is also laden with errors and useless data points. Polls are as accurate as ever, but they promise more precision than they can deliver. A campaign's earned media operation can be fraught with peril and frustration. Local news outlets are struggling to stay afloat. They lack the resources they need to cover local elections, so candidates counting on the press's "free" media exposure will be disappointed. Federal and statewide candidates can attract attention in the increasingly dominant national media, but only if their race is competitive. And the coverage they garner probably will not meet their needs: it will focus more on the strategic aspects of the race than their policy platforms and qualifications for office. Chances are, the tone of their coverage will be more negative than positive. That is especially true if the candidate stumbles, underperforms, fails to meet expectations, or gets embroiled in a scandal. Campaigns can attempt to shape their media coverage, but these efforts are often futile.

Campaigns have far more control over their paid media. They make all decisions related to the production and content of their advertising and other forms of sponsored communication. They direct the timing and distribution of paid messaging. But campaigns have no control over how voters perceive their paid messaging, and indeed whether they receive it at all. Many of those persuadable voters are just not paying attention. And campaigns have no say over how their opponent will respond. The opposing campaign is also running their own spots. Nor can the campaign prevent news organizations from scrutinizing their advertising for accuracy and fairness. Campaigns stand to benefit from advertising sponsored by allied groups and the party, but their ability to shape this communication is inhibited by legal prohibitions against coordination.

Campaigns do matter, just not as much as some electioneering practitioners like to think. An attention-grabbing ad run during the final week can yield a one-point bump—enough to decide a tight race. A late-breaking damaging scandal can have the opposite but equally consequential effect (as evidenced by the likely impact of the "Comey letter" on the 2016 presidential election). Social media enable the candidate to communicate directly with their supporters and empower them to do their own electioneering. They also provide platforms for microtargeted advertising. Face-to-face canvassing by enthusiastic volunteers can be more effective than anything else a campaign does, especially if they have access to accurate data about who is answering the door. But the rest is largely out of the campaign's hands. In the end, managing the chaos of running for office is partly a matter of accepting and coming to terms with the lack of control.

REFERENCE

Gallup. 2019. "Presidential Approval Ratings—Donald Trump." https://news. gallup.com/poll/203198/presidential-approval-ratings-donald-trump.aspx.

Index

Clinton, Bill: advertising and, 134–35, 138; appearances by, 188; earned media and, 107; national conditions and, 18, 21; opposition research and, 74; reelection of, 220

Clinton, Hillary: generally, 16, 114, *148*; advertising and, 119, 121, 126, 132, 134, 136, 140–42; analytical journalism and, 96–97; campaign finance and, 204–5, 212–13; data and, 5–55; earned media and, 107; email server and, 94–95, 150–51; "fake news" and, 167–68; field offices, 181–82; gaffes and, 90; ground game and, 182–83; mobilization and, 29; motivated reasoning and, 32; in nomination phase, 6; opposition research and, 74, 76; persuasion and, 29, 31; polling and, 64; scandals and, 94–95; social media and, 149–50

closed primaries, 8

CNN, 99

Coleman, Marshall, 21

Coleman, Norm, 127, 130

Colorado, mail voting in, 22, 189

Comey, James, 94–95, 150

comparative ads, 125

Comstock, Barbara, 5

confidence level, 65

Congressional Leadership Fund (CLF), 208–9

contrast ads, 125

conventions, 9–10

Cook Political Report, 12, 142

Cooper, Terry, 73

counter-opposition research, 70–71

crosstabs, 62–64

Crowley, Joe, 5, 128–29

Cruz, Heidi, xv

Cruz, Ted: campaign finance and, xvi; earned media and, xiv; ground game and, xv, 179–80; lack of electoral success, viii; paid media and, xiv; social media and, xv, 162; targeting and, 41–42

Cuccinelli, Ken, *1*, 9, 36

Culberson, John, 5

Cunningham, Joe, 126

Daily Caller, 100

Daily Wire, 100

"Daisy" ad, 119

D'Amico, Steven, 76

dark money, 206

data, 50–58; databases, 52; "digital profile," 50; mobilization and, 50; overview, 50–52; parties, role of, 52–54; persuasion and, 50; predictive modeling, 51–52; race and, 55–57; religion and, 56–57; usefulness of, 54–58; voter files, 51; voter identification, 52

Davis, Danny, 54

Davis v. Federal Election Commission (2008), 204

Dayton, Mark, 108

Dean, Howard, 53, 75, 89, 92

DeLauro, Rosa, 5

Delaware, advertising in, 139

Democratic Party. *See specific topic or individual*

Denham, Jeff, 13

Denver Post, 98

DeSantis, Casey, 130

DeSantis, Ron, 61, 130

"dialing for dollars," 210–11

digital advertising, 121–24

direct voter contact, 151

"dirty tricks," 72, 93